Simply *More* Delicious

A COLLECTION OF NEW AND TREASURED RECIPES

The Miriam Hospital Women's Association
Providence, Rhode Island

The Miriam Hospital Women's Association supports The Miriam Hospital through fundraising, volunteerism, providing health education, developing public interest and encouraging goodwill toward the hospital.

Proceeds of this book will enable the MHWA to name a patient room in the new Victor and Gussie Baxt Building as part of The Miriam's capital campaign.

Additional copies can be obtained by sending $25.95 plus $1.82 sales tax and $8.23 shipping and handling ($36.00) to the address below:

The Miriam Hospital Women's Association

164 Summit Avenue

Providence, Rhode Island 02906

http://cookbook.miriamhospital.org

Telephone (401)793-3520

Fax (401) 793-2521

The painter of the cover art, Faye MG Stolzman, has named the original painting "Molly's Gift" because it is inspired by her mother, Molly Granoff. "Thank you Mom for passing on your passions for cooking and art. Thank you Miriam Hospital Women's Association for enabling me to contribute to this incredible legacy that is *Simply More Delicious.*"

WIMMER
COOKBOOKS

A CONSOLIDATED GRAPHICS COMPANY

800.548.2537   wimmerco.com

The Miriam Hospital Women's Association's original cookbook, *Simply Delicious*, made its debut in 1975 with a printing of 5,000 copies which quickly sold out. After second and third printings, a total of 22,500 cookbooks were sold, but requests for the cookbook continued to roll in. Many of our committee members received their copy of *Simply Delicious* as young brides and have prepared its recipes for years. Countless recipes have become family favorites, requested by college students when they return home. Mothers and grandmothers have passed their cookbooks down to a new generation. Many have added notations in the margins of their favorite recipes and these well-used cookbooks are cherished all the more for this. Despite these acts of kindness, the demand for *Simply Delicious* persisted. We also realized that we wanted to provide a copy of the cookbook to our children and children-in-laws.

Because *Simply Delicious* has been unavailable since 1988, we've decided to update and reprint our bestseller. We have kept many beloved favorite recipes and added new ones to reflect a change in healthful eating practices and a wider variety of foods available. We've also added a vegetarian section and a section just for kids. Additionally, since Rhode Island has so many outstanding restaurants, we've prevailed upon some of our nationally renowned chefs to share some of their recipes with us. We proudly present 500 lovingly tested recipes in our new cookbook, which we have entitled *Simply More Delicious.*

The Miriam Hospital Women's Association has a long and proud history. In tribute to the work of these women, *Simply More Delicious* tells the story of how a group of dedicated and brave women saw the need and had the drive to found a hospital over 110 years ago. And since that time, generations of Rhode Island women have continued to support The Miriam Hospital through fundraising, volunteering, providing health education, developing public interest and encouraging goodwill toward the hospital.

We are proud to be a part of this tradition of women and hope that you will enjoy the recipes and the telling of our history as well. Your purchase of *Simply More Delicious* will enable the Miriam Hospital Women's Association to further support the capital campaign of the hospital and name a new patient room in the new Victor and Gussie Baxt building at The Miriam Hospital.

Robin Engle and Leslie Sax
Co-Editors

We would like to thank the following people for their significant role in the publication of *Simply More Delicious.*

Cookbook Steering Committee

Donna Frank	Diane Lazarus	Harriet Samors
Susan Froehlich	Joyce Leven	Evelyn Seigle
Sharon Gaines	Terry Lieberman	Karen Trinkle
Marcia Hirsch	Marianne Litwin	Pamela Vogel
Susan Adler Kaplan	Judi Matt	DeeDee Witman
Mary Kitzes	Susan Odessa	

Table of Contents

This recipe was in *Simply Delicious*

Measurements and Equivalents

1 tablespoon fresh herbs	=	1 teaspoon dried herbs
1 tablespoon fresh ginger	=	1 teaspoon powdered ginger
Dash cayenne or red pepper	=	few drops hot pepper sauce
1 teaspoon	=	⅓ tablespoon
3 teaspoons	=	1 tablespoon
½ tablespoon	=	1½ teaspoons
1 tablespoon	=	3 teaspoons or ½ fluid ounce
2 tablespoons	=	⅛ cup or 1 fluid ounce
3 tablespoons	=	1½ fluid ounces
4 tablespoons	=	¼ cup or 2 fluid ounces
8 tablespoons	=	½ cup or 4 fluid ounces
12 tablespoons	=	¾ cup or 6 fluid ounces
16 tablespoons	=	1 cup or 8 fluid ounces or ½ pint
⅓ cup	=	5 tablespoons + 1 teaspoon
⅜ cup	=	¼ cup + 2 tablespoons
½ cup	=	8 tablespoons or 4 fluid ounces
⅔ cup	=	10 tablespoons + 2 teaspoons
⅝ cup	=	½ cup + 2 tablespoons
¾ cup	=	12 tablespoons or 6 fluid ounces
⅞ cup	=	¾ cup + 2 tablespoons
1 cup	=	16 tablespoons or ½ pint or 8 fluid ounces
2 cups	=	1 pint or 16 fluid ounces
1 pint	=	2 cups or 16 fluid ounces
1 quart	=	2 pints or 4 cups or 32 fluid ounces
1 gallon	=	4 quarts or 8 pints or 16 cups or 128 fluid ounces

Source: *The New Food Lover's Companion,* Second Edition

Simply *More* To Begin With

The Miriam Hospital Women's Association has a proud and unusual history. It traces its roots to 1897 and predates The Miriam Hospital itself by 28 years.

From the beginning, food played an important role.

The Miriam Hospital Women's Association started as a women's charitable lodge, affiliated with a national Jewish fraternal lodge, B'rith Abraham. When the parent group demanded that all lodges open membership to men and women jointly, our ladies disaffiliated, preferring to remain a women's organization. Our women took on the mission of facilitating the transition of recent immigrants by providing grass roots social services.

The members of this small women's group assumed responsibility of feeding those who were ill and needy in the Jewish immigrant community. The women cooked Kosher food in huge pots on the two burner stove in the back of Mary Grant's millinery shop on Prairie Avenue in Providence, Rhode Island. Each woman was assigned a day to bring Kosher meals to the hospital and to visit with and serve the Jewish patients. On Friday afternoons, the women brought candles to women patients so that they might usher in the Sabbath.

Our women raised funds to provide the needy with medical and dental care, convalescent care, eyeglasses, dental appliances, wheelchairs, special diets, transportation and housekeeping services. In 1904 they completed their first subscription of $250 to the Rhode Island Hospital to ensure a free bed for needy Jewish patients — a subscription which was renewed annually for the next 20 years. To maintain this annual subscription, members went door to door to collect pennies, nickels and dimes to meet the quarterly installment fee.

They also made contributions to St. Joseph's Hospital and the Providence Lying-In Hospital in payment for services to the Jewish poor.

Artichoke Dip

2-3   **(14 ounce) cans quartered or halved artichokes**

2   **cans diced chili peppers**

½-¾   **cup mayonnaise**

1-1½   **cups shredded orange Cheddar cheese**

  freshly grated Parmesan

Preheat oven to 375°. Place artichokes in a large bowl and add the diced chili peppers, mayonnaise and shredded Cheddar cheese. Mix thoroughly. Place in a medium to large casserole. Sprinkle a small amount of fresh Parmesan over the top.

Bake approximately 35 to 45 minutes until slightly browned and bubbling at the edges. Serve with tortilla chips or scoops.

15 SERVINGS

Sautéed Artichoke Hearts

This may be used as a vegetable or an hors d'oeuvre.

1   **package frozen artichoke hearts, defrosted**

1   **egg**

3-4   **tablespoons Parmesan cheese**

1   **cup seasoned bread crumbs**

  butter and/or oil for sautéing

Beat eggs with Parmesan cheese. Dip artichoke hearts in egg mixture, then in bread crumbs.

Sauté until golden brown.

4 TO 6 SERVINGS

Hot Bean Dip

1   (16 ounce) can refried beans
1   cup reduced fat sour cream
1   cup salsa
½   teaspoon salt
1   teaspoon black pepper
½   cup (2 ounces) shredded Cheddar
      cheese

Preheat the oven to 325°. Combine beans, sour cream, salsa, salt and pepper in a large bowl. Transfer to a 4 cup shallow baking dish, sprinkle cheese on top. Bake 10 to 15 minutes, or until completely heated. Can be prepared ahead of time, but don't heat until ready to serve.

Serve with tortilla chips and vegetables.

Warm Blue Cheese Dip

1   cup chopped pecans
3   tablespoons melted butter, divided
2   (8 ounce) packages cream cheese
2   (4 ounce) packages blue cheese
1   cup soft bread crumbs
¼   cup chopped parsley

Preheat oven to 350°. In small skillet, toast pecans in 2 tablespoons butter. Cool.

Place cheeses in a food processor and process until smooth. Stir in pecans. Place mixture in a greased shallow casserole. Combine bread crumbs, parsley and 1 tablespoon butter. Sprinkle on top of cheese. Bake for 25 minutes.

Serve warm with crackers and pear slices.

Glazed Bologna

1	large circumference, whole bologna (3-4 pounds)
1	cup ketchup
⅓	cup melted margarine
1½	tablespoons Worcestershire sauce
1½	tablespoons prepared mustard
1½	teaspoons onion salt

Preheat oven to 350°. Score bologna diagonally, ¼ inch deep.

Place in pan. Cover with foil and bake for 1-1¼ hours.

Combine remaining ingredients for sauce. Brush on frequently for last 15 minutes of cooking.

Slice ¼ inch thick. Cut each slice into quarters and place on a plate with toothpicks and Dijon mustard.

24 SERVINGS

Fresh Tomato Bruschetta

8	ripe plum tomatoes, seeded and diced
2	tablespoons finely minced garlic
½	cup coarsely chopped fresh basil
¼	cup finely chopped fresh parsley
1	tablespoon fresh lemon juice
½	tablespoon extra virgin olive oil
1	teaspoon finely minced fresh tarragon
¼	teaspoon crushed red pepper flakes
2	baguettes, cut in ½ inch thick slices
6	cloves garlic, cut in half

In a bowl, mix all ingredients except bread and garlic cloves. Add salt and pepper to taste. Set aside, unrefrigerated for 3 hours.

Preheat oven to 350°. Toast bread on a baking sheet. Rub cut side of garlic on each slice and top with tomato mixture.

Caponata

Can be made 2 days ahead.

5   tablespoons olive oil

1-1½ pounds eggplant, unpeeled, cut
       into ½ inch cubes

1   medium onion, cubed

4   large garlic cloves, chopped

1   (14½ ounce) can diced tomatoes in
       juice with Italian seasonings

3   tablespoons red wine vinegar

2   tablespoons drained capers

⅓   cup shopped fresh basil

     toasted pine nuts

Heat oil in a heavy large pot over medium heat. Add eggplant, onion, and garlic cloves. Sauté until eggplant is soft and brown, about 15 minutes. Add diced tomatoes with juice, then red wine vinegar and drained capers. Cover and simmer until eggplant and onion are very tender, stirring occasionally. Cook about 12 minutes. Season caponata to taste with salt and pepper. Mix in fresh basil. Transfer caponata to serving bowl. Sprinkle with toasted pine nuts. Serve warm, at room temperature or cold. Cover and chill.

Mom's Cheese Ball

1   (8 ounce) package cream cheese,
       softened

5   ounces Bleu cheese

⅛   teaspoon garlic salt

2   tablespoons chopped green pepper

2   tablespoons chopped pimento

     chopped walnuts

Using your hands, combine cheeses and blend together well. Add next 3 ingredients and blend them into cheese mixture. Form a ball and chill in refrigerator until it can be handled easily. Then roll in chopped walnuts. Refrigerate, preferably 24 hours and serve with crackers of your choice.

# Cheese Pennies

4	**tablespoons butter**
1	**cup grated Cheddar cheese**
½	**cup sifted flour**
¼	**teaspoon salt**
	dash cayenne pepper
¼	**teaspoon dry mustard**
	caraway seeds
	poppy seeds

Preheat oven to 350°. Cream butter until light and fluffy. Add cheese and beat. Sift dry ingredients together, and add. Mix well.

Shape into a roll about 1¼ inches wide. Wrap in waxed paper and refrigerate until firm. Slice dough into ¼ inch rounds and place on cookie sheet. Sprinkle top with caraway or poppy seeds.

Bake for 8-10 minutes, or until lightly browned. Cool on rack. Store in airtight container. Serve with cocktails, soups or salads.

Cheese Wafers

May be served warm or cold.

2	**cups flour**
1	**cup soft butter**
2	**cups grated Parmesan cheese**
1½	**teaspoons salt**
⅛	**teaspoons pepper**
	dash cayenne
2	**tablespoons poppy seeds**
2	**tablespoons water**
1	**egg slightly beaten**

Preheat oven to 400°. Combine flour and butter, using fork or pastry blender. Add cheese, salt, pepper, cayenne and poppy seeds. Sprinkle with water and shape into ball.

Roll out on unfloured board to ¼ inch thickness. Cut into rounds with 2 inch cutter.

Place on ungreased cookie sheet, brush with beaten egg and bake for 12-15 minutes or until golden brown. Cool on racks.

40 PIECES

 **Duffy's Cheese Ball**

½ **pound cream cheese**
½ **pound Cheddar cheese**
⅓ **cup chopped scallions**
⅓ **cup chopped stuffed green olives**
¼ **cup chopped black olives**
2 **tablespoons dry sherry**

Bring cheeses to room temperature and mix all ingredients well. Roll into a ball and chill.

Serve with plain crackers.

Turkey Bacon with Goat Cheese and Pear

16 **thin slices turkey bacon, about 2 inches in length**
16 **teaspoons soft fresh goat cheese (from 5 ounce log)**
2 **very ripe small pears, halved, cored, cut into ¼ inch thick slices**
   fresh thyme leaves

Preheat oven to 450°. Place turkey bacon slices in single layer on large rimmed baking sheet. Sprinkle with pepper. Bake until crisp, about 10 minutes. Using spatula, slide turkey bacon onto platter. Top each with 1 teaspoon goat cheese and 1 pear slice. Sprinkle with thyme and serve.

 **Tiny Cheese Tarts**

   dough, for 9 inch double crust pie
4 **eggs, beaten**
6 **ounces Swiss cheese, grated**
4 **ounces Cheddar cheese, grated**
2 **tablespoons grated Parmesan cheese**
⅔ **cup milk**
¾ **teaspoon salt**
¼ **teaspoon pepper**
   dash of nutmeg

Preheat oven to 425°. Line miniature muffin tins with dough which has been rolled quite thin. Refrigerate.

Combine remaining ingredients, stir well, and fill each section ⅔ full.

Bake for 15 minutes. Serve warm.

4 DOZEN

Goat Cheese Torta

2   **(8 ounce) packages cream cheese, softened**

7-8   **ounces mild goat cheese**

1   **teaspoons snipped fresh oregano or 1 teaspoon dried oregano, crushed**

⅛   **teaspoon freshly ground pepper**

¼   **cup prepared pesto**

½   **cup sun-dried tomatoes, packed in oil**

1-2   **tablespoons slivered almonds, toasted**

Line 1 quart loaf pan with clear plastic wrap.

Combine cream cheese and goat cheese, garlic, oregano, and pepper. Use food processor or beat with electric mixer until smooth.

Assemble as follows: spread ⅓ cheese mixture on the bottom of the pan. Top with pesto, spreading evenly. Layer with another ⅓ cheese mixture. Drain sun-dried tomatoes, reserving one tomato for garnish. Chop remaining tomatoes and spread evenly over cheese mixture. Top with remaining cheese.

Cover with plastic wrap and spread evenly over cheese mixture. Press gently to pack cheese. Chill several hours.

Uncover. Invert onto serving plate and remove plastic wrap. Garnish with thin slices of sun-dried tomato, toasted almonds and fresh oregano or parsley.

Parmesan Twists

These freeze well, in spiral form, unbaked

1 cup grated Parmesan cheese
1 cup sifted flour
  pinch of salt
1 teaspoon paprika
7 tablespoons sour cream
¼ cup butter

Blend cheese, flour, salt and paprika. Add sour cream and butter and work to make smooth dough. Chill 30 minutes.

Divide dough into 4 parts. Roll each section into a rectangle on floured board and cut into 5 x 1 inch strips. Twist into spirals.

Bake on an ungreased jelly-roll pan at 350° for 15 minutes or until golden.

Serve warm.

4 TO 5 DOZEN

Irene's Chicken Appetizer in Lettuce Wraps

1½ pounds boneless chicken breasts
⅓ cup hoisin sauce
4 teaspoons rice vinegar
1 tablespoon soy sauce
  lettuce

GARNISH
  basil
  mint leaves
  thinly slice scallion
  salted peanuts
  sliced jalapeño pepper, optional

Use one half of the sauce to marinate the chicken for 2 hours. Grill the chicken about 5 minutes each side. Let rest 10 minutes. Chop the chicken into small cubes. Mix the chicken cubes with the rest of the sauce.

Spoon the chicken into lettuce leaves. Garnish with basil, mint leaves, thinly sliced scallions, salted peanuts and sliced jalapeño pepper.

Barbecued Drumettes

2   pounds drumettes
       (drumstick side of chicken wing)
       garlic powder
½   cup honey
½   cup soy sauce
½   cup ketchup

Preheat oven to 375°. Place drumettes in pan, sprinkle with garlic powder, and bake for 15 minutes. Remove from oven.

Combine remaining ingredients, pour over chicken, and bake for 1 hour, basting as needed.

4 TO 5 SERVINGS

Chicken Nut Puffs

1   cup chicken broth (or bouillon)
½   cup salad oil
1½   teaspoons seasoned salt
1   teaspoon celery seed
1   tablespoon chopped parsley
2   teaspoons Worcestershire sauce
1   cup flour, sifted
4   eggs
1½   cups diced chicken
⅓   cup chopped almonds, optional

Combine broth, oil and seasonings in saucepan and bring to boil. Add flour and cook over low heat, beating rapidly until mixture leaves sides of pan and forms a smooth compact ball. Remove from heat.

Add eggs, one at a time, beating well after each addition until mixture is shiny. Stir in chicken and nuts.

Drop by teaspoonfuls onto greased baking sheets. Bake at 450° for 10-15 minutes until browned. Serve hot.

Puffs may be frozen and used as needed. Just heat and serve.

ABOUT 100 PUFFS

Teriyaki Chicken Wings

2   **pounds chicken wings**
      Teriyaki marinade
¼   **cup ketchup**
¼   **cup brown sugar**
¼   **cup white vinegar**
      head of lettuce

Marinate the chicken wings in Teriyaki for at least 2 hours. Preheat oven to 350°. Place chicken wings on a cookie sheet that has been sprayed with vegetable spray. Place the wings in oven for 30 minutes. Turn wings and cook for 15-25 minutes longer or until brown. Total cooking time is 1½ hours.

10 SERVINGS

Crusty Chicken Wings

2   **pounds chicken wings, disjointed**
½   **cup butter**
2   **teaspoons herb-seasoned salt, divided**
3   **cups Panko bread crumbs**

Melt margarine in small saucepan and add 1 teaspoon seasoned salt. Spread potato flakes on piece of waxed paper.

Dip wings in seasoned margarine, shaking off excess. Roll in Panko until completely coated. Place in 13 x 9 x 2 inch baking pan, sprinkle with remaining seasoned salt, and bake at 375° for 35 minutes or until chicken is golden brown and crisp.

6 SERVINGS

Deviled Eggs with Capers and Tarragon

Can be made four hours ahead.

6	hard-boiled eggs
2	tablespoons extra virgin olive oil
1	tablespoon mayonnaise
1½	teaspoons Dijon mustard
2	tablespoons minced celery
4	teaspoons chopped fresh tarragon
1	tablespoon minced drained capers
2	teaspoons minced shallot
	sliced celery

Shell eggs then cut in half lengthwise. Transfer yolks to small bowl and mash with a fork. Mix in oil, mayonnaise and mustard. Stir in minced celery, tarragon, capers and shallot. Season to taste with salt and pepper.

Spoon yolk mixture into whites. Garnish each with a celery slice. Cover loosely and refrigerate.

Almond Stuffed Figs

	dried figs
	almonds
	orange zest
1	cup dry red wine
¼	cup honey

Preheat oven to 350°. Remove stems from the dried figs and form a cup. Chop almonds and stuff them inside the dried figs.

In a small saucepan, heat the red wine and honey until dissolved.

Grease an ovenproof casserole with butter. Place figs (open side up) in the dish. Pour wine/honey mixture on top of the figs to cover them. Top with orange zest.

Cover the pan with aluminum foil and bake for 35 minutes. The mixture may be basted while baking.

Stuffed Grape Leaves

Johnson and Wales University College of Culinary Arts

80	grape leaves

STUFFING

1⅓	cups canned tomatoes
¼	cup tomato paste
2	tablespoons chopped green pepper
½	teaspoon allspice
½	teaspoon black pepper
2½	teaspoons salt
1	teaspoon paprika
1	pound ground lamb or half beef/ lamb
1¼	cups uncooked rice

STOCK

2	cups chicken stock
½	cup tomato juice
4	tablespoons lemon juice
1½	teaspoons salt
2	cloves garlic, crushed

Wash grape leaves in 3 changes of cold water.

Combine stuffing ingredients and mix thoroughly.

Spread out grape leaves, dull side up. Place 1½ tablespoons stuffing in lower quarter of each leaf and roll about ¾ inch thick and 3 inches wide.

Place a plate upside down in a pot. Arrange stuffed grape leaves in layers in pot on top of plate, alternating rows.

Combine ingredients for stock, heat to boiling and pour over stuffed grape leaves. Simmer until rice is done. Drain and serve with wedge of lemon and parsley garnish.

8 TO 12 SERVINGS

Chafing Dish Dogs

¾	cup prepared mustard
1	jar (10 ounce) currant jelly
2	pounds frankfurters, sliced on diagonal

Melt mustard and jelly over low heat. Add frankfurters.

When ready to serve, transfer to chafing dish.

Guacamole

1	tablespoon chopped onion
1	tablespoon chopped, seeded jalapeño peppers
1	tablespoon chopped fresh cilantro
½	teaspoon sea salt
2	ripe avocados
½	cup peeled, seeded and chopped tomatoes
1	teaspoon lime juice

In a food processor, pulse the onions, jalapeños, cilantro and salt until coarse. Halve and pit the avocados. Scoop the flesh into the onion mixture and pulse gently. Add tomatoes and lime juice and mix by hand.

Serve with corn chips or soft, heated corn tortillas.

Guacamole with Fresh Corn and Chipotle

Can be made 4 hours ahead.

2	large ripe avocados (about 1½ pounds), halved, pitted, peeled
1	tablespoon fresh lime juice
1	ear of fresh cooked corn
1	plum tomato, seeded, diced
2	green onions, chopped
1	canned chipotle chile, finely chopped
¼	cup sour cream

Mash avocados with lime juice in medium bowl. Using sharp knife, remove corn kernels from cob and add to avocado mixture. Stir in tomato and green onions. Combine chipotle and sour cream in small bowl; whisk to blend. Stir sour cream mixture into avocado mixture. Season with salt.

Place plastic wrap directly onto surface of guacamole and refrigerate. Bring to room temperature before serving.

Hummus

1   **can (20 ounces) chickpeas**
½   **cup fresh lemon juice**
2   **cloves garlic, chopped**
⅓   **cup tahini (sesame seed purée)**
     salt and pepper to taste

Drain chickpeas, reserving liquid. In blender, combine peas, lemon juice and garlic. Blend on medium speed until smooth. If necessary, add a little of reserved liquid.

Add tahini and continue blending until combined. Adjust seasoning.

Serve with pita bread cut into triangles.

6 SERVINGS

Vegetarian Chopped Liver

1   **large onion**
1   **can peas, drained (save juice)**
1   **cup chopped, walnuts**
     (can be chopped ahead and
     stored in the freezer)
2   **hard-boiled eggs**

Slice onion and then sauté. Process onions, peas, and walnuts in that order in the food processor. Add some juice if needed and then add eggs. Process until smooth, and add black pepper to taste. May be frozen or kept refrigerated at least one week.

Grilled Chicken Liver Crostini

Al Forno Restaurant's adaptation of a traditional Tuscan dish.

1   pound chicken livers, trimmed

2   large onions (8-10 ounces), peeled

2-3 tablespoons virgin olive oil

12 tablespoons unsalted butter, at
    room temperature

2   leaves fresh sage

¼   teaspoon minced fresh rosemary

⅛   teaspoon minced fresh ginger

½   cup freshly grated Parmigiano-
    Reggiano

¼   teaspoon kosher salt, optional

1   teaspoon minced fresh garlic

1   loaf Italian bread, cut into
    ½-inch-thick rounds

¼   cup chopped fresh Italian parsley

Prepare a charcoal grill, setting the grill rack about 4 inches above the coals.

Skewer the chicken livers and slice the onions horizontally ⅝ inch thick. Brush the livers and onion slices all over with the olive oil.

Grill the onion slices about 8 minutes per side, or until they are lightly charred but cooked through. Grill the livers 2-3 minutes per side so that they are medium-rare or still pink inside.

On a cutting board, coarsely chop the livers and onions. Combine them in a bowl with 4 tablespoons butter, the sage, rosemary, ginger and Parmigiano. Mash with fork until you have a chunky consistency. Taste and add salt if necessary.

Fold the garlic into the remaining 8 tablespoons of butter and spread it on both sides of bread slices. Grill the bread, toasting both sides. Spread each slice with some of the liver paste and serve immediately, garnished with parsley and additional Parmigiano.

8 TO 10 APPETIZER SERVINGS

Reprinted with permission from On Top of Spaghetti by Johanne Killeen and George Germon, published by William Morrow, an Imprint of Harper Collins Publishers.

Sweet and Sour Meatballs

2   **pounds ground beef**
1   **(16 ounce) can whole cranberry sauce**
1   **(12 ounce) jar chili sauce**
1   **bay leaf**
1   **small onion, grated**
    salt and pepper to taste

Season meat as desired and form into balls.

Put sauces in medium (3 quart) pot, add bay leaf and onion, and bring sauce to low boil.

Drop meatballs into hot sauce and cook on low for 1-1½ hours.

Serve as appetizer or main course over rice.

60 MEATBALLS

Tiny Meatballs with Marmasoy Dip

1   **egg**
½   **cup bread crumbs**
2   **tablespoons prepared horseradish**
1   **cup water chestnuts, chopped fine**
1   **pound ground beef**
½   **cup water**

DIP

⅓   **cup orange marmalade**
1   **clove garlic, minced**
¼   **cup soy sauce**
2   **tablespoons lemon juice**
⅓   **cup water**

Preheat oven to 350°. Beat egg and water. Add crumbs, beef, water chestnuts and horseradish. Mix gently. Shape into balls 1 inch in diameter. Place balls on jelly-roll pan and bake for 12 minutes. Serve in chafing dish with dip in a separate bowl.

DIP

Place all ingredients in pan and heat to boiling. Serve hot.

40 TO 45 MEATBALLS

Mushrooms with Anchovy Stuffing

1	pound mushrooms
¼	cup olive oil
1	(2 ounce) can flat anchovy fillets
1	garlic clove, finely minced
1	teaspoon fresh lemon juice
¾	cup bread crumbs
¼	cup minced parsley
	black pepper to taste

Preheat oven to 350°. Wash mushrooms. Remove and chop stems and sauté in 3 tablespoons of the oil for 3 minutes. Chop anchovies, mix with remaining ingredients, add chopped stems and mix well.

Fill caps with mixture. Place in shallow baking pan and sprinkle with remaining oil.

Bake for 15 minutes.

30 MUSHROOMS

Mushroom Hors d'Oeuvres

1¼	cups mushrooms, chopped
½	cup chopped onions
2	tablespoons butter
1	teaspoon flour
½	teaspoon seasoned salt
¼	teaspoon thyme
	dash of cayenne
1	package refrigerated crescent rolls (8 triangles)

Preheat oven to 400°. Sauté mushrooms and onions in butter. Stir in flour and seasonings. Cool.

Separate triangles and cut each in half. Roll to enlarge each half.

Put some of mushroom mixture on each triangle, fold over and crimp with fork to seal edges.

Bake for 15-20 minutes or until brown.

16 SERVINGS

Marinated Mushrooms

1	pound fresh mushrooms
1	teaspoon salt
	freshly ground black pepper to taste
1	teaspoon oregano
5	tablespoons wine vinegar
1	tablespoon lemon juice
1	cup olive oil
2	cloves garlic, split

Slice mushrooms. Add remaining ingredients, mixed together and toss lightly. Let stand at room temperature several hours. To keep more than a day or two, refrigerate in a covered container.

Serve with toothpicks for hors d'oeuvres.

ABOUT 1½ QUARTS

Roquefort Mushrooms

2	dozen mushrooms, bite size
	bowl of salted water
	lemon juice
¼	cup sour cream
2	ounces blue cheese
2	teaspoons Worcestershire sauce
2	teaspoons grated onion
½	teaspoon curry powder
¼	cup chopped pecans or Macadamia nuts
	tiny tips of watercress

Rinse mushrooms and place in salted water with a few drops of lemon juice for 10 minutes. Drain. Remove stems and blot mushrooms dry.

Blend remainder of ingredients and fill caps with mixture. Chill.

Garnish with watercress.

2 DOZEN

Stuffed Mushrooms

20	large mushroom caps
4	tablespoons melted butter
1	small onion, minced
1	cup bread crumbs
	salt and pepper to taste
	pinch oregano
½	cup grated Havarti cheese
3	tablespoons dry sherry

Preheat oven to 400°. Wipe mushrooms with damp paper towel and dip in butter. Place close together in shallow pan.

Pour remaining butter into frying pan and cook onions until golden. Add crumbs, seasonings and cheese. Mix well and add sherry.

Spoon mixture into mushrooms and bake for 10 minutes.

20 MUSHROOMS

Olive Spread with Walnuts

Can be prepared up to 3 days ahead.

1¾	cups pitted Kalamata olives, rinsed
¼	cup plus 3 tablespoons of toasted walnuts, chopped, divided
¼	cup olive oil
2	teaspoons coarse grain Dijon mustard
1	garlic clove minced
1	teaspoon chopped fresh thyme
1	teaspoon chopped fresh oregano
1	teaspoon chopped fresh sage
	pinch of cayenne pepper

Finely chop olives and 3 tablespoons of walnuts in the food processor. Add olive oil, mustard, garlic, thyme, oregano, sage and cayenne pepper. Process until coarsely puréed. Stir in remaining ¼ cup walnuts.

Serve with French bread toasted with olive oil until golden brown.

Marinated Olives

1	(7 ounce) can green pitted olives, drained
1	(7 ounce) can pitted black olives, drained
1	tablespoon chopped fresh parsley
1	clove garlic, crushed
3	tablespoons olive oil
¼	teaspoon salt
	dash of freshly ground pepper

Combine ingredients in a sterile jar. Refrigerate, covered, several days to develop flavor.

ABOUT 1 PINT

Caramelized Onion Dip

1	tablespoon vegetable oil
2	cups thinly sliced onion
¾	cup mayonnaise
¾	cup sour cream
1	teaspoon salt
1	teaspoon ground black pepper
	potato chips for serving

Heat oil in a heavy medium saucepan over a medium-low heat. Add onions. Cover and cook until onions are a rich golden brown, stirring frequently. Approximately 20 minutes. Be patient, the onions need to caramelize and turn a deep golden brown. Remove from heat and let cool.

Whisk together mayonnaise and sour cream in a medium bowl to blend. Stir in the cooled caramelized onions, salt and pepper. Cover dip and refrigerate until flavors blend, about 2 hours.

Garlic Pita Chips

1   package regular size pita bread
    vegetable spray
1   (6 ounce) container fresh shredded
    Parmesan cheese
    garlic powder

Preheat oven to 400°. Cut pita bread in half so you have two circles. Spray each half with vegetable spray. Put the sprayed halves together and then cut the circles in half and then in thirds.

Place the pieces sprayed side up on a cookie sheet. Sprinkle each chip with cheese and then garlic powder. Cook for 8-10 minutes or until slightly toasted.

Cheesy Sweet Potatoes

1   pound sweet potatoes, peeled
2½   ounces finely grated Parmigiano-
     Reggiano (about 1 cup)
2   egg whites
2   teaspoons chopped fresh rosemary
¾   teaspoon cracked black pepper
     parchment paper

Preheat oven to 425°. Finely grate sweet potatoes into a bowl. Squeeze grated sweet potatoes in batches to release as much moisture as possible and place in another bowl: fluff with a fork. Stir in cheese, egg whites, rosemary and pepper. Line a large cookie sheet with parchment paper. Spoon 1 rounded tablespoon batter onto cookie sheet and flatten into a thin 2 to 2½ inch round. Repeat with remaining batter, leaving 1 inch between rounds. Bake until edges and underside are crisp and browned, 13-15 minutes. Remove from oven, let cool slightly and remove from parchment.

# Polish Pirogi

FILLING

4	large potatoes
2	medium onions, chopped
12	ounces farmer cheese
	salt and pepper to taste

DOUGH

1	egg
2	cups flour
⅔	cup water
¼	teaspoon salt

FILLING

Boil and mash potatoes. Cool. Fry onions until golden brown. Mix all ingredients for stuffing and set aside.

DOUGH

Mix all ingredients (add more flour if necessary). Roll out dough and cut circles with 2½ inch diameter glass. Fill with about 1 teaspoon stuffing. Fold dough, pressing edges together well. Prepare all pirogi before boiling.

Place pirogi in a large pot of boiling water (not too many at one time). Stir lightly until they rise to surface. Boil for about another minute. Remove and rinse briefly under cold water. Spread out on a plate and boil the next batch.

Pirogis are best when fried in butter before serving, so they acquire a crisp, golden brown outside. They may be made several days before use and refrigerated.

4 TO 6 SERVINGS

Corn Salsa

1	jar fresh salsa
1	avocado, mashed
2	cold ears of corn with the corn removed or 1 can of corn
1	chopped green pepper
	fresh cilantro, chopped

Mix all ingredients together and serve.

Fruit Salsa

1   cup frozen raspberries
2   peaches (fresh or canned), peeled
      and chopped
2   kiwifruit, peeled and chopped
1   teaspoon lime zest
2   teaspoons lime juice
1   teaspoon sugar
2   bags cinnamon pita chips

Mix fruits, lime zest, lime juice and sugar. Refrigerate for 1 hour to combine flavors. Serve with cinnamon pita chips.

Nova Scotia Roll-Ups

½   cup cream cheese
½   cup sour cream
⅓   cup white horseradish, drained
6   slices Nova Scotia salmon
      capers
      lemon slices
      parsley

Beat cream cheese and sour cream, add horseradish and mix well. Spread mixture on salmon slices and roll up.

Place on plates and garnish with remaining ingredients.

May be served with slices of buttered pumpernickel bread.

6 SERVINGS

Spinach Balls

2   (10 ounce) packages frozen chopped
      spinach, cooked and well drained
2   cups stuffing mix
1   cup grated Parmesan cheese
6   eggs, beaten
      salt and pepper to taste
¾   cup butter, room temperature

Combine all ingredients well. Roll into walnut size balls. Freeze.

Preheat oven to 350°. Place spinach balls on baking sheet while still frozen. Bake for 10 minutes.

70 PIECES

Spanakopita

- ½ cup plus 1 tablespoon unsalted butter, divided
- 1 pound baby spinach
- ½ pound feta, crumbles (scant 2 cups)
- ½ teaspoon freshly grated nutmeg
- ½ teaspoon salt
- ½ teaspoon pepper
- 10 phyllo sheets, thawed if frozen

Melt 1 tablespoon butter in a 12 inch heavy skillet over moderate heat, then cook spinach, stirring until wilted and tender, about 4 minutes. Remove from heat and cool, about 10 minutes. Squeeze handfuls of spinach to remove as much liquid as possible, then coarsely chop. Transfer to a bowl and stir in feta, nutmeg, salt and pepper.

Preheat oven to 375°. Melt remaining ½ cup butter in a small saucepan, then cool. Cover phyllo stack with 2 overlapping sheets of plastic wrap and then a dampened kitchen towel.

Take 1 phyllo sheet from stack (keeping remaining sheets covered) and arrange on a work surface with long side nearest you and brush with some butter. Top with another phyllo sheet and brush with more butter. Cut buttered phyllo stack crosswise into 6 (roughly 12 by 2¾ inch) strips.

Put a heaping teaspoon of filling near 1 corner of a strip on end nearest you, then fold corner of phyllo over to enclose filling and form a triangle. Continue folding strip (like a flag), maintaining triangle shape. Put triangle, seam side down, on a large baking sheet and brush top with butter. Make more triangles in same manner, using all of phyllo.

Bake triangles in middle of oven until golden brown, 20 to 25 minutes. Then transfer to a rack to cool slightly.

Barbecued Meat Strips

1½ pounds boneless sirloin steak
⅔ cup soy sauce
¼ cup brown sugar
¼ cup dry sherry
1 tablespoon oil
1 teaspoon ginger
1 garlic clove, minced

Cut steak into strips 6 inches long, 1½ inches wide and ⅛ inch thick. This is easier to do if steak is partially frozen.

Combine remaining ingredients for marinade. Pour over steak and marinate 1 hour or more. Thread on skewers.

Barbecue on grill 4 inches above heat or broil in oven a little closer to heat. Turn often until steak is done as desired.

12 SERVINGS

Teriyaki Round Steak Roll-Ups

1½ pounds top round steak, ¾ inch thick
1 tablespoon brown sugar
1 teaspoon ginger
1 (13½ ounce) can pineapple chunks, drained (reserve syrup)
½ cup soy sauce
½ cup salad oil
1 clove garlic, minced

Partially freeze steak for easy slicing. Cut meat into strips 3 inches long by ⅛ inch thick. Place in plastic bag. Mix brown sugar and ginger in small bowl. Stir reserved pineapple syrup into brown sugar mixture. Stir in soy sauce, salad oil and garlic. Pour over meat. Tie bag tightly and refrigerate overnight.

Cut pineapple chunks in half. Roll each steak strip around pineapple half. Secure with wooden toothpick. Broil 3-4 inches from heat, 2 minutes on each side.

60 TO 80 ROLL-UPS

Tuscan Marinated Vegetable Platter

This appetizer platter from Chef Lori Buannano at the Rhode Island Convention Center was a favorite for many who attended the 2008 Miriam Hospital Gala.

ARTICHOKES

	artichokes, jar or canned, in their own natural juice
½	cup olive oil
3	cloves roasted garlic
1	tablespoon chopped fresh parsley
1	cup red wine vinegar
½	cup honey
½	tablespoon thyme

MUSHROOMS

1	cup red wine vinegar
4	whole bay leaves
½	tablespoon thyme
	garlic cloves
	red pepper flakes
	salt
	pepper
½	cup basil oil
½	tablespoon chopped fresh basil
1	red bell pepper, julienned
	mushrooms, cleaned

EGGPLANTS

1-2	fresh eggplants
	rosemary oil
½	tablespoon oregano
½	cup basil oil
1	tablespoon hopped fresh basil
	salt and pepper to taste

Prepare and marinate each vegetable separately. The quantities of the vegetables vary with personal preferences and you can marinate as much as you would like.

Artichokes: Mix artichoke marinade ingredients together and toss gently with drained artichokes. Cover and refrigerate overnight.

Mushrooms: Make a broth with the red wine vinegar, bay leaves, thyme, red pepper flakes and salt and pepper. Cook mushrooms. Chill and marinate overnight with mixture of basil oil, fresh chopped basil, julienne of red pepper and salt and pepper to taste.

Eggplants. Slice the eggplants lengthwise, drizzle with rosemary oil, and roast for 30 minutes. Chill and julienne the roasted eggplant. Season to taste with salt and pepper. Marinate with basil oil, oregano and fresh basil and refrigerate overnight.

WHITE BEANS

1	(15 ounce) can white beans, rinsed and drained
4	cloves roasted garlic
½	tablespoon fresh basil
1	cup diced tomato
½	cup virgin olive oil
	salt and pepper to taste

White Beans: Combine beans with remaining ingredients. Cover and refrigerate overnight.

Arrange on a platter and serve with rustic breads.

Smoked Salmon Crostini

Whole Foods Market

24	thin rounds of bread, cut on the diagonal from a baguette
	extra virgin olive oil
8	ounces cream cheese, softened
1½	tablespoons finely chopped dill
2	tablespoons very finely chopped red onion
1	teaspoon fresh ground black pepper
8	ounces pre-sliced smoked salmon
2-3	tablespoons capers
	fresh dill sprigs for garnish
	lemon wedges to garnish platter

Preheat oven to 350°. Brush the bread on one side with olive oil and place oil side up, on a baking sheet. Bake 8-10 minutes until just crisp and slightly golden. Do not over toast. Set aside to cool.

In a small bowl, blend together cream cheese, dill, onion and black pepper. Place in a pastry bag with a large tip or use a small spoon to place a dollop on the center of each toast. Cut salmon slices in half or thirds and fold a bite-sized slice over each toast. Garnish with capers and fresh dill sprigs. Place on a large platter with lemon slices.

2 DOZEN

Mini Tomato and Mozzarella Skewers

Can be prepared, covered and chilled for up to 8 hours.

20-25   bocconcini (mini marinated
       mozzarella balls)
2   tablespoons chopped fresh
       parsley
1   tablespoon chopped fresh chives
20-25   small cherry tomatoes
40   small fresh basil leaves
       skewers or toothpicks

Cut the bocconcini in half and put in a bowl with olive oil, parsley and chives plus ¼ teaspoon salt and ½ teaspoon of fresh ground black pepper. Cover and refrigerate for a least 1 hour, preferably over night.

Cut each cherry tomato half and thread one half on a small skewer or toothpick, followed by a basil leaf, then bocconcini, another basil leaf and the other half of the tomato. Repeat with more skewers and the remaining ingredients and serve.

Vegetable Crescent Squares

1   package crescent rolls
1   (8 ounce) package cream cheese
1   dollop mayonnaise
1   bunch green onions, chopped
1-2   cups chopped vegetables of your
       choice (some examples are carrots,
       green pepper or broccoli)

Flatten out crescent roll into a rectangle. Bake on a cookie sheet according to package directions. After crescent roll cools 1-2 minutes, move to a cooking rack to finish cooling.

Soften cream cheese. Mix cream cheese with mayonnaise and green onions. Spread mixture onto crescent roll. Put chopped vegetables onto cream cheese mixture. Use a spatula to gently press vegetables down. Refrigerate for 1 to several hours. Cut into small squares before serving.

Simply *More* Soups

A "pushke" or collection box was used in 1914 to collect coins for the vital work
of the Miriam Hospital Association.

"Yes, Esther dear, I'll bring you all the kosher meals you want.
Yes, Chicken Soup, too, especially Chicken Soup."

In the late 1800's, the immigrant communities of Providence, Rhode Island witnessed starvation and congestion. Facilities for providing organized care for the indigent sick were inadequate. Hospitals were considered dreadful, terrible places where those in charge neither understood nor cared to understand the patient's problems. It was considered a loss of respect to allow a relative to be taken to a hospital.

All their activities to care for the indigent sick strengthened the resolve of the women of the "Miriam Society No. 1" to establish a Jewish hospital where Jewish patients could feel comfortable, but "with a non-sectarian spirit where all could come for healing". In 1907 the women, now reorganized as The Miriam Hospital Association, received a charter from the Secretary of State, for the purpose of "...building, maintaining, and operating a Hebrew Hospital." They undertook solicitation of annual subscriptions for a building fund and began to build a bank account.

The women went from house to house, often climbing two and three flights of stairs, with little tin collection boxes, called "pushkes" in which to collect coins on behalf of the building fund. They collected membership dues of $1 per year, payable in monthly installments.

Simply More Soups

Asparagus and Leek Chowder

Sensational!

3	cups sliced mushrooms, about ½ pound
3	large leeks sliced
1	(10 ounce) package frozen cut asparagus, thawed
6	tablespoons butter or margarine
3	tablespoons flour
½	teaspoon salt
	dash pepper
2	cups chicken broth
2	cups light cream
1	(12 ounce) can white corn, drained
1	tablespoon chopped pimiento
	dash crushed saffron

In a large saucepan, cook mushrooms, leeks and asparagus in butter until tender but not brown, about 10 minutes. Stir in flour, salt and pepper. Add broth and cream to mixture. Cook, stirring until thickened and bubbly. Stir in remaining ingredients. Heat through but do not boil. Adjust seasoning.

6 TO 8 SERVINGS

Broccoli Soup

4	cups broccoli
1	cup chopped onion
3	cups chicken broth
1	teaspoon thyme
1	bay leaf
¼	teaspoon garlic powder
4	tablespoons butter
4	tablespoons flour
½	teaspoon salt
½	teaspoon pepper
2	cups milk

Place broccoli, onion, broth, thyme, bay leaf and garlic powder in a saucepan and bring to a boil. Simmer for 10 minutes. Remove bay leaf and pour mixture into blender or food processor. Process for 30 seconds.

Using the same saucepan, melt the butter and slowly blend in flour. Add salt and pepper and mix well. Slowly stir in the milk and heat until it begins to bubble. Pour in broccoli purée and bring back to a boil. Reduce heat and simmer until ready to serve.

This soup can be frozen.

4 TO 6 SERVINGS

Avegolemeno

Greek Lemon Chicken Soup

½   cup round or short grain rice
6   cups chicken broth
1   tablespoon olive oil
¼   teaspoon Greek oregano, optional
2   eggs
2   tablespoons lemon juice
6-8 very thin lemon slices
½   cup diced cooked chicken, optional
     salt and pepper to taste
     chopped fresh parsley for garnish

Boil rice in chicken broth, olive oil and oregano until tender.

Beat eggs with lemon juice and add ½ cup hot broth to eggs, beating constantly. Meanwhile, simmer lemon slices gently in broth.

Remove soup from heat, add egg mixture back into pot and stir well to get desired creamy effect. Add chicken. Reheat if necessary on low heat, being careful not to boil and cause eggs to curdle.

Garnish each serving with a slice of lemon and chopped parsley.

6 SERVINGS

Butternut Squash, Cabbage and Cannellini Bean Soup

Capriccio's Restaurant in Providence, Rhode Island

¼   cup unsalted butter
1   small white onion, diced
3   celery stalks, diced
1   large butternut squash, shredded
1   medium carrot, diced
½   head white cabbage, shredded
12   cups good chicken stock
1   (32 ounce) can cannellini beans

Add butter, onion, celery, carrot, cabbage and squash to an 8 quart pan. Sweat and cook for 5 minutes, stirring occasionally. Add chicken stock and cannellini beans. Bring to a boil.

Lower the heat and let simmer for 1 hour. Season to taste with salt and pepper.

1 GALLON

The restaurant cooks its cannellini beans in house, but the chef provided the canned equivalent here for easy home cooking.

Black Bean Soup

1	pound black beans
¼-½	cup olive oil
2	medium yellow onions, diced
4	garlic cloves, crushed
2	quarts water
1	tablespoon plus ½ teaspoon ground cumin
½	tablespoon oregano
2	bay leaves
½	tablespoon salt
1	teaspoon pepper
1	tablespoon parsley flakes
½	medium red pepper diced
½	tablespoon brown sugar
½	tablespoon lemon juice
2	tablespoons sherry, optional
	sour cream for garnish, optional

Soak black beans in water overnight. Drain in colander.

In large soup pot, sauté onions and garlic in olive oil until tender. Add drained beans and water to the pot. Stir in 1 tablespoon cumin and other seasonings. Bring to a boil, reduce heat and cook, uncovered and stirring occasionally, for about 2 hours until beans are tender and liquid is reduced by at least half. Stir in red pepper, ½ teaspoon cumin, brown sugar, lemon juice and sherry. Cook for another 30 minutes, stirring frequently. Serve plain or with a dollop of sour cream.

10 SERVINGS

Carrot Ginger Soup

2	tablespoons olive oil
1	medium onion, chopped
3	tablespoons finely chopped fresh gingerroot
2	cloves garlic, minced
3	cups chopped carrots
1	medium potato, peeled and chopped
8	cups broth
	salt to taste
	white pepper to taste
	dash of sherry, optional
	chopped fresh parsley for garnish

In a large pot, sauté onion, ginger and garlic in olive oil until onion is tender, but not browned. Add carrots, potato and broth. Bring to a boil, cover and reduce heat. Cook for 35-45 minutes or until vegetables are tender. Cool slightly.

Purée the soup in batches in a blender or food processor. Add salt and white pepper to taste. Add sherry if desired. Rewarm if necessary. Garnish with chopped parsley.

4 TO 6 SERVINGS

Chicken Gumbo

An easy, delicious version of a Cajun classic.

1   (16 ounce) can cut okra, drained
1   onion, chopped
1   green pepper, chopped
3   tablespoons margarine
4   cups chicken stock
1   (16 ounce) can tomatoes
1   bay leaf
    salt and pepper to taste
1   cup diced cooked chicken
1   tablespoon snipped parsley
3   cups hot cooked rice

In a large saucepan, melt margarine and sauté okra, onion and green pepper until onion is tender. Add flour, stir well. Slowly add broth, stirring constantly. Add tomatoes and bay leaf. Simmer for 15 minutes. Season to taste. Add chicken and parsley. Heat through and serve in bowls over rice.

6 SERVINGS

Matzo Balls

4   extra large eggs, at room
     temperature
½   teaspoon salt
¼   teaspoon pepper
⅓   cup hot water
¼   cup vegetable oil
1½   cups matzo meal
2   quarts water
1   tablespoon salt

Beat eggs, salt and pepper with fork. Stir in water and chicken fat. Add matzo meal and beat with a wire whisk. Refrigerate for 20 minutes. Put water and salt in large soup pot and set on heat to boil.

Wet hands in cold water and take approximately 2 tablespoons of mixture in palm. Form gently into balls. Drop into boiling water and cook 20 minutes. Remove with slotted spoon and serve in chicken soup.

10 TO 12 SERVINGS

Chicken Soup

1	whole chicken, cut up if desired
3-4	quarts water
4	carrots, cut into thirds
1-2	parsnips, cut in thirds
3	stalks celery with leaves
1	onion, left whole with skin
1	turnip, optional
2-4	garlic cloves
	handful of parsley
1	teaspoon whole peppercorns
	salt to taste

Wash chicken thoroughly and cut off excess fat. Place chicken pieces in a large soup pot and cover with water. Bring to a boil and reduce to medium or medium-high heat. Skim off foam.

Add vegetables, herbs and spices. Bring to a second boil and then reduce to a low, gentle simmer. Cook for several hours until chicken is tender.

With a slotted spoon, remove chicken to a separate bowl. Strain out vegetables and herbs and discard. Strain through cheesecloth if you want a very clear broth. Wash soup pot well and return broth to pot. Refrigerate overnight. Skim off excess fat when cooled.

Pull meat off bones and use in soup or for other purposes such as chicken salad.

Prior to serving, add chopped chicken and desired vegetables such as freshly chopped carrots, celery and parsnips. Gently simmer until vegetables are softened.

Serve with noodles and/or matzo balls.

Vegetarian Chili

Mary M. Flynn, PhD, RD, LDN is a research dietician at The Miriam Hospital and Brown University.

¾ cup extra virgin olive oil

1 medium red pepper, chopped

1 medium green pepper, chopped

1 medium red onion, chopped

   salt to taste

2 teaspoons chipotle chili pepper or chili powder

½ teaspoon celery salt

1 (28 ounce) can crushed tomatoes

1 (16 ounce) can kidney beans, drained and rinsed

1 (16 ounce) can black beans, drained and rinsed

4 cups cooked brown rice

Heat olive oil in a large pan over medium heat. Add the peppers and onions, stir to combine with the oil and cook for about 15-20 minutes or until vegetables are translucent. Add salt if desired.

Sprinkle the cooked vegetables with chili pepper and celery salt. Stir to mix in evenly. Add tomatoes and beans. Stir to combine. Reduce heat to medium low and simmer for at least 45 minutes, stirring occasionally. Serve with brown rice.

6 SERVINGS

The chili can also be simmered all day in a crockpot.

Cucumber Soup

2 large cucumbers, peeled

3 cups chicken broth

2 cups plain yogurt

1½-2 teaspoons chopped dill or curry powder

   salt and freshly ground pepper to taste

Halve cucumbers, remove seeds and cut into 1 inch pieces. Purée cucumbers with 1 cup broth in blender. Add remaining ingredients and serve very cold.

6 TO 8 SERVINGS

Betsy's Easy Elegant Escarole Soup

1   head escarole
5   cups chicken broth
      grated Parmesan cheese

Wash escarole thoroughly. Drain. Break up with hands.

Boil broth, add escarole and cook 20 minutes.

Top each serving with grated cheese.

6 SERVINGS

Jane's Gazpacho

Comes directly from Madrid. Caraway seeds add a unique touch.

1   teaspoon caraway seeds
2¾   teaspoons coarse salt
4-5   cloves garlic
6-8   slices old white bread
6   tomatoes, fresh or canned
½   onion
½   green pepper
1   cucumber
4   tablespoons wine vinegar, divided
5-6   generous tablespoons olive oil, divided
2   cups water, divided
1   teaspoon ketchup
      lemon juice to taste
      pinch of sugar
      salt to taste

GARNISH

1   tomato, diced
1   cucumber, diced
1   green onion, chopped fine
1   onion, chopped
      croutons

Crush caraway seeds, salt and garlic with mortar and pestle.

Soak bread in water. Cut vegetables small enough to go in blender.

Add to blender: 4-5 slices bread with half of water squeezed out, tomatoes, onion, green pepper, cucumber, 2 tablespoons vinegar, 3 tablespoons olive oil, 1 cup water, half of herb mixture, ketchup to color and lemon juice. Blend until liquefied. Repeat until all ingredients are used. Add sugar and salt to taste. As you prepare this, you must keep tasting, adjusting amounts of vegetables and seasonings to your own taste.

Serve garnishes in separate bowls.

6 TO 8 SERVINGS

New Rivers Fresh Tomato Soup

This uncooked tomato soup from Bruce Tillinghast at New Rivers in Providence is simply the essence of garden fresh tomatoes. Don't even attempt this soup with hot house tomatoes.

3	pounds ripe large garden tomatoes, washed and unpeeled
1	generous teaspoon chopped garlic
1	teaspoon salt
	fresh ground pepper to taste
	juice of half a lemon or 2 tablespoons of balsamic vinegar, red or white.
¼	cup (approximately) extra virgin olive oil
	basil oil for garnish
6	large fresh basil leaves for garnish
	mixture of petals from 6 nasturtium flowers, optional

Coarsely chop the tomatoes, remove and discard any fibrous core. Toss with the garlic, salt, fresh ground pepper and lemon juice or vinegar. Macerate for 2 hours in the refrigerator.

In a blender, purée the chilled tomatoes and juices until smooth. Strain into a bowl to remove seeds and put mixture back into the blender. With the blender running add the olive oil to emulsify the soup. The amount of olive oil needed will vary with the water content of the tomatoes. The more water, the more oil needed. The color of the soup will actually get lighter as if cream has been added. The soup is actually vegan. Adjust the seasoning with salt, pepper and lemon juice or balsamic vinegar.

Serve chilled with basil leaves cut in a fine chiffonade (thin ribbons). Add the nasturtium petals if using and drizzle with the basil oil.

4 TO 6 SERVINGS

If you make the soup ahead of time, it may separate. It will emulsify again in the blender. You can leave it in the blender in the refrigerator just in case.

Lentil Soup

Mary M. Flynn, PhD, RD, LDN is a research dietician at The Miriam Hospital and Brown University.

½   **cup extra virgin olive oil, divided**
½   **cup red onion, chopped**
½   **cup chopped carrots**
     salt and pepper to taste
½   **cup celery**
1½ **cups dry lentils**
6   **cups vegetable broth**
     sprig of fresh thyme
2-3 **bay leaves**

Heat 4 tablespoons olive oil on medium heat in a large soup pan. Add the onions, stir to coat with oil and cook for about 5 minutes. Add the rest of the olive oil and the carrots and celery. Stir to mix in, reduce heat to low and cook for about 25 minutes. Salt and pepper the vegetables if you like.

Add the vegetable broth, lentils and herbs. Raise heat to medium high and bring to a boil. Reduce heat to low, cover and cook for 45 minutes. You can add cooked brown rice, potatoes or barley to the soup.

8 SERVINGS

Red lentils make a thicker soup.

Red Pepper Soup

2   **red peppers, cored, seeded and chopped**
1½ **cups water**
1   **low sodium chicken bouillon cube**
¼   **teaspoon thyme**
1   **cup low-fat buttermilk**
     ground black pepper

In medium saucepan, combine peppers, water, bouillon and thyme. Bring to a boil, cover and simmer over medium-low heat for 10 minutes. Cool slightly. Transfer to a blender and purée until smooth. Add buttermilk and blend until combined.

Return to saucepan and heat through, but do not boil or cover. Refrigerate 4 hours, or until completely chilled. Dust with freshly ground black pepper before serving.

3 SERVINGS

Minestrone Soup

1   **(17 ounce) can cannellini beans, or ⅔ cup dried beans soaked overnight**

1   **tomato, squashed**

1   **bay leaf**

1   **peeled tomato**

      sea salt

      ground black pepper

      olive oil

2   **small red onions, chopped**

½   **head fennel, chopped**

3   **stalks celery, chopped**

3   **carrots, peeled and chopped**

3   **garlic cloves, minced**

      fresh basil, leaves and stems separated

2   **(14 ounce) cans plum tomatoes**

2   **zucchini, sliced and quartered**

¾   **cup red wine**

½   **head Swiss chard, washed and sliced with stalks**

2   **cups chicken or vegetable stock**

2   **ounces pasta**

      Parmigiano-Reggiano cheese

Add beans to a pot of water with bay leaf, squashed tomato and potato, cook until tender. Dried beans must be cooked for an hour; fresh beans 25 minutes. Drain and reserve half a glass of cooking water. Discard bay leaf, tomato, and potato. Season with salt, pepper and a bit of oil.

While beans are cooking, heat a little olive oil in a large saucepan. Add onions, carrots, celery, fennel, garlic and basil stems. Cook slowly on low heat with the lid ajar for 20 minutes until soft. Add tomatoes, zucchini and red wine; simmer 15 minutes.

Add Swiss chard, stock and beans. Put dried pasta into plastic bag and smash gently with rolling pin. Empty contents into soup, simmer until pasta is cooked.

At this point, soup may seem a bit thick. If so, add additional stock or reserved cooking water. To serve, garnish with torn basil leaves, a little olive oil drizzled on top and grate Parmigiano-Reggiano cheese.

6 TO 8 SERVINGS

Mushroom Bisque

1 pound fresh mushrooms
1 quart chicken broth
1 medium onion, chopped
7 tablespoons butter, divided
6 tablespoons flour
3 cups milk
1 cup heavy cream
1 teaspoon or more salt
   white pepper to taste
   Tabasco sauce to taste
2 tablespoons sherry, optional

Wash mushrooms and cut off stems. Slice 6 caps and reserve. Discard any dried ends from stems. Grind or chop fine remaining caps and stems. Simmer, covered, in broth with onion for 30 minutes.

Sauté sliced mushroom caps in 1 tablespoon butter and reserve for garnish.

Melt remaining butter in saucepan, add flour and stir with wire whisk until blended. Meanwhile bring milk to boil and add all at once to butter-flour mixture, stirring vigorously with whisk until sauce is thickened and smooth. Add cream.

Combine mushroom-broth mixture with sauce and season to taste with salt, pepper and Tabasco sauce. Reheat and add sherry before serving. Garnish with sliced caps.

8 SERVINGS

Vichyssoise

6 leeks, carefully cleaned and finely chopped
3 onions, finely chopped
¼ pound butter
2 quarts chicken stock
1 pound potatoes, peeled and sliced
1 teaspoon salt
1 teaspoon white pepper
1 cup heavy cream
1 cup sour cream
   chopped chives for garnish

Sauté leeks and onions in butter until just soft. Add stock, potatoes, salt and pepper. Cook until potatoes are tender.

Put mixture into blender and blend smooth. Add creams. Blend and chill or serve hot. Top each serving with a sprinkle of chives.

8 SERVINGS

Baked Onion Soup Arboretum

The Arboretum was a favorite restaurant in East Providence, Rhode Island and heralded new cuisine.

6	cups sliced Spanish onions
½	cup sweet butter
2	tablespoons flour
1½	quarts beef stock
2	bay leaves
	salt
	coarsely ground black pepper
½	cup dry white wine
	French bread, cut in 1 inch slices and oven toasted
6	slices Gruyère or Swiss cheese

Sauté onions in butter until soft and golden, stirring occasionally. Sprinkle flour over onions and mix. Add beef stock. Bring to a boil. Reduce heat, add bay leaves and cover. Let simmer 30-45 minutes. Taste and correct seasoning, adding salt and pepper to taste. Remove bay leaves. Add wine.

Preheat oven to 350°. Fill individual serving bowls or large casserole with soup. Top with toasted French bread and cheese slices. Bake until cheese browns lightly, about 15-20 minutes.

6 SERVINGS

Pumpkin Soup

4	green onions, chopped
1	onion, chopped
2	carrots, pared and sliced
3	tablespoons butter
1	(29 ounce) can pumpkin
5	cups chicken broth
	salt to taste
½	teaspoon garlic powder
2	tablespoons flour
1	tablespoon softened butter
1	cup whipping cream
½	cup small croutons for garnish

Sauté onions and carrots in melted butter until soft. Add broth and pumpkin. Add salt and garlic powder. Simmer 30 minutes.

Mix flour and softened butter and stir into soup. Bring to a boil. Remove from heat and cool slightly. Put mixture in blender and purée.

Return soup to saucepan, add cream and heat just to boiling point.

Serve garnished with croutons. May also be served cold.

8 SERVINGS

Spicy Creole Peanut Soup

This soulful soup from Bruce Tillinghast at New Rivers in Providence is great on a chilly winter night.

2	tablespoons vegetable oil
1	medium Spanish onion, diced small
3	medium celery ribs, diced small
1	large garlic clove, diced
1	tablespoons whole celery seed
2	tablespoons flour
¼	teaspoon cayenne pepper
2	(11½ ounce) cans of V-8 or tomato juice, or 1 of each
24	ounces whole milk (or use tomato juice can to measure almost equal amount)
1	(16-18 ounce) jar of smooth peanut butter
	salt
	lemon or lime juice
	Tabasco sauce
	toasted peanuts, chopped
	celery leaves from the center of the bunch, chopped

In a heavy bottom pan, heat the oil. Add the onion, celery, garlic and sauté until translucent.

Add the celery seed and the flour and stir to heat, and then add the tomato or V-8 juice. When hot add the peanut butter and cayenne. Heat, stirring until the peanut butter is melted. Add the milk in a constant stream stirring to incorporate. (The flour and peanut butter should keep the milk from curdling.) Lower the heat and simmer for 15 minutes, stirring occasionally so the bottom does not scorch. Do not boil. The onions and celery should retain a bit of crunch.

Adjust the seasoning. There is plenty of salt in the tomato juice and peanut butter so you may want to use a little lemon or lime juice to perk up the flavor. Add Tabasco to suit your taste and heat level.

Garnish the soup with chopped toasted peanuts and some chopped leaves from the center of the celery bunch.

Serve with a crisp curly endive or frisèe salad.

SERVES 6 TO 8

Tomato and Garlic Bisque

Red Stripe Restaurant in Providence

5   **pounds native large ripe tomatoes, vine ripened preferred**

2   **cloves garlic, peeled and mashed**

12   **stems fresh flat leaf parsley**

2   **quarts chicken stock**

½   **cup extra virgin olive oil**

1   **quart heavy cream**

1   **handful finely chopped basil leaves**

      salt

      pepper

Preheat oven to 375°. Cut tomatoes in half and arrange on a large baking tray along with garlic cloves, parsley stems, and olive oil. Sprinkle liberally with salt and pepper and bake for 30 minutes.

When roasted tomatoes are done, strain off excess juices and place mixture in blender. Blend on high for 1 minute until all ingredients are incorporated. Strain through a colander to catch tomato seeds and parsley stems.

On the stovetop, combine chicken stock and roasted tomato purée mixture. Cook over medium heat for 20 minutes, and then slowly add heavy cream. Reduce heat to low and let flavor of soup maturate.

To serve, place in bowl and top with freshly chopped basil and serve with crusty Italian bread.

6 TO 8 SERVINGS

Simply *More* Salads & Molds

Mary Grant has been called "the Mother of The Miriam Hospital."

In Russia, while only in her mid-teens, Mary Grant found herself responsible for her six younger brothers and sisters. Her father had left for America in hopes of earning enough money to send for his family and start a new life. While he was gone, his wife died in childbirth. It was up to Mary, as the eldest of the siblings, to care for the family. By working long days and nights as a milliner, and selling the family's remaining possessions, Mary was able to scrape together enough money for their passage to America. In 1885, she rejoined her father who had settled in New York. Determined to keep her family together, she married Louis Grant, a jeweler from Providence, Rhode Island who promised to love and care for them all. They moved to Willard Avenue, an immigrant community in South Providence, where she opened a millinery shop. Soon, Mary Grant and some of her friends established the "South Providence Ladies Aid Society". Small contributions were collected which enabled the society to offer interest free loans to people in the community to help them start small businesses. Soon there were many successful neighborhood businesses established and Mary became a neighborhood celebrity equally popular with both Irish and Jewish residents.

Her hat shop became a meeting place for her women's grass roots neighborhood assistance group. In 1897 she and the other women members of "Miriam Lodge No. 13" dedicated their days to providing care for those indigent immigrants who had become ill in this new land. Two years later, the women applied for a charter from the State of Rhode Island as "Miriam Society No.1". Mary Grant was elected president.

Arugula and Fennel Salad

Simple and very delicious.

1	pound arugula
½	fennel bulb, slice or shaved
½	Vidalia onion, thinly sliced
	juice of 1 lemon
3	tablespoons olive oil
1	teaspoon salt
	freshly ground black pepper to taste
	fresh Parmesan cheese

Wash and thoroughly dry arugula and place in a salad bowl. Add fennel and onion to salad.

Prepare dressing by whisking together lemon juice, olive oil and salt. Toss salad with dressing. Add freshly ground black pepper to taste. Top with fresh Parmesan cheese.

4 SERVINGS

 Antipasto Salad

1	(14 ounce) can chickpeas, drained
1	(6 ounce) jar marinated artichoke hearts, drained and quartered
1	(2 ounce) can anchovy fillets, drained and cut up
1	(4 ounce) jar pimientos, drained and diced
½	pound salami, cut into ¼ inch cubes
8	ounces mozzarella cheese, cut into ¼ inch cubes
12	pitted ripe olives
½	head iceberg lettuce, broken
1	celery heart, thinly sliced

DRESSING

6	tablespoons olive oil
5	tablespoons wine vinegar
1	teaspoon salt
½	teaspoon pepper

Combine dressing ingredients and shake well.

Combine salad ingredients in large bowl. Add dressing and toss lightly.

8 TO 10 SERVINGS

Bean Salad

1	(15 ounce) can cut green beans
1	(15 ounce) can red kidney beans
1	(15 ounce) can chickpeas
1	(8 ounce) can pitted ripe olives
1	red onion, thinly sliced
½	cup minced green pepper
½	cup olive oil
⅓	cup red wine vinegar
¼	cup Burgundy wine
½	cup sugar
¼	teaspoon dry basil
¼	teaspoon garlic powder
	salt to taste

Drain all beans well. Mix with all other ingredients. Cover and refrigerate several hours or preferably overnight.

12 SERVINGS

Black Bean, Corn and Mango Salad

A great accompaniment to grilled entrées.

3	ears corn
1	(15 ounce) can black beans, rinsed and drained
1	large ripe mango, peeled and diced
½	cup chopped red onion
½	cup diced red pepper
3	tablespoons lime juice
1	tablespoon olive oil
½	teaspoon dry cumin
¼	teaspoon salt or to taste
1	clove garlic, crushed
2-3	tablespoons chopped fresh cilantro
	dash cayenne pepper

Cook corn and cut kernels off the cob. Allow to cool and place in a large bowl. Add black beans, mango, red onion and red pepper. In a small bowl, whisk together lime juice, olive oil and spices. Stir in garlic and cilantro. Toss with corn, black beans and mango. Refrigerate at least one hour before serving.

8 SERVINGS

Can be served as a salsa with chips.

Roasted Beet Carpaccio with
Walnut Oil, Wild Arugula and Gorgonzola

Bacaro Restaurant in Providence

2   **cups aged red wine vinegar**
3   **shallots, minced**
3   **pounds beets**
     wild arugula
     radicchio
     crumbled Gorgonzola
     walnut oil

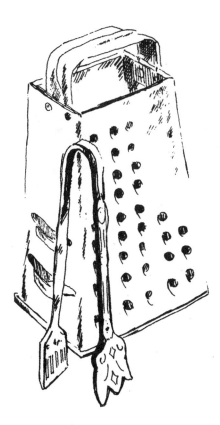

Prepare mignonette for the beets: Mix red wine vinegar and shallots together and allow to sit for 1 hour.

Preheat oven to 350°. Trim the beets, leaving the rootlets and 1 inch of the stem intact. Wash the beets and lay them on a piece of aluminum foil which is large enough to wrap the beets. Bring the 2 outside edges of the foil together and crimp. Crimp the left side of the foil to make a bag. Add 1 cup of water into the bag and crimp the last edge. Place beets in large baking pan. Roast for 1 hour or until the beets are easily pierced with a paring knife. Remove from the oven and allow to cool. Slip skins off the beets.

Slice the beets thin on a mandolin. Place around the plate, slightly overlapping. Brush the beets with the mignonette. Lightly salt the beets. Place a small salad of wild arugula and radicchio in the center of the plate. Sprinkle crumbled Gorgonzola over the beets. Drizzle walnut oil over the rocket.

Broccoli Salad

4	cups chopped fresh broccoli
½	cup raisins
¼	cup sunflower seeds, optional
½	cup chopped red onion
¼-½	cup soy imitation bacon bits
1	cup Miracle Whip
½	cup sugar
2	tablespoons apple cider vinegar

Mix first 5 ingredients together. In a small bowl, whisk together mayonnaise, sugar and apple cider vinegar. Toss with other ingredients. Refrigerate overnight.

8 SERVINGS

Asian Cabbage Salad

I	medium red or green cabbage, shredded
6	scallions, sliced
¼	cup slivered almonds
¼	cup toasted sesame seeds
1	package ramen noodles

DRESSING

⅓	cup rice wine vinegar
⅓	cup peanut oil
4-5	drops sesame oil
¼	teaspoon garlic powder
¼	cup sugar
1	teaspoon salt
¼	teaspoon pepper
	seasoning packet from ramen noodles

Mix dressing ingredients. Toss with cabbage, scallions, almonds and sesame seeds. Marinate at least 1 hour. Crumble ramen noodles and add just before serving.

6-8 SERVINGS

May substitute shredded napa cabbage for other cabbage.
May add diced chicken for a luncheon dish.

Perfect Cole Slaw

2	pounds cabbage
1	medium onion, diced
1	carrot, shredded
1	green pepper, diced
1	cup mayonnaise
1	teaspoon salt or to taste
¼	teaspoon pepper or to taste
3	tablespoons or more white vinegar
2	tablespoons or more sugar

Shred cabbage. Rub with a little salt. Add vegetables. Add remaining ingredients and mix well. Refrigerate several hours before serving.

12 SERVINGS

Purple Cabbage Salad

16	ounces shredded purple cabbage
⅓	cup chopped scallions
⅓	cup pine nuts
1	(8 ounce) bag shredded carrots
1	(11 ounce) can Mandarin oranges, reserving liquid
¼-½	cup dried cranberries

DRESSING

4	tablespoons brown sugar
½	teaspoon ground pepper
¼	teaspoon sea salt
4	tablespoons red wine vinegar
1	tablespoon reserved Mandarin orange juice
½	cup vegetable oil
1	teaspoon chicken bouillon
½	teaspoon garlic powder

Mix dressing ingredients in a jar and shake until mixed. Mix salad ingredients together and toss with dressing. Refrigerate at least 1 hour to allow flavors to mix.

8-10 SERVINGS

Caesar Salad

1-2 garlic cloves
1½ teaspoons salt, divided
4 anchovies
¼ teaspoon Worcestershire sauce
¼ teaspoon dry mustard
   juice of 1 lemon
3 tablespoons white wine vinegar
⅓ cup olive oil
1 raw or coddled egg, optional
½-1 cup shredded Parmesan cheese
   freshly ground black pepper
3-4 hearts of romaine lettuce
   croutons for garnish
   anchovies for garnish, optional

Coarsely chop garlic and mash together with a pinch of salt, preferably with a mortar and pestle, to make a soft paste. Put mixture into mixing bowl. Coarsely chop anchovies and mash into a paste and add to bowl. Add Worcestershire, mustard, salt, lemon and vinegar and then whisk in olive oil. Whisk in egg, Parmesan and black pepper. Keep adding Parmesan until mixture is very thick. If tasting, the dressing should be a very strong mix of garlic, anchovies and vinegar.

Chop lettuce into bite size pieces and toss with dressing. Adjust seasoning if necessary. Garnish with croutons and anchovies.

8 SERVINGS

Dressing can be made and refrigerated up to 4 hours in advance. Bring to room temperature for 20 minutes, whisk ingredients again, and toss salad.

Carrot Salad

3 large carrots, coarsely shredded
¼ cup olive oil
1 tablespoon vinegar
1 clove garlic, minced
   salt and pepper to taste

Mix all ingredients together and chill.

6 SERVINGS

Cauliflower Salad

1	medium cauliflower, separated into flowerets
2	medium zucchini, sliced
⅔	cup oil and vinegar dressing
	leaf lettuce
	pimiento or red pepper

Cook each vegetable in boiling salted water for 10 minutes, or until crispy tender. Remove with slotted spoon to shallow glass dish in separate mounds and pour on dressing. Cover and refrigerate 4-5 hours to blend flavors.

Line salad bowl with leaf lettuce and arrange ring of cauliflower around edge. Fill center with zucchini and garnish with pimiento cut in star (or other) shape.

8 SERVINGS

Cauliflower Spinach Salad

6	tablespoons olive oil
3	tablespoons wine vinegar
1	clove garlic, crushed
	salt and pepper
	dash of basil
3	cups fresh spinach, torn in bite size pieces
2	cups raw cauliflowerets
½	avocado, sliced and sprinkled with lemon juice
2	(11 ounce) cans Mandarin oranges, well-drained
½	cup dry roasted peanuts

Combine oil, vinegar, garlic and seasonings. Toss with remaining ingredients.

6 SERVINGS

# Chicken Salad

4	cups cubed cooked chicken (white meat)
1½	cups chopped celery
3	green onions, diced
1	(6 ounce) can water chestnuts, sliced
2	pieces candied ginger, minced
1	teaspoon salt
½	cup mayonnaise
½	cup toasted slivered almonds

Mix together chicken, celery, onions, water chestnuts, ginger and salt. Fold in mayonnaise. Chill. Serve garnished with almonds.

8 SERVINGS

Italian Couscous Salad

1	(16 ounce) package couscous
1	pint grape or plum tomatoes, halved and chopped
½	English seedless cucumber, chopped
1	medium summer squash, chopped
1	medium zucchini, chopped
1	(15 ounce) can cannellini or garbanzo beans, drained and rinsed

Cook the couscous according to package directions and let cool. Refrigerate for at least 2 hours or overnight.

In a large bowl, combine the chilled couscous with all the vegetables and beans. Add the dressing, toss well and serve.

8 SERVINGS

DRESSING

¼	cup olive oil
2	tablespoons balsamic vinegar
1	clove garlic, minced
6	basil leaves, chopped
1	tablespoon Parmesan cheese

Corn Salad

5	ears corn
½	cup diced red onion
3	tablespoons cider vinegar
3	tablespoons olive oil
½	teaspoon kosher salt
½	teaspoon freshly ground black pepper
½	cup basil leaves, chiffonade cut

Cook corn and place in ice water to shock. Cut kernels off the cob. Toss with remaining ingredients. Serve cold or at room temperature

4 TO 6 SERVINGS

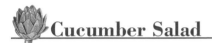
Cucumber Salad

2	large cucumbers
2	onions
½	cup mayonnaise
½	cup sour cream or plain yogurt
2	tablespoons vinegar
½	teaspoon salt
¼	teaspoon pepper
	pinch of sugar

Slice unpeeled cucumbers paper thin. Slice onions thinly and separate into rings. Blend cucumbers and onions with remaining ingredients. Refrigerate a few hours or overnight.

8 SERVINGS

Marinated Cucumbers

2	large cucumbers, peeled
1	large onion, sliced paper thin
2	tablespoons vinegar
½	teaspoon salt
¼	teaspoon pepper
1	tablespoon sugar

Score cucumbers lengthwise with fork and slice paper thin. Put in bowl with onion slices. Mix remaining ingredients together and pour over vegetables. Chill several hours before serving.

6 SERVINGS

Grilled Flank Steak Salad

A great summer entrée salad from Eastside Marketplace, Providence, Rhode Island.

MEAT PREPARATION

2	pounds certified Angus flank steak
½	cup Brianna's Ginger Mandarin Dressing
¼	cup soy sauce
¼	cup rice wine vinegar
	McCormick Montreal Steak Seasoning

SALAD

1	(5 ounce) bag Portofino Salad blend or other lettuce mix
1	(15 ounce) can Mandarin oranges, drained
1	avocado, peeled and sliced into wedges
1	small red onion, peeled and slice into thin rings
1	pint grape tomatoes, washed

SALAD DRESSING

⅓	cup Stonewall scallion oil
¼	cup rice wine vinegar
1	teaspoon dry mustard
	salt and pepper to taste

Place flank steak in gallon size zip-top plastic bag. Pour in ½ cup Ginger Mandarin dressing, soy sauce, and rice wine vinegar. Seal and marinate in refrigerator for 24 hours. Flip bag half-way through process.

One half hour before serving, drain the meat and discard the marinade. Sprinkle both sides of meat with Montreal steak seasoning. Preheat the grill. Whisk salad dressing ingredients together. Toss with lettuce mix and arrange on a platter. Grill the flank steak to medium rare, approximately 10-15 minutes. Let meat rest for 5-10 minutes and then carve on a diagonal into thin slices. Arrange meat over the tossed salad. Top with Mandarin oranges and arrange the remaining vegetables on the platter. Serve immediately.

6 SERVINGS

Creamed Herring

1	(32 ounce) jar herring in wine sauce
1	red onion, chopped
1	(8 ounce) container sour cream

Drain and discard liquid from jar of herring. Combine herring with red onion and sour cream. Refrigerate overnight.

12 SERVINGS

Tasty Macaroni Salad

2	cups elbow macaroni
½	cup mayonnaise
1	tablespoon lemon juice
1	teaspoon salt
1	teaspoon sugar
1	tomato, diced
1	cup diced celery
¼	cup finely chopped onion or scallions
¼	cup chopped green pepper
¼	teaspoon celery salt
	pepper to taste
	salad greens
3	tablespoons chopped pimiento
	radish roses for garnish

Cook macaroni according to package directions. Drain. Rinse with cold water and drain again.

Mix mayonnaise with lemon juice, salt and sugar. Combine with macaroni and all but last 3 ingredients. Chill.

Serve on salad greens. Garnish with pimiento and radish roses.

6 TO 8 SERVINGS

Lemon Orzo Pasta Salad

Tom's Market in Coventry, Rhode Island

1	pound orzo pasta, cooked
2	lemons
½	cup fresh spinach
½	teaspoon lemon pepper seasoning
½	cup cubed feta cheese
½	cup vegetable oil
	salt to taste
	pepper to taste

Zest lemons being careful not to remove bitter white pith. Set aside lemon zest.

Cut spinach leaves into fine ribbons. Combine cooked orzo, spinach, lemon zest, lemon pepper, and feta cheese. Toss together with the oil. Season with salt and pepper to taste.

8 SERVINGS

 # Salad Niçoise

1	clove garlic
1	(7 ounce) can tuna, drained and flaked
2-3	anchovy fillets, chopped
2	tablespoons capers
1-2	sprigs parsley, chopped
1-2	pinches basil
1	cup olive oil
¼	cup wine vinegar
2	teaspoons salt
	freshly ground black pepper
½	head iceberg lettuce, torn
4-5	leaves romaine lettuce, torn
½	head Boston lettuce, torn
½	small green pepper, cut into strips
1	sweet onion, sliced
4	radishes, sliced

GARNISH

2	hard-boiled eggs, sliced
2	tomatoes, cut into wedges
6	black olives
6	green olives
3	whole anchovy fillets, halved
4	raw mushrooms, sliced, optional

Rub inside of salad bowl, preferably wooden, thoroughly with cut garlic clove. Discard garlic. In bowl, mix tuna, anchovies, capers, parsley, basil, oil, vinegar, salt and pepper. Let stand ½ hour.

Add vegetables and toss thoroughly. Correct seasonings. Garnish.

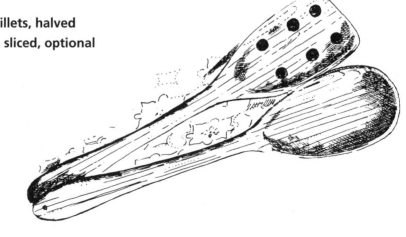

Warm Nut and Cranberry Salad

1   cup walnuts
1   cup pecans
¼   cup canola oil
1   tablespoon butter
⅓   cup pure maple syrup
      kosher salt to taste
1   (8 ounce) bottle Annie's organic Shiitake Mushroom Dressing
      balsamic vinegar
2   bags mesclun salad mix or other salad greens, 20-24 ounces total
1   (15 ounce) can white cannellini beans, drained and rinsed, optional
1   cup crumbled blue cheese
1   cup dried cranberries
1   package croutons

Mix walnuts and pecans together in large saucepan covered with canola oil. Add butter, cook over low-medium heat, stirring continuously, for 5 minutes. Add maple syrup and keep mixing so it doesn't burn. Cook a few more minutes until caramelized. Add a little kosher salt. Nuts can be prepared a day ahead, kept in a sealed container and reheated in oven at 250°.

Make dressing by pouring out most of the oil in the Annie's Shiitake Mushroom dressing and fill with balsamic vinegar. Mix well.

Put mesclun salad in a shallow bowl. Lightly dress and toss. Sprinkle blue cheese, cranberries and croutons on top and lightly mix in. If using beans, add before mixing. Pour warm nuts on top.

8 SERVINGS

Nut mixture is also great served over grilled chicken.

Quinoa Salad with Lemon Tahini Dressing

Quinoa contains all 8 essential amino acids, making it a complete protein.

1   cup dry quinoa
2   cups water or broth
1   (15 ounce) can chickpeas, drained
     and rinsed
⅔   cup diced cucumber
1   cup cherry tomatoes, cut in half or
     quarters
½   cup chopped fresh parsley
¼   cup finely chopped red onion
     mixed salad greens
     crumbled feta cheese

DRESSING

1   clove garlic, minced
¼   cup tahini
     zest of 1 lemon
⅓   cup fresh lemon juice
2-4 tablespoons hot water
     pinch sea salt
     pepper to taste

Combine quinoa and water or broth in medium saucepan. Bring to a boil, reduce heat, cover and simmer 10-15 minutes until water is absorbed and grain appears soft and translucent. Allow to cool. While cooling, make dressing. Whisk together ingredients, thinning as necessary with hot water. Toss cooled quinoa, chickpeas, cucumber, tomatoes, parsley and onion with dressing and chill.

Serve over mixed salad greens with crumbled feta cheese.

4 TO 6 SERVINGS

Sun-Dried Tomato Pasta Salad

A kick-off luncheon favorite from Tom's Market in Coventry, Rhode Island

1	pound penne pasta
1	cup vegetable oil
1	cup yellow roasted peppers, chopped
¼	cup scallions, chopped
1	cup quartered artichoke hearts
¼	cup sun-dried tomatoes, cut into fine strips
½	pound mozzarella cheese, cut into small cubes
½	teaspoon dried basil
½	teaspoon dries oregano
½	teaspoon sugar
¼	teaspoon salt
½	cup sun-dried tomato vinaigrette
1	chicken breast, grilled and sliced

Cook pasta. Cool. Toss with oil to prevent sticking. Toss pasta with remaining ingredients, except chicken. Top with grilled, sliced chicken breast.

6 TO 8 SERVINGS

Spinach Salad

1	(10 ounce) package spinach, cleaned and torn
2	hard-boiled eggs, chopped
½-1	cup sliced mushrooms
6	slices turkey bacon, cooked and chopped

Mix dressing ingredients together in a blender. Combine salad ingredients in bowl and toss with dressing as needed.

4 TO 6 SERVINGS

DRESSING

½	cup oil
¼	cup honey
¼	cup cider vinegar
1	teaspoon salt
½	teaspoon celery seed

All of the dressing will not be used. Refrigerate in a jar and shake before using. It is also good on a mixed green salad with fruit and nuts.

 **Salad Supreme**

1	avocado, peeled and sliced
2	tablespoons fresh lemon juice
1	head lettuce or other greens
2-3	tomatoes, quartered
1	red onion, sliced and separated into rings
1	(6 ounce) jar marinated artichokes, drained
1	tablespoon capers
¼	cup pimiento strips
1	cup chickpeas, drained
1	cucumber, thinly sliced
1	green pepper, cut into rings
1	cup pitted black olives
1	cup garlic or cheese croutons
	Caesar dressing
	salt and pepper to taste

Sprinkle avocado with lemon juice in a bowl. Reserve juice for salad. Mix all ingredients, except dressing, avocado, and croutons in salad bowl. Add dressing, avocado, lemon juice and croutons just before serving.

10 SERVINGS

Spinach or Romaine Salad with Strawberries

½	cup mayonnaise
2	tablespoons cider vinegar
¾	cup sugar
¼	cup milk
2	tablespoons poppy seeds
12	ounces romaine lettuce or spinach, torn
1	purple onion, sliced
1	pint strawberries, sliced

Combine mayonnaise, vinegar, sugar and milk in blender and blend well. Add poppy seeds and blend.

Toss lettuce, strawberries and red onions with dressing and serve.

6 SERVINGS

Spinach Salad with Cranberries, Feta and Pecans

1   cup chopped pecans

3   tablespoons butter

½   cup sugar

1   tablespoon coarsely ground black pepper

8   ounces mixed greens or spinach

¾   cup dried cranberries

½   pound crumbled feta cheese

DRESSING

1   teaspoon sugar

4   cloves garlic

1   teaspoon dried oregano

¼   cup chopped red onions

¼   teaspoon salt

¼   teaspoon pepper

½   cup red wine vinegar

1   cup chopped parsley

½   cup oil

To sugar the pecans, sauté them in melted butter. Mix sugar and coarse black pepper in bowl. Add nuts. Mix well and set aside.

Mix dressing ingredients.

Wash greens. Place in large bowl with cranberries, feta cheese and pecans. Toss with dressing and serve.

8 TO 10 SERVINGS

Sweet Potato Salad

Tom's Market in Coventry, Rhode Island

1   pound sweet potatoes, cut into large cubes

    vegetable oil to coat potatoes

1   tablespoon Italian seasoning

½   teaspoon granulated garlic

½   teaspoon onion powder

    salt and pepper to taste

½   cup cubed feta cheese

¼   cup chopped mild banana pepper rings

¼   cup Devine honey balsamic dressing

Preheat oven to 350°. Toss cubed sweet potatoes with oil and seasonings. Roast on a baking sheet coated with vegetable cooking spray until lightly browned, approximately 20-25 minutes.

Cool potatoes. Toss with feta cheese, hot peppers, dressing and salt and pepper to taste.

4 SERVINGS

Tabbouleh

1   cup bulgur
1½ cups boiling water
¼   cup olive oil
½   cup fresh lemon juice, or less
2   teaspoons salt, divided
1   small garlic clove, minced
½   cup finely chopped fresh mint or
    2 tablespoons dried mint
1½ cups chopped Italian parsley
4   scallions, minced
2   tomatoes, seeded and diced
1   small cucumber, peeled, seeded and
    diced, optional
½   teaspoon pepper

Combine bulgur with boiling water, olive oil, lemon juice and ½ teaspoon salt. Allow to stand at room temperature for at least 30 minutes until water is absorbed. Add remaining ingredients, including 1 teaspoon salt. Toss gently. Serve immediately or cover and refrigerate. Flavor improves if tabbouleh is allowed to sit for several hours.

6 TO 8 SERVINGS

Great served with small romaine leaves as scoopers.

Balsamic and Basil Vinaigrette

A recipe from Ira Brandstein, Director of Food and Nutrition at The Miriam Hospital.

2   tablespoons fresh basil leaves,
    minced
1¼ teaspoons minced garlic
¾   teaspoon salt
¼   teaspoon ground black pepper
1¼ teaspoons sugar
1   teaspoon Dijon mustard
½   cup balsamic vinegar
1½ cups olive oil

In a blender or food processor, combine all ingredients except olive oil and process until well blended. Add oil in a slow, steady stream until incorporated. Refrigerate at least one hour before serving. Stir well before each use.

2 CUPS

Vegetable Pasta Salad

½	pound penne or other tubular pasta
½	cup low fat cottage cheese
¼	cup reduced fat mayonnaise
1	tablespoon cider vinegar
1	tablespoon olive oil
1	clove garlic, minced
1	cup broccoli florets, steamed until tender, but crisp and green
1	cup cut asparagus pieces (1 inch), steamed until just tender
1	cup chopped tomatoes
½	cup peeled, seeded and diced cucumber
¼	cup chopped celery
2	scallions, thinly sliced on the diagonal
1	dill pickle, diced
1	tablespoon minced fresh dill
	salt and pepper to taste

Cook pasta until al dente. Drain, rinse and set aside.

Combine cottage cheese, mayonnaise, vinegar, olive oil and garlic in a food processor and process until smooth.

Mix together pasta, puréed cheese mixture and the remaining ingredients in a large serving bowl. Chill for 20 minutes to allow the flavors to blend.

6 SERVINGS

Green Goddess Dressing

1	cup mayonnaise
1	clove garlic
4	anchovies
6	scallions, cut up
¼	cup fresh parsley
1	tablespoon lemon juice
1	tablespoon tarragon vinegar
½	teaspoon salt
¼	teaspoon pepper
1	cup sour cream

Combine all ingredients except sour cream in blender and blend. Stir in sour cream.

This dressing is delicious with a salad of romaine lettuce, artichoke hearts and sieved hard-boiled eggs.

Mock Caesar Salad Dressing

2	ounces lemon juice
5	ounces vegetable oil
1	teaspoon Dijon mustard
1	clove garlic, crushed
1-2	teaspoons sugar
¼	teaspoon freshly ground black pepper
¼	cup Parmesan cheese

Mix all ingredients with hand blender or shake well in jar. Refrigerate well.

Great served with romaine lettuce, red onions, sliced mushrooms and croutons.

Works well with "soy" Parmesan cheese to make a dairy-free Caesar salad.

Cranberry Fruit Mold

A Thanksgiving tradition.

2	(16 ounce) cans whole cranberries
1	(20 ounce) can crushed pineapple
2	navel oranges, peeled and diced
1	(12 ounce) bottle maraschino cherries, cut into small pieces
½	cup chopped walnuts
3	(3 ounce) packages cherry gelatin
2	(3 ounce) packages lime gelatin
5	cups boiling hot water

In large bowl, mix fruits and nuts. In a second bowl, combine all 5 packages of gelatin with hot water. Stir until gelatin is dissolved. When gelatin has cooled to lukewarm, add it to the first bowl of fruit and nuts. Pour into 2 quart mold and refrigerate until set.

12 TO 14 SERVINGS

Diet Gelatin Compote

Sounds too easy to be great.

2   (3 ounce) packages red sugar free gelatin
2   cups boiling water
1   pint sour cream
1   (16 ounce) can whole cranberry sauce

Dissolve gelatin in boiling water. Cool. Blend in sour cream until mixture is smooth.

Add cranberry sauce and mix well. Pour into glass bowl or compote and refrigerate until set. Serve in glass compote.

8 TO 12 SERVINGS

Drunken Jello

1   (3 ounce) package lime gelatin
1   cup boiling water
½   cup cold water
½   cup green crème de menthe
¼   cup heavy cream
    fresh mint for garnish

Dissolve gelatin in boiling water. Add cold water and crème de menthe and refrigerate until partly congealed.

Whip mixture together with cream, adding cream gradually until color is medium green. Pour into parfait glasses and refrigerate.

Garnish with fresh mint.

4 TO 6 SERVINGS

 Lemon Mold

1   (3 ounce) package lemon gelatin
½   cup sugar
⅛   teaspoon salt
1   cup boiling water
1   (6 ounce) can frozen lemonade
      concentrate
1   cup heavy cream, whipped
      fresh fruit

Mix gelatin, sugar and salt in bowl. Add boiling water and stir until dissolved. Stir in lemonade concentrate. Chill until consistency of jelly, then fold in whipped cream. Pour into 4 cup ring mold and chill until set.

When ready to serve, unmold and fill center with assorted fresh fruits.

4 TO 6 SERVINGS

 Orange Blossom Mold

2   envelopes unflavored gelatin
1½   cups cold water
1   cup sugar
2   (6 ounce) cans frozen orange juice
      concentrate
2   cups heavy cream, whipped
      green grapes, fresh strawberries or
      blueberries for garnish

Sprinkle gelatin over cold water in saucepan. Place over low heat and stir until dissolved. Remove from heat, add sugar and stir to dissolve. Stir in frozen juice. Fold in whipped cream. Pour into 6 cup mold and refrigerate until firm. Unmold on serving platter and garnish with fresh fruit.

Simply *More* Brunch & Breads

The first Miriam Hospital opened on Parade Street in 1926.

By the end of WWI, membership in the Miriam Hospital Association had grown to 1900. The women began to search for a site suitable for a medical facility. Their search was rewarded when they found a group of four adjoining buildings on Parade Street, consisting of a maternity hospital which occupied the corner building and a boarding house which occupied the other three.

On November 12, 1921, a deposit of $1,000 was placed on the property, with a total purchase price of $27,000. The women enlisted help from other Jewish organizations in the state. During a one week period at the end of 1924, a group of 450 volunteers canvassed door to door to obtain donations for the new hospital. They raised $80,000, surpassing their target. This amount allowed debts to be settled and renovations to begin.

It would take four years for the renovations to be completed and medical equipment to be purchased or donated. On November 16, 1925, The Miriam Hospital admitted its first patient. The hospital received its charter from the Rhode Island legislature and officially opened in March 1926 with 63 beds and 14 bassinets.

Baked French Toast

Prepare the day ahead.

1	**loaf French bread**
3	**eggs**
3	**tablespoons sugar**
1	**teaspoon vanilla extract**
2¼	**cups milk**
½	**cup flour**
6	**tablespoons dark brown sugar**
½	**teaspoon cinnamon**
¼	**cup butter**
1	**cup fresh or frozen blueberries**
1	**cup sliced strawberries**

Grease 13 x 9 inch pan. Diagonally cut bread into 1 inch slices and place in baking dish. Set aside.

In a medium bowl, lightly beat eggs, sugar and vanilla extract; stir in milk until blended. Pour mixture over bread in pan, turning slices to coat well. Cover and refrigerate overnight.

Preheat oven to 375°. In a small bowl, combine flour, brown sugar and cinnamon. Cut in butter until mixture resembles coarse crumbs. Turn bread slices over in pan. Scatter blueberries over bread and sprinkle evenly with crumb mixture. Bake 40 minutes or until golden brown. Cut into squares and top with sliced strawberries.

4 TO 6 SERVINGS

Baked French Toast with Praline Topping

1	(13-16 ounce) loaf bread
8	eggs
2	cups half and half
1	cup milk
2	tablespoons sugar
1	teaspoon vanilla extract
¼	teaspoon cinnamon
¼	teaspoon nutmeg

PRALINE TOPPING

1	cup butter or margarine
1	cup brown sugar
1	cup pecans
2	tablespoons corn syrup
½	teaspoon cinnamon
½	teaspoon nutmeg

Slice bread and line a buttered 9 x 12 inch pan. Beat all ingredients until blended. Pour over bread to completely cover. Cover and refrigerate overnight.

Preheat oven to 350°.

Mix praline topping ingredients together and top bread and eggs. Bake for 40 minutes. Serve with maple syrup.

6 TO 8 SERVINGS

 ## Joan's Soufflé

16	slices Pepperidge Farm white bread
8	ounces sharp Cheddar cheese, grated
½	cup butter
6	eggs
2	cups milk
1	teaspoon salt

Remove crusts and cube bread. Butter 2 quart soufflé dish. Layer bread, cheese, bread, cheese in dish.

Melt butter and let cool. Beat eggs with fork or wire whisk. Combine butter, eggs, milk and salt. Pour over bread and cheese. Refrigerate overnight.

Remove from refrigerator 1 hour before cooking. Preheat oven to 400°. Set dish in pan 1 inch full of hot water. Bake for 45 minutes, or until brown and bubbly.

6 TO 8 SERVINGS

Minnie's Cheese Blintzes

BATTER

5	eggs, well beaten
1	cup flour
2	cups water

CHEESE FILLING

2¼	pounds farmer cheese
1	pound cream cheese
3	tablespoons sugar
2	eggs, beaten

Mix eggs with water and stir in flour. Mix until smooth to form smooth batter. Set aside.

Mix ingredients for filling and set aside.

Drop large spoonful of batter into hot, greased 7 or 8 inch frying pan and rotate pan until bottom is covered. Cook until lightly browned on bottom and set on top. Invert on floured board or cloth. Repeat until all batter is used.

Place 1 heaping spoonful of filling in center of each pancake and fold like an envelope. Fry or bake as desired. Serve with sour cream.

ABOUT 32

Blintz Soufflé

¼	cup butter or margarine
12	frozen blintzes, any flavors
4	eggs, well beaten
1 ½	cups sour cream
1	teaspoon vanilla extract
¼	cup orange juice
¼	teaspoon salt
¼	cup sugar
	pinch nutmeg for topping

Preheat oven to 350°. Melt butter in a 12 x 8 inch baking dish. Reserve half of melted butter and set aside. Place frozen blintzes in pan on top of butter, alternating different flavors. Add remaining ingredients to beaten eggs and pour over blintzes. Sprinkle with nutmeg and reserved melted butter. Bake until puffed and lightly browned, about 45-60 minutes.

Can also be made the day before and refrigerated overnight.

6 TO 8 SERVINGS

Blintz Pie

½   cup butter
½   cup sugar
2   eggs
¾   cup milk
1¼   cups flour
1   teaspoon baking powder
½   teaspoon salt

FILLING

1   pound ricotta cheese
1   egg
2   tablespoons melted butter
1   tablespoon sugar
    dash salt

Preheat oven to 350°. Mix butter and sugar until creamy. Add eggs, milk, flour, baking powder, and salt. Pour half of batter into greased 8 inch square pan. In separate bowl, mix together filling ingredients and spoon over first batter layer. Pour remaining batter on top and gently spread across pan. Bake for 1 hour.

8 SERVINGS

Puffy Apple Pancake

2   tablespoons butter or margarine
½   cup plus 2 tablespoons sugar, divided
¼   cup water
6   medium Granny Smith or Pippin apples, peeled, cored and cut into 8 wedges
3   large eggs
¾   cup milk
¾   cup flour
¼   teaspoon salt

Preheat oven to 425°. In a 12 inch oven safe skillet over medium heat, bring butter, ½ cup sugar and water to a boil. Add the apple wedges and cook about 15 minutes until apples are golden and the sugar mixture begins to caramelize.

In a blender, mix eggs, milk, flour, salt and 2 tablespoons sugar at medium speed until batter is smooth. Pour batter over cooked apple mixture.

Place skillet in the oven and bake for 15 minutes or until puffy and golden in color. Serve immediately.

2 TO 3 SERVINGS

Country Breakfast Casserole

3 cups frozen shredded hash brown potatoes
1 cup shredded Cheddar or Monterey Pepper Jack cheese
½ cup sliced mushrooms
¼ cup diced tomatoes
¼ cup diced red or green bell pepper
¼ cup sliced green onion
4 eggs, beaten
1 (12 ounce) can evaporated milk
1 teaspoon salt
¼ teaspoon pepper
1 teaspoon basil
½ teaspoon paprika

Preheat oven to 350°. Spray 2 quart square baking dish. Arrange potatoes evenly in the bottom of the dish. Lightly sauté mushrooms and bell pepper. Sprinkle potatoes with cheese, mushrooms, bell peppers, tomatoes and green onion. In medium mixing bowl, combine eggs, milk, salt, pepper, basil, and paprika. Pour egg mixture over potato mixture. Dish may be covered and refrigerated at this point for several hours or overnight. Bake uncovered for 40-45 minutes (or 55-60 minutes if made ahead and chilled) until center appears set. Let stand 5 minutes before serving.

Recipe can be doubled and cooked in a 13 x 9 inch casserole.

6 SERVINGS

Garlic Grits

1 cup quick cooking grits
4 cups water
1 teaspoon salt
4 tablespoons butter or margarine
1 cup grated Cheddar cheese
1 clove garlic, crushed, or garlic powder to taste
2 eggs, beaten
Tabasco sauce to taste

Preheat oven to 400°. Cook grits in salted water according to package directions. Add butter, cheese and garlic. Stir well and allow to cool slightly. Slowly stir beaten eggs into grits. Season with salt and Tabasco to taste. Pour into greased 1½ quart casserole. Bake for 20 minutes.

4 TO 6 SERVINGS

Lemon Ricotta Cheese Griddle Cakes

A recipe from Rue De L'Espoir Restaurant in Providence, Rhode Island.

10	eggs, separated
¾	cup butter, melted
2½	cups ricotta cheese
¾	teaspoon vanilla extract
¾	cup flour
½	cup sugar
¾	teaspoon salt
	lemon zest

Beat egg whites until they form glossy peaks. Set aside.

Fold together egg yolks, butter, ricotta cheese and vanilla extract. In separate bowl, whisk together flour, sugar, salt and lemon zest. With rubber spatula, incorporate dry ingredients into wet ingredients. Gently fold whipped egg whites into batter. Spray sauté pan with vegetable oil cooking spray. On medium heat, make griddle cakes in the sauté pan, being careful not to overcrowd the pan.

Mel's Rhode Island Johnnycakes

1	cup white stone ground cornmeal
1	cup vigorously boiling water
1	tablespoon butter, melted
½	teaspoon salt
1	egg
1	teaspoon sugar
⅛-¼	cup milk

Slowly add boiling water to cornmeal and mix until smooth. Add butter, salt, egg and sugar. Add milk, a little at a time, and mix.

Heat skillet. Johnnycakes are best cooked on a very hot skillet. Grease skillet generously. Cook 6-8 minutes on each side. Serve with hot maple syrup.

5 TO 6 SERVINGS

For thin, lacy johnnycakes, use more milk; for thicker ones, less.

Tomato Quiche

1	(9 inch) pie crust
2	large ripe tomatoes, cut in ½ inch slices
¼	cup flour
	salt to taste
	freshly ground pepper to taste
	oil
½	cup sliced black olives
1	cup minced scallions, divided
3	slices provolone cheese
2	eggs, lightly beaten
1	cup grated Cheddar cheese
1	cup heavy cream

Preheat oven to 425°. Bake pie crust for 8 minutes. Cool.

Lower oven to 375° Dip tomatoes slices in flour seasoned with salt and pepper. Sauté quickly in a small amount of oil and drain on paper towel.

Arrange olives and all but 2 tablespoons of scallions on bottom of pie crust. Add provolone and then tomatoes. Stir eggs and Cheddar cheese into heavy cream and pour into pie crust. Bake for 40-45 minutes or until filling is set and brown. Sprinkle remaining scallions on top, if desired. Cool 5 minutes before cutting.

6 SERVINGS

Tarte à l'Oignon

2	onions, diced
¼	cup butter
1	cup sour cream
2	eggs, beaten
½	tablespoon salt
	dash of pepper
½	pound Swiss cheese, broken into bits
	baked 9 inch pie crust

Preheat oven to 350°. Brown onions in butter until golden. In bowl, mix sour cream, eggs, salt, pepper and cheese. Add browned onion and butter. Pour into pie crust and bake for 30 minutes, or until golden brown.

6 TO 8 SERVINGS

Vegetable Quiche

1   pie crust, uncooked
9-10 large eggs
1   cup heavy cream
1   cup milk
     salt and pepper to taste
1   cup shredded yellow Cheddar
        cheese
1   cup shredded white Cheddar cheese
2   cups broccoli florets, fresh or frozen,
        cooked

Preheat oven to 400°. Roll out pie crust and line pie plate. Beat eggs; add cream, milk, salt and pepper. Place broccoli or other vegetable on bottom of pie crust. Top with cheeses. Pour egg mixture on top. Bake for 45 minutes or until center is firm.

If making the night before. Allow to cool, cover with foil and refrigerate. Reheat uncovered at 325° for 10 minutes.

6 SERVINGS

You can substitute any vegetable, such as asparagus or spinach.

Zucchini Pie

½   cup margarine, melted
4   cups zucchini, sliced
1   large onion, chopped
2   tablespoons parsley
¼   teaspoon salt
¼   teaspoon pepper
¼   teaspoon garlic powder
¼   teaspoon sweet basil
¼   teaspoon oregano
2   eggs
2   cups shredded mozzarella
1   (8 ounce) can refrigerated crescent
        dinner rolls
1-2 tablespoons Dijon mustard

Preheat oven to 375°. Sauté zucchini and onion in margarine over a low flame until zucchini is soft. If zucchini and onions are soupy, drain some liquid. Add spices and mix well.

In a large bowl, beat eggs. Add mozzarella cheese and mix well. Add zucchini mixture.

Make pie crust out of crescent rolls and line 9 inch pie plate. Spread Dijon mustard over crust. Add zucchini-egg mixture. Cook 18-20 minutes.

6 SERVINGS

 ## Bagels

1½ cups warm water
1 package yeast
4 tablespoons sugar, divided
1 tablespoon salt
4½-6 cups flour, unsifted

Rinse bowl with hot water to warm. Pour in warm water, sprinkle yeast and stir until dissolved. Stir in 3 tablespoons sugar, salt and enough flour for soft dough. Turn out on lightly floured board and knead for 10 minutes, adding flour as needed until dough is smooth and elastic. Cover and let rise for 15 minutes. Punch down and roll on floured board to a 5 x 9 inch rectangle 1 inch thick. Cut into 12 equal strips. Roll each strip until ½ inch thick. Moisten ends and join to form bagels. Cover to rise 20 minutes.

Preheat oven to 375°. Bring 1 gallon of water to boil in deep pot. Add 1 tablespoon sugar and lower heat. Simmer 4 bagels exactly 7 minutes. Simmering longer than 7 minutes can cause sogginess. Remove with fork and cool on towel while you cook remaining bagels. Bake on ungreased cookie sheet for 30-35 minutes.

1 DOZEN

¼ cup milk
¼ cup hot water
4 packages yeast
10 cups unsifted flour
1½ cups butter
½ cup margarine
1 pint sour cream
1½ teaspoons salt
2 cups sugar, sugar
8 large eggs, divided
½ cup raisins
½ cup chopped walnuts, optional
 cinnamon to taste

Combine cold milk with hot water for a lukewarm mixture and pour over yeast in bowl. Mix gently until smooth and runny.

Place flour in large mixing bowl and make well in center. Pour yeast mixture into well.

Melt butter and margarine slowly so they do not get too hot. Add sour cream and pour into well. Then add 1 ½ cups sugar, salt and 7 eggs. Mix thoroughly with hands, gradually mixing flour from sides into well. Mix until dough comes away from sides of bowl. If dough is too sticky to do this, add a little more flour. Put dough into large bowl. Cover with aluminum foil and dish towel and refrigerate overnight.

Prepare raisins the night before. Soak in warm water for a few minutes. Drain and chop. Chop fine (large blade of grinder may be used). Add cinnamon to taste, ½ cup sugar and nuts if desired.

The next day bring dough and raisin mixture to room temperature (about 2 hours). Preheat oven to 350°. Divide dough into four pieces. Roll one piece about ⅜ inch thick and cut into 3 x 3 inch squares. Put 1 teaspoon raisin filling in center of each square, roll up diagonally and close. They should look like little pillows.

The remaining dough may be prepared in this manner or according to the following variations. Directions apply to ¼ of dough at a time.

VARIATION 1: Roll out, fill and make into one large roll. Bake on a greased cookie sheet.

VARIATION 2: Roll out, cut into strips, fill and roll into pinwheels for cinnamon buns, and set into greased muffin tins.

VARIATION 3: Roll into balls and bake in greased muffin tins.

VARIATION 4: Roll out and fill and shape into loaf. Bake in greased loaf pan.

Put separate pieces close together on greased cookie sheets. Cover these, rolls and dough in pans, with dish towels and let rise at room temperature about 1 hour.

Brush tops with well-beaten egg and bake for about 20 minutes or until golden brown.

Basic Raised Dough with Variations

1	**package yeast**
¼	**cup warm water**
¼	**cup milk, scalded**
¼	**cup sugar**
½	**teaspoon salt**
¼	**cup shortening**
2¼-2½	**cups flour, divided**

CHEESE FILLING

1⅓	**pounds farmer cheese**
⅔	**pound cream cheese**
1	**egg**
2	**tablespoons sugar**

In large bowl, dissolve yeast in water and milk. Stir in sugar, salt, shortening, egg and 1¼ cups flour. Beat until smooth. Stir in remaining flour to make a soft ball. On floured bowl, knead for about 5 minutes until smooth and elastic. Place greased side up in a greased bowl. Cover with plastic wrap. Let rise in warm place until double in bulk.

Preheat oven to 350°. Roll out. See variations.

VARIATION 1: Cut dough in half and roll out in a circle. Brush with melted butter, sugar, cinnamon and raisins. Cut in wedges and roll up into crescents. Let stand ½ hour covered and bake for 20-30 minutes.

VARIATION 2: Cut dough in half. Roll out into an oblong shape. Brush with butter and spread with cheese mixture. Roll up and cut into pinwheels and turn broad side down on cookie sheet. Let stand ½ hour and bake for 20-30 minutes.

VARIATION 3: Proceed as above using prune butter as filling.

Bread Machine Challah

¾ cup warm water

2 eggs

4 tablespoons margarine

3 tablespoons sugar

3 tablespoons honey

1 tablespoon soy milk powder

1¼ teaspoons salt

3¼ cups white bread flour

¾ tablespoon dry yeast

1 egg yolk mixed with 2 tablespoons water

sesame seeds

In bread machine, place water, margarine, 2 eggs, sugar, honey, soy powder, salt and flour. Make a small well in the flour and add yeast. Set machine on dough setting and start.

When bread machine finishes, remove dough, placed on a floured board, form into a ball and cut in half. Cover half of the dough with a damp towel and cut the other half into 4 equal pieces. Form each piece into a 1-inch diameter rope. Braid the 4 strands into a loaf and cover with a damp towel. Repeat with the remaining dough. Let the covered loaves rise for 40 minutes.

Preheat oven to 375°. Brush loaves with egg yolk and water mixture and sprinkle with sesame seeds. Bake 15-20 minutes until golden and cool on a wire rack.

2 SMALL LOAVES

A dairy version may be made by using butter instead of margarine and using ½ cup warm milk and ¼ cup warm water, and eliminating soy powder.

Challah

3 envelopes yeast
⅓ cup warm water
⅔ cup sugar
1½ cups water
½ cup orange juice
¾ cup vegetable oil
1 tablespoon salt
4 eggs
8 cups flour, divided
1 beaten egg yolk
1 cup raisins, optional

Combine yeast and warm water and allow to proof 10 minutes. Combine sugar, water, orange juice, oil and salt. Beat in 4 eggs. Add yeast. Add 4 cups flour and mix. Add remaining flour and knead. Place in lightly oiled bowl. Cover with a warm, damp towel. Allow to rise until doubled in bulk, about 1 hour.

Knead 2-3 minutes, recover with warm, damp towel, and allow to rise for another ½ hour. Divide into 3 sections and allow to rest for 10 minutes. Each section will make one loaf. Each can be divided into 3 pieces, braided and placed in a loaf pan or coiled into a round loaf and placed on a baking sheet. Cover with a warm, wet towel and let rise another hour.

Preheat oven to 350°. Brush loaves with beaten egg yolk. Bake for ½ hour.

3 LOAVES

Passover Rolls

3 cups hot water
8 cups matzo farfel
8 eggs, beaten
6 tablespoons margarine
salt and pepper

Preheat oven to 375°. Mix matzo farfel, margarine, salt and pepper in a bowl. Pour water over mixture and allow to cool. Add eggs and mix. Pour into greased muffin tins. Bake for 45 minutes.

2 DOZEN

Cheese Popovers

½	teaspoon salt
1	cup sifted flour
2	eggs, well beaten
1¼	cups milk
¼	cup grated Cheddar cheese

Preheat oven to 425°. Add salt to flour. Combine eggs and milk and add to flour mixture, stirring until well blended. Fold in cheese. Heat well greased muffin tins in oven until very hot. Fill tins half-full with batter and bake for 20-25 minutes. Prick popovers with fork during last 5 minutes to allow steam to escape. Serve hot.

12 POPOVERS

Jackie's Popovers

3	eggs
1	cup milk
1	cup sifted flour
1	teaspoon salt

Preheat oven to 450°. Combine ingredients and beat with an electric mixer until smooth. Fill greased muffin tin ¾ full. Bake for 30 minutes, then lower heat to 375° and bake for an additional 10-15 minutes or until firm to the touch.

8 SERVINGS

Corn Bread Casserole

2	large onions, chopped
6	tablespoons butter or margarine
2	eggs
2	tablespoons milk
2	(17 ounce) cans cream style corn
1	(16 ounce) package cornmeal muffin mix
½	pint sour cream
2	cups shredded Cheddar cheese

Preheat oven to 425°. Oil 9 x 13 inch pan. Sauté onion in butter. In a medium bowl, mix eggs and milk until well blended. Add corn and muffin mix. Mix well. Spread batter in prepared pan. Spoon sautéed onion over top. Spread sour cream over onion. Sprinkle with cheese. Bake for 35 minutes until puffed and golden. Let stand 10 minutes before cutting.

12 SERVINGS

May be frozen.

Apple Muffins with Pecan Streusel

Rue De L'Espoir Restaurant in Providence, Rhode Island.

2 cups flour

¾ cup sugar

1 tablespoon baking powder

1 egg

1 cup milk

½ cup oil

2 cups diced apple

STREUSEL

½ cup pecans

1 tablespoon butter

¾ cup brown sugar

1 teaspoon ground cinnamon

1 teaspoon flour

Preheat oven to 400°. Mix flour, sugar and baking powder together and make a well in the center of the bowl. Add egg, milk and oil and mix gently. Fold apples into batter. Spoon batter into muffin tins that have been coated with vegetable cooking spray.

Make streusel by placing pecans in food processor and pulsating until coarsely chopped. Add sugar, cinnamon, flour and butter and continue to pulsate until just crumbly. Sprinkle on top of muffin batter. Bake for 20-25 minutes.

6 MUFFINS

Date and Apricot Loaf

1 cup dates, cut into bits

1 cup dried apricots, cut into bits

1½ cups sugar

¼ cup butter, melted

1¾ cups boiling water

2 eggs, slightly beaten

2½ cups sifted flour

pinch of salt, optional

1 cup chopped walnuts or pecans

Preheat oven to 350°. Put dates, apricots, sugar and butter in a large bowl. Pour boiling water over them and allow to cool. Add two slightly beaten eggs and mix well. Add flour and salt and stir. Stir in chopped nuts. Bake in a greased glass loaf pan for 1 hour and 20 minutes.

1 LOAF

Banana Nut Bread

Simple, moist and dense with no oil or butter.

3	ripe bananas, well mashed
2	eggs, well beaten
2	cups flour
½	cup sugar
1	teaspoon salt
1	teaspoon baking soda
½	cup chopped walnuts

Preheat oven to 350°, Grease loaf pan. Mix bananas and eggs. Stir in next 4 ingredients. Add walnuts and blend. Bake for 1 hour.

1 LOAF

Try adding chocolate chips.

Belle's Banana Bread

4	tablespoons sour cream
1	teaspoon baking soda
½	cup butter, at room temperature
1	cup sugar
2	eggs
1	teaspoon vanilla extract
2-3	bananas, very ripe
1½	cups flour

Mix sour cream and baking soda together and allow to sit ½ hour in refrigerator.

Preheat oven to 350°. Cream butter and sugar. Add eggs, one at a time, mixing between each addition. Add vanilla extract and mix. Mash bananas and add to the mixture. Add the sour cream and stir. Slowly add the flour until well incorporated. Bake in an ungreased loaf pan in the middle of the oven for 60-65 minutes.

1 LOAF

Blueberry Muffins

1 cup milk
1 tablespoon lemon juice or vinegar
3 cups plus 2 tablespoons flour, divided
1 teaspoon salt
1 cup plus 1 tablespoon margarine
2 cups plus 2 tablespoons sugar
5 extra large eggs
1 teaspoon baking soda
1 tablespoon baking powder
2 teaspoons vanilla extract
2⅔ cups cake flour, unsifted
2 pints blueberries or frozen blueberries without syrup

Preheat oven to 400°. Make soured milk by combining 1 tablespoon lemon juice or vinegar with enough milk to make 1 cup. Let stand for 5 minutes before using.

Cream 1 cup plus 1 tablespoon flour with salt, margarine, and sugar. Add eggs all at once and beat for 3 minutes. Add remaining flour, baking soda and baking powder. Beat well. Blend in soured milk, vanilla extract and cake flour and beat until thoroughly mixed. Fold in blueberries.

Grease muffin tins or use paper cups and fill completely with batter. Sprinkle sugar on top. Bake for 25 minutes.

2 DOZEN

The batter can be refrigerated for 2-3 days and the cooked muffins freeze well.

Pumpkin Bread

½ cup canola oil
1½ cups sugar
2 eggs
¾ teaspoon nutmeg
¾ teaspoon cinnamon
¾ teaspoon salt
¾ cup canned pumpkin or squash
½ cup water
1¾ cups flour
1 teaspoon baking soda
½ cup raisins, optional
½ cup walnuts, optional

Preheat oven to 350°. Mix together oil, sugar, eggs, nutmeg, cinnamon and salt. Stir in remaining ingredients. Pour into greased loaf pan. Cook for approximately one hour.

1 LOAF

Lemon Bread

1½ cups sugar
½ cup butter, melted
1½ teaspoons lemon extract
¾ cup lemon juice, divided
2 eggs
1½ cups unsifted flour
1 teaspoon baking powder
1 teaspoon salt
½ cup milk
grated rind of 1 lemon

Preheat oven to 350°. Combine 1 cup sugar, butter, lemon extract, and ¼ cup lemon juice. Beat in eggs one at a time, until smooth. Sift dry ingredients and stir in alternately with the milk. Add the lemon rind. Pour into greased 8 inch loaf pan and bake for about 1 hour or until a toothpick inserted in the center comes out clean.

Mix ½ cup sugar and ½ cup lemon juice. Pierce top of cooked bread with fork tines and pour lemon juice and sugar mixture over bread. Cool in pan 1 hour, then remove. Wrap in foil and let stand 24 hours before cutting. This will stay fresh in the refrigerator for several months. Can be frozen.

1 LOAF

Wheat Bread

2 cups white flour
2 cups whole wheat flour
1 cup sugar
2 teaspoons salt
1 quart buttermilk
4 teaspoons baking soda

Preheat oven to 375°. Grease 2 loaf pans. Stir together flours, sugar and salt. Combine buttermilk and baking soda and stir into dry ingredients. Pour into pans.

Place loaf pans in oven. Reduce temperature to 350° and bake about 1 hour.

2 LOAVES

Chocolate Chip Pumpkin Bread

3   cups flour
2   cups sugar
½   teaspoon salt
2   teaspoons baking powder
2   teaspoons baking soda
1   cup oil
1   (15 ounce) can pumpkin
4   eggs
1   teaspoon allspice
1   cup chopped nuts, optional
2   cups chocolate chips

Preheat oven to 350°. In a large bowl, mix all ingredients together. Grease and flour 3 coffee cans. Fill each halfway. Bake for 1 hour.

3 COFFEE CAN LOAVES

Zucchini Bread

3   eggs
1   cup vegetable oil
2   cups sugar
2   cups grated zucchini
3   teaspoons vanilla extract
2   cups sifted all-purpose flour
1   teaspoon salt
¼   teaspoon baking powder
1   teaspoon baking soda
3   teaspoons cinnamon
¾   cup chopped nuts

Preheat oven to 350°. Beat eggs until foamy. Add oil, sugar, zucchini and vanilla extract. Mix lightly. Add dry ingredients, mix well. Stir in chopped nuts. Pour into 2 well greased loaf pans. Bake for about 1 hour and 20 minutes.

2 LOAVES

Simply *More* Meats

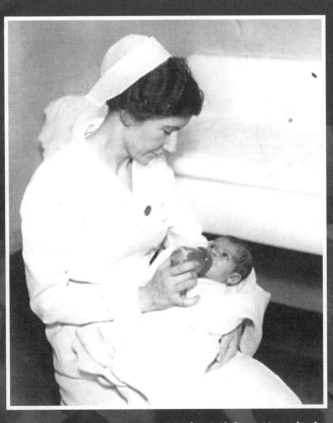

In the original Nursery at the Miriam Hospital.

The women of the Miriam Hospital Association worked to enhance the day to day operations of the hospital. They visited wards, established a medical library for physicians and a general library for patients and arranged for holiday celebrations.

Rules as to Admission of Patients

Patients are admitted regardless of creed or nationality. Contagious cases are not admitted.

Patients suffering with chronic or incurable diseases cannot be admitted except in cases where temporary relief is indicated and then only for a limited time.

Admission: Daily from 8:00 A.M. to 6:00 P.M. Urgent cases at any hour. Patients should apply in person at hospital for examination.

RATES

PRIVATE ROOMS:

Single Room — $ 40.00 to $ 50.00 per week.

Two-bed Room — $ 31.50 to $40.00 per week.

Three-bed Room — $ 28.00 per week.

WARDS:

General Wards (Adults) — $ 21.00 per week.

Children's Ward — $14.00 per week.

Children's Ward (Private) — $ 21.00 per week.

Obstetrical Ward — $ 60.00 flat for 14 days.

OPERATING ROOM:

Major Operations — $ 12.00.

Minor Operations — $ 5.00.

Ward patients — $ 5.00.

LABORATORY:

Private Patients — $ 5.00.

No Laboratory charge for General Ward patients.

FIRST ANNIVERSARY ISSUE OF THE MIRIAM HOSPITAL 1927

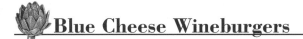

Beef and Broccoli

2	tablespoons peanut oil
1	teaspoon salt
1-2	cloves, crushed garlic
1	tablespoon fresh minced gingerroot
1½	pounds sirloin tips or flank steak, sliced paper thin diagonally
1	head broccoli, cut into flowerets
2	tablespoons medium dry sherry
1	tablespoon medium soy sauce
5	tablespoons chicken stock
1	tablespoon cornstarch, dissolved in 2-3 tablespoons cold water
	cooked rice

Heat wok over high heat until a drop of water skitters over surface. Add oil, drizzling down side of wok. When oil is hot, add salt, garlic and ginger. Remove garlic and ginger before they burn.

Add beef, stir-frying just enough to remove redness. Remove from wok. Add broccoli and stir-fry. (If necessary, add more oil before adding broccoli.) When broccoli turns a bright green, cover wok and cook 2-3 minutes, until broccoli is tender but still crisp.

Uncover, add beef. Add sherry, soy sauce, and chicken stock, stir-frying over high heat. Add cornstarch in water. Stir-fry 10-30 seconds until slightly thickened and glossy.

4 TO 6 SERVINGS

Serve with rice and Chinese tea (no sugar!)

Blue Cheese Wineburgers

2	pounds lean ground beef
½	cup dry red wine
2	teaspoons salt
¼	teaspoon pepper
1	teaspoon grated onion
½	cup crumbled blue cheese

Combine first 5 ingredients. Cover and chill for several hours to blend flavors.

Shape into 12 thin patties. Place cheese over 6 patties. Top with remaining patties, pressing edges together. Grill or broil to rare or medium.

6 SERVINGS

Café Zelda Burger

Chef John Philcox shares this recipe from Café Zelda in Newport, Rhode Island

2 tablespoons butter, divided

2 tablespoons olive oil, divided

12 ounces white mushrooms

1 large Spanish onion

3 pounds lean ground beef

salt and freshly ground black pepper

6 Portuguese bolo rolls, split

6 thick slice mild Cheddar cheese

6 romaine leaves

6 tomato slices

Cut the onion in half lengthwise, and cut into ¼ inch slices. Cut the mushrooms in ¼ inch slices.

Divide the butter and oil evenly between two sauté pans. Heat over medium high heat until butter is melted. Cook mushrooms in one pan until they are just done, about 5 minutes. Cook onions in the other pan until they are soft and caramelized, about 15-20 minutes.

Form the ground beef into 6 patties. Season with salt and pepper, and cook on your grill until they're done to your liking. Lightly toast the rolls on the grill. Top burgers with onions, mushrooms and a slice of cheese. Cover the grill for a few seconds to melt the cheese. Serve immediately with romaine leaves and tomato slices.

6 SERVINGS

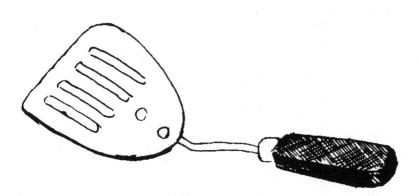

Short Ribs

16	ounces tomato sauce
4	tablespoons honey
4	tablespoons cider vinegar
2	tablespoons Worcestershire sauce
4-5	pounds beef short ribs
1	large onion, finely chopped
1	clove garlic, minced
	salt and pepper

Preheat oven to 375°. Mix tomato sauce, honey, vinegar and Worcestershire sauce in a saucepan. Heat until bubbly and remove from heat. Sprinkle ribs on all sides with salt and pepper. Put ribs in Dutch oven, sprinkle with onion and garlic. Pour in tomato sauce mixture. Cover, and bake for 3-3½ hours until tender.

6 SERVINGS

 Holly's Brisket

2	packages dehydrated onion soup
½	cup honey
1	cup ketchup
2	teaspoons Worcestershire sauce
1	cup hot water
	dash dry mustard
	dash Tabasco sauce
1	large single brisket

Preheat oven to 325°. Combine ingredients for sauce and pour over brisket. Bake, covered for 3-4 hours, basting frequently. Add desired vegetables during last hour.

8 SERVINGS

For best results cook brisket a day before serving and reheat.

Beloved Brisket

Brisket
2-3 onions, sliced, divided
1 cup orange juice
½ cup red wine
4 tablespoons ketchup
1 teaspoon sugar

Place half of the onions on the bottom of the pan and place brisket on top of the onions, cover the meat with remaining onions.

Mix remaining ingredients and pour mixture over the meat. Marinate 5 hours or overnight.

Prick meat. Bake at 325° for 3 hours. Cover with foil for first 2 hours, and cook the last hour uncovered.

Cholent

3 tablespoons chicken fat or oil
3 onions, diced
2 cups dry kidney beans
2 pounds brisket or short ribs
2 pounds potatoes, peeled and quartered
water to cover
1 tablespoon salt
½ teaspoon pepper
1 teaspoon paprika

Heat the fat in large, heavy pot and sauté onions for 5 minutes. Add remaining ingredients, starting with kidney beans and meat, and cover with water ½ inch above top of ingredients.

Cover and cook slowly over low heat for 5-6 hours or in low oven over night. Check frequently, so as not to burn, adding more water if necessary. When finished, contents should be thick and almost all liquid absorbed.

6 SERVINGS

Chili Taco Casserole

1	(11 ounce) package corn chips, crushed
4	tomatoes, chopped
1	onion, sliced
1	head lettuce, torn into bite-sized pieces
3	(1 pound) cans chili with beans
2	pounds sharp Cheddar cheese, shredded

Layer ingredients in order given, divided evenly into 2 greased 3 quart casseroles.

Bake at 425° for 25 minutes until hot and bubbling and cheese is melted.

24 SERVINGS

Flemish Beef

4	pounds blade steak
2	tablespoons fat
3	cloves garlic, crushed
2	tablespoons butter
6	cups sliced onions
1	teaspoon salt
½	teaspoon pepper
1	cup beef stock
1½	(12 ounce) bottles imported beer
4-5	sprigs parsley
2	bay leaves

Preheat oven to 350°. Cut beef in pieces ½ inch thick, 2 inches wide and 3 inches long.

Heat oil in heavy skillet, add garlic and brown beef quickly. Remove beef to casserole.

Add butter to skillet and sauté onions until golden. Season with salt and pepper.

Make two layers each of beef and onions in casserole.

Rinse out skillet with beef stock, making sure you get all the brown pieces sticking to the pan and pour over beef and onions. Add beer, parsley and bay leaves. Cook, covered for 2½-3 hours. Serve over noodles or spaetzle.

6 TO 8 SERVINGS

Fondue Bourguignonne

A favorite at each holiday season.

3   pounds top round or tenderloin, in bite sized cubes

vegetable oil-enough to fill fondue pot a little more than half full

1   garlic clove, split, optional

chopped onion

RÉMOULADE SAUCE

2   cups mayonnaise

½   cup finely chopped dill pickles

2   tablespoons finely chopped capers

1   tablespoon prepared mustard

1   tablespoon chopped parsley

1   tablespoon chopped chives

TOMATO SAUCE

4   tablespoons butter

4   tablespoons flour

1   teaspoon garlic powder

1   cup ketchup

1   cup sherry

2   tablespoons wine vinegar

2   beef bouillon cubes dissolved in 4 tablespoons boiling water

2   teaspoons brown sugar

2   teaspoons prepared mustard

salt and pepper to taste

dash of cloves

2   tablespoons onion juice

Serve chunks of raw beef on individual plates. Heat oil just before serving (add garlic if you like) and transfer to fondue pot. Place sauces, salt and chopped onion in small serving bowls. All guests cook their own meat, piece by piece, on long forks in fondue pot and help themselves to sauces, salt and onion.

RÉMOULADE SAUCE

Combine all ingredients. Be sure to drain and dry capers and pickles on paper towels before chopping.

TOMATO SAUCE

Melt butter in saucepan. Stir in flour and garlic powder. When bubbling, stir in ketchup, sherry, vinegar, bouillon, brown sugar and mustard. Bring to boil and simmer five minutes. Add rest of seasonings, stirring constantly. Serve cold.

MUSTARD SAUCE

2	**cups mayonnaise**
4	**tablespoons prepared mustard**
⅔	**cup chili sauce, strained, or ketchup**
½	**cup shredded onion**
2	**tablespoons white horseradish**
2	**teaspoons oregano**
¼	**teaspoon cayenne**
⅔	**cup sour cream**

MUSTARD SAUCE

Combine all ingredients except sour cream. Beat with fork to blend thoroughly. Stir in sour cream.

6 SERVINGS

Use any other sauce you like, such as Béarnaise or Hollandaise. Above sauces will keep for weeks in refrigerator.

Glazed Corned Beef

1	**corned beef (6-7 pounds)**
1	**onion**
1	**clove garlic**
3	**bay leaves**
3	**stalks celery with leaves**
1	**carrot**
	whole cloves
1	**cup dark brown sugar**
1	**scant teaspoon vinegar**
½	**teaspoon dry mustard**
1	**heaping teaspoon flour**
1	**(11 ounce) can Mandarin oranges**
	ginger ale

Put corned beef in pot and cover with water. Boil for 5 minutes and pour off water. Cover with cold water again. Add onion, garlic, bay leaves, celery and carrot. Boil slowly for 4 hours or until tender. Drain well. Place in baking pan, score fat, and stud with whole cloves.

Preheat oven to 350°. Mix brown sugar, vinegar, mustard and flour and pour over beef. Arrange oranges on glaze and cover bottom of pan with ginger ale. Bake for 1 hour, basting often.

8 TO 10 SERVINGS

Mother's Meatloaf

1¼   pounds lean ground sirloin
1   large egg, beaten
⅓   cup bread crumbs
    paprika
    garlic powder
    onion powder
½   teaspoon prepared mustard
¾   cup of tomato juice
¼   cup chopped onion
¼   cup finely chopped green pepper
1   cup ketchup
1   cup water

Preheat oven to 350°. Thoroughly mix ground sirloin, egg, bread crumbs, mustard and 4 shakes each of paprika, garlic powder and onion powder. Mix in tomato juice. Shape into oblong loaf and place in center of 8 inch square casserole. Cover top loosely with onions and peppers. Bake 30 minutes. Remove from oven and pour mixture of ketchup and water over top. Baste a couple of times. Bake another "hour or so" and serve sliced, covered with sauce.

4 SERVINGS

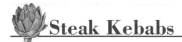# Steak Kebabs

SAUCE

½	cup dry white wine
½	cup ketchup
1	tablespoon prepared mustard
1	tablespoon Worcestershire sauce
1	clove garlic, minced
½	teaspoon whole rosemary
2	tablespoons vinegar
2	tablespoons brown sugar

KEBABS

2	pounds beef round steak 1½ inches thick, cut into 1½ inch cubes
12	cherry tomatoes
1	(4 ounce) can mushroom caps
1	green pepper, cut into 1½ inch strips
1	(16 ounce) can boiled onions, drained

Combine sauce ingredients in bowl. Add meat and marinate for a few hours, turning occasionally. Alternate the meat, tomatoes, mushrooms, peppers and onions on skewers. Place on grill and broil for 8-10 minutes, turning frequently.

4 SERVINGS

Beef Tenderloin

1	beef tenderloin roast, 4-6 pounds, trimmed
½	cup red wine
¼	cup soy sauce
6	cloves garlic, minced
	dash dry mustard

Preheat oven to 450°. Line pan with foil. Put tenderloin in pan. Mix ingredients together and pour over tenderloin. Roast for 15 minutes. Turn oven off; do not open door. Leave in 35-40 minutes for rare, and 45-50 minutes for medium.

Mama Joni's Italian Meat Sauce

6	cups chopped onion
6-8	cloves garlic, crushed
½	cup olive oil, or enough for sautéing meat
3	pounds ground beef
3	(32 ounce) cans Italian plum tomatoes with liquid (remove bay leaf)
6	(6 ounce) cans tomato paste
6	cups water
2	bay leaves
	salt to taste
	freshly ground black pepper to taste
1	teaspoon oregano or to taste
1	teaspoon basil
1	teaspoon sugar

Sauté onion and garlic in oil until brown. Add ground beef, broken up, and sauté just until pink.

Transfer meat to heavy 9 or 10 quart Dutch oven. Add remaining ingredients. Simmer, uncovered, for 3-4 hours, stirring occasionally. Correct seasonings after about an hour.

ABOUT 9 QUARTS

Sauce should be thick. Freeze what you don't need immediately.

TT's Flank Steak

½	cup soy sauce
2½	tablespoons brown sugar
2	tablespoons lemon juice
1	teaspoon ground ginger
½	teaspoon garlic salt
	flank steak

Combine all ingredients and whisk together. Place flank steak in a dish. Pour marinade over steak. Refrigerate over night turning flank steak at least once. Grill flank steak to desired doneness.

Marinated Stuffed Flank Steak

2	pounds flank steak
½	teaspoon rosemary
¼	teaspoon ground tarragon
3	cloves garlic
	pinch basil
½	teaspoon thyme
1	bay leaf
1	tablespoon grated onion
½	cup oil
½	cup water
½	cup red wine vinegar
	your favorite stuffing or see below

Cut steak in half crosswise and make a pocket in each half. Combine remaining ingredients and heat until well blended. Cool. Pour over meat and marinate overnight. Remove meat from marinade and dry. Fill with stuffing. Close openings with skewers. Cook over slow coals 20 minutes on each side, basting with marinade. Cut into slices across grain.

STUFFING

4	cups herbed bread cubes
¾	teaspoon ground sage
1	teaspoon grated onion
¼	teaspoon salt
⅛	teaspoon pepper
2	tablespoons butter
⅓	cup beef or chicken stock

Combine ingredients and mix lightly.

4 TO 5 SERVINGS

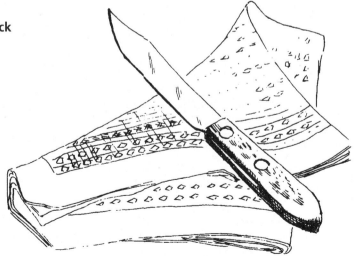

111

Dynamites

2½ pounds lean ground beef
1-2 teaspoons olive oil
1 large green pepper, chopped
1 large red pepper, chopped
3-4 stalks of celery, chopped
1 large Vidalia onion, chopped
   celery salt to taste
   sea salt to taste
   ground pepper to taste
   crushed red pepper to taste
1 (8 ounce) can tomato paste
1-2 tablespoons extra virgin olive oil

Brown ground beef in sauté pan, drain thoroughly and place in slow cooker. Add 1-2 tablespoons extra virgin olive oil to sauté pan, heat and add peppers, onion and celery, sauté until just soft. Add sautéed vegetables, celery salt, sea salt, ground pepper, and little bit of crushed red pepper into a slow cooker.

Add can of tomato paste. Add some water to the can to scrape out all of tomato paste. Stir well. If mixture seems very thick, add a little more water.

Cook for 1½ hours on high heat in slow cooker. As Dynamites heat up, taste for desired level of spice at this point, turn temperature to low for 1 hour. If mixture is still thick, add a little bit more water, very sparingly as to not make it thin.

Add crushed red pepper a little at a time to desired taste.

Serve in fresh torpedo rolls.

Peachy Bean and Frankfurt Casserole

2 (16 ounce) cans baked vegetarian beans
6 knockwurst, each cut in 4 pieces
4 gingersnaps, crushed
¼ cup maple syrup
2 tablespoons peach jam
4 tablespoons margarine

Preheat oven to 300°. Combine all ingredients and place in 2 quart casserole. Cook covered for 2 hours, and uncovered for 1 hour until dark brown.

8 SERVINGS

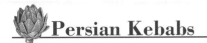
Persian Kebabs

3	pounds cubed beef or lamb
1	(32 ounce) container plain yogurt
1	cup lemon juice
4	large onions, diced
½	cup dry red wine
	salt and pepper
	garlic powder
	paprika

Mix yogurt and remaining ingredients. Place beef or lamb cubes in marinade. Marinate in refrigerator overnight, or longer. Skewer and charcoal broil or broil in oven broiler.

12 SERVINGS

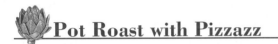
Pot Roast with Pizzazz

4-6	pounds single brisket or top rib
	freshly ground pepper
	garlic powder
	seasoned salt
1	package dehydrated onion soup
2	cups boiling water
½	bottle chili sauce
½	large bunch fresh dill, or 2 tablespoons dried
4-6	carrots, cut into sticks
2	large potatoes, quartered

Preheat oven to 300°. Generously sprinkle meat with pepper, garlic powder and seasoned salt. In heavy pan sear meat on high heat until almost burned. Remove meat. Draining excess fat.

Add onion soup, boiling water, chili sauce, dill and meat. Cover and cook at 300° for 2-2½ hours, or until meat is tender. Remove meat and set aside. Add vegetables and cook until tender, about 40 minutes. Remove vegetables.

Let pan with gravy cool for a few minutes. Place it in freezer until fat solidifies. Remove fat.

Slice meat and return it with vegetables to pan. Heat and serve.

4 TO 6 SERVINGS

Stuffed Cabbage

1	head cabbage
1	pound ground turkey, beef or veal
4	tablespoons uncooked rice
4	tablespoons grated onion
2	tablespoons ketchup
1	egg
1	teaspoon salt
½	teaspoon pepper
1	(28 ounce) can tomatoes
1	(10¾ ounce) can tomato soup
	juice of 1 lemon
½	cup brown sugar
¼	cup raisins

Cut a wedge from the core of the cabbage. Place cabbage in a large pot of boiling water with the cored side down. Simmer until the leaves begin to separate and then pull off leaves.

In a mixing bowl, mix meat, rice, onion, ketchup, egg, salt and pepper. Put 1 tablespoon of meat mixture at the base of each cabbage leaf. Fold sides in and roll like an envelope.

In a small bowl, mix together tomatoes, tomato soup, lemon juice and brown sugar. Line shallow casserole with half of this mixture. Add cabbage rolls and pour remaining mixture on top. Cover and bake for 1 hour.

Uncover and add raisins and baste. Bake two more hours.

4 TO 6 SERVINGS

Luscious Liver

2	green peppers, cut up
½	pound mushrooms
1	onion, sliced fine
1½	pounds beef liver
¼	teaspoon salt
⅛	teaspoon oregano
¼	teaspoon basil
⅛	teaspoon garlic powder
¾	cup red or white wine, dry
1	red tomato, quartered

Sauté the mushrooms and peppers. Drain well. Brown the onion in oil. Brown the liver quickly in pan, turning once. Add remainder of ingredients. Simmer 15 minutes. Serve over rice or potatoes.

Beef Stroganoff

4-5 tablespoons butter
1 large onion, sliced
2 pounds mushrooms, sliced
1 heaping tablespoon flour
4 heaping tablespoons sour cream
2 pounds beef tenderloin
  salt to taste
  dash of nutmeg, optional

All ingredients should be at room temperature.

Melt 2 tablespoons butter and sauté onions. Remove onions from pan and sauté mushrooms. Mix mushrooms, onions and flour together and let cool. Stir in sour cream. Let mixture stand at least 2 hours or refrigerated overnight.

Cut meat into thin strips 3 inches long. About 20 minutes before serving, heat sour cream mixture in double boiler. Brown meat rapidly on both sides in remaining butter. Allow meat to cool for a few minutes and stir into sour cream mixture. Add pan juices. Season with salt and nutmeg. If mixture is too thick, add 1-2 tablespoons water swished through meat pan.

Serve over noodles.

4 TO 5 SERVINGS

Stir-Fried Beef with Vegetables

An authentic Chinese recipe. Stir-fried in a wok, this food is low in calories and high in vitamins and minerals.

2   tablespoons peanut oil

1   teaspoon salt

1-2   cloves garlic, crushed

1   tablespoon fresh minced gingerroot

1½   pounds sirloin tips, flank steak, chicken breasts, chicken livers, or veal, sliced very thin

2-3   stalks celery, sliced diagonally into ¼ inch pieces

1   green pepper, sliced into ½ inch by ½ pieces

3-4   onions, thinly sliced, then cut in half

¼-½   pound mushrooms, sliced or a small package dried Chinese mushrooms, soaked in water

1   tablespoon medium dry sherry

5   tablespoons chicken stock or bouillon

1   tablespoon cornstarch in 2-3 tablespoons cold water

OPTIONAL

     bok choy

     thinly sliced water chestnuts

     sliced bamboo shoots

     fresh bean sprouts

     fresh Chinese pea pods

     any other vegetable you'd like

Heat dry wok over high heat until a drop of water bubbles over surface. Add oil, drizzling down side of wok. When oil is hot add salt, garlic and ginger. Remove garlic and ginger before they burn.

Add meat or chicken, stir-frying just enough to remove pinkness. Remove and set aside. Stir-fry vegetables, adding a little more oil if necessary. Start with tough vegetables such as celery and pepper. When vegetables are seared and lightly coated with oil, cover for 2-3 minutes, until they are tender but still crisp.

Return meat to wok. Add sherry and stock, stir-frying. Add cornstarch and water mixture, and stir-fry 30 seconds, or until slightly thickened and glossy.

6 SERVINGS

Serve with rice and Chinese tea.

# Lamb Curry

This is a very simple recipe — use leftover lamb with equal success!

2	tablespoons minced onions
1	clove garlic, minced
2	tablespoon curry powder
½	teaspoon marjoram
⅛	teaspoon cayenne
½	teaspoon salt
3	tablespoons butter
2	pounds boned leg of lamb, cubed
½-1	cup beef bouillon
	lemon to taste
	cooked rice
	chutney
	chopped onions
	peanuts
	coconut

Sauté the onions, garlic and seasonings in butter. When onion is soft, add meat and brown. Slowly add bouillon and simmer until tender, about 1 hour. When done add lemon juice to taste. Serve with rice, garnishes of chutney, chopped raw onion, peanuts, coconut, etc.

Lamb and Eggplant

2	tablespoons oil
3	pounds lamb cubes
6	onions, chopped
1	large eggplant, peeled and cubed
1	teaspoon paprika
1	teaspoon ground allspice
1	teaspoon salt
½	teaspoon pepper
1	teaspoon sugar
1	(16 ounce) can Italian tomatoes
1	cup dry red wine

Preheat oven to 350°. In a large casserole heat oil and brown meat. Add onions and cook until translucent. Add remaining ingredients. Cover and bake for 1½ hours, or until lamb is tender.

6 SERVINGS

Orange Mint Glazed Leg of Lamb

1   leg of lamb, 5 pounds
3   cloves garlic, slivered
1   teaspoon salt
¼   teaspoon pepper
1   teaspoon rosemary
½   cup orange juice
¼   cup orange liqueur
½   cup chopped mint or ½ cup mint jelly

Preheat oven to 300°. Make slits in lamb and insert garlic slivers. Place on rack in open roasting pan, fat side up. Season and bake for 30-35 minutes per pound. An hour before end of cooking time, combine orange juice and liqueur and pour over lamb, topping with mint. Baste often for good glaze.

4 TO 6 SERVINGS

Baked Lamb Shanks and Barley

6   lamb shanks
     salt and pepper
1   large onion, diced
1   stalk celery with leaves, diced
3   carrots, sliced
1   clove garlic, minced
¼   cup oil
¾   cup pearl barley (large size)
1   cup consommé or 1 bouillon cube dissolved in 1 cup boiling water
1   cup sherry
2   bay leaves
     dash of thyme

Preheat oven to 350°. Place lamb shanks in roasting pan or large casserole. Roast, uncovered, for 30 minutes. Pour off excess fat. Season with salt and pepper; set aside.

Sauté onion, celery, carrots and garlic in 2 tablespoons oil until onions are golden. In another skillet add remaining oil and lightly toast barley, stirring constantly so it does not burn. Add consommé and sherry. Combine sautéed vegetables and barley in roasting pan with lamb shanks on top. If necessary, add additional hot consommé to be sure barley is covered with liquid. Add bay leaves and thyme. Cover pan. Bake for 2 hours, stirring occasionally.

6 SERVINGS

Penne and Tomato-Lemon-Braised Lamb Shoulder

Al Forno Restaurant in Providence, Rhode Island

1	lemon
⅔	cup freshly squeezed lemon juice
1½	cups tomato paste, preferably organic (two 6 ounce cans)
½	teaspoon sea salt
1	(5-6 pound) bone-in lamb shoulder
5-6	sprigs fresh thyme
	freshly ground black pepper
1	pound dried penne
	freshly grated Pecorino Romano

Preheat oven to 350°. Remove the yellow zest from lemon with a sharp vegetable peeler, being careful to leave bitter white pith behind. Set aside. (You can squeeze the peeled lemon as part of the volume of the juice.)

Stir together lemon juice, tomato paste, salt and 2 cups water; add the lemon zest.

Place the lamb in a roaster with a tight fitting lid that is just large enough to hold the meat snugly. Pour the tomato and lemon mixture over the meat. Add the thyme and a liberal amount of black pepper. Drape a piece of moistened parchment paper directly over the lamb and liquid. Cover the roaster and bake for 1 hour. Lower the oven temperature to 325° and roast an additional hour, or until lamb is very tender-almost falling off the bone. Taste the sauce and add more salt if necessary. Keep the lamb warm while you prepare the pasta course.

Bring a large pot of water to a boil. Generously salt the water and drop in the penne. Cook, stirring often, until al dente. Drain the pasta and transfer it to a heated serving bowl. Nudge the lamb to one side of a roaster and tip the pan a bit to ladle enough of tomato-lemon sauce over the penne to coat it nicely. There should be a little puddle of sauce on the bottom of the bowl. Sprinkle a liberal amount of Pecorino Romano over the pasta and toss. Serve right away with the extra cheese passed at the table.

For the main course, slice the lamb, place on a heated platter, and nap it with some of the remaining sauce. Serve with or without vegetable accompaniment.

8 SERVINGS

Reprinted with permission from *On Top of Spaghetti* by Johanne Killeen and George Germon, published by William Morrow, an Imprint of Harper Collins Publishers.

Backyard Lamb Shanks

6	meaty lamb shanks
1	cup tomato juice
½	cup lemon juice
½	cup dill pickle juice
1	large onion, finely chopped
1	green pepper, finely chopped
1	teaspoon salt
1	teaspoon coarsely ground pepper
1	teaspoon cumin
1	teaspoon marjoram

Place lamb shanks in deep bowl. Combine remaining ingredients and pour over meat. Marinate for 4 hours. Grill over slow coals, brushing with marinade and turning occasionally, about 1 hour, or until tender (do not overcook).

Veal Marsala

½	cup bread crumbs
½	cup flour
1	teaspoon salt
⅛	teaspoon pepper
⅛	teaspoon paprika
¼	teaspoon oregano
¼	teaspoon basil
2	pounds Italian style veal cutlets
4	tablespoons oil
4	tablespoons butter
½	pound mushrooms, slice
1	cup Marsala wine

Preheat oven to 350°. Blend crumbs, flour, seasonings and herbs together. Dredge veal in this mixture. Heat 1 tablespoon oil in large skillet; add 1 tablespoon butter and sauté cutlets, a few at a time, until brown on both sides. (Add oil and butter as needed for browning.) Transfer veal to flat baking pan. When all veal is browned, melt remaining butter and sauté mushrooms. Add wine and cook 1 minute. Pour over meat and bake for 15 minutes or until tender. Serve immediately.

6 SERVINGS

Veal à la Marietta

4   onions, sliced

½   cup olive oil

4   cloves garlic, crushed

5   pounds veal leg or rump, cut in 1½ inch cubes

5   large fresh red peppers, coarsely chopped

5   large fresh green peppers, cut into 1 inch strips

2   (28 ounce) cans whole Italian tomatoes, put through sieve or food mill

     salt and freshly ground pepper

     oregano

OPTIONAL

     mint flakes

     grated Parmesan cheese

½   pound fresh mushrooms, sliced

Sauté onion in oil for about 2 minutes. Add garlic and cook 1 minute longer. Add veal cubes, cover, and brown well on all sides over medium heat. Add seasonings to taste.

Transfer to Dutch oven and add peppers and tomatoes. Cook covered, stirring occasionally, for 30 minutes or until peppers are tender. Correct seasonings. Add mushrooms and cook about 15 minutes more or until peppers are brown.

TO SERVE

Served with fettuccine or other pasta, green salad, garlic bread and perhaps some zucchini, this is a perfect party dish. It doubles, triples or quadruples well. It may be made 2 or 3 days in advance and refrigerated, or weeks in advance and frozen.

10 TO 12 SERVINGS

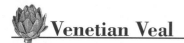

4	pounds veal cubes
1	teaspoon salt
½	cup flour
1	pound mushrooms, sliced
2	tablespoons butter
1	cup olive oil
1	teaspoon pepper
1	tablespoon parsley, chopped
1	cup tomato sauce
1	cup chicken stock
½	cup Madeira wine
2	tablespoons lemon juice
	grated Parmigiano-Reggiano for garnish

Preheat oven to 350°. Spread pieces of veal on a sheet of wax paper and sprinkle with salt. Place flour in bowl, add meat and turn in flour to coat well. Sauté mushrooms in butter to brown. Remove to casserole. Add olive oil to pan and brown veal cubes. Remove veal to casserole. Add remaining ingredients. Bake for 1 hour or until tender. Adjust seasoning. Serve with grated cheese.

8 SERVINGS

Simply *More* Poultry

Food continued to play an important role.
A committee of the Miriam Hospital Association supervised
the preparation and serving of kosher foods for Passover.

Two Separate Kitchens

There are two separate kitchens in accordance with the sanitary law, and the most modern arrangements are employed. The food is prepared and served from the Main kitchen — there is no rehandling or reheating of food. The service is so planned and systematized that no time is lost and the food is served hot.

The Miriam Hospital consistently aims to serve palatable food in accordance with the dietary laws.

FIRST ANNIVERSARY ISSUE OF THE MIRIAM HOSPITAL 1927

Chicken Amaretto

1	package frozen puff pastry shells
6	boneless chicken breast halves
	pinch garlic powder
	pinch curry powder
½	cup margarine
½	pound fresh mushrooms, thickly sliced
¼	cup amaretto liqueur
	grated rind and juice of 1 lemon
1½	cups chicken broth
1	tablespoon cornstarch
	chopped tomato and parsley

Bake pastry shells according to package directions and keep warm.

Cut chicken into 1 inch strips, sprinkle with salt and pepper. Mix flour, garlic powder and curry powder. Roll chicken strips in flour mixture. Brown chicken pieces on both sides in skillet with margarine. Add mushrooms and amaretto. Simmer 5 minutes. Mix chicken broth and cornstarch. Stir lemon rind and juice in skillet and cook over low heat until mixture bubbles and thickens. Spoon mixture in pastry shells. Sprinkle on top with the chopped tomato and parsley.

 # Baked Chicken Breasts

4	boneless chicken breast halves
	onion powder
	parsley flakes
	salt and pepper
12	tablespoons butter, divided
2	eggs
⅓	cup milk
1	cup cornflake crumbs
½	cup sherry or Rhine wine

Preheat oven to 350°. Flatten each piece of chicken, season, and top with pat of butter. Roll and secure with toothpick.

Beat eggs with milk. Dip chicken in egg mixture and roll in cornflake crumbs.

Place in baking dish with 1 pat of butter under each piece. Melt 4-6 tablespoons butter and pour over breasts. Bake for 30 minutes. Pour sherry or wine over chicken and bake 30 minutes more.

4 SERVINGS

Chicken and Artichokes

An unusual combination with a refreshing taste.

6   chicken cutlets
     seasoned bread crumbs
½   cup oil
3-4 garlic cloves
     salt and pepper to taste
¼   cup tarragon vinegar
3   tablespoons fresh parsley, finely
     chopped
2   (8½ ounce) jars artichoke hearts,
     drained and halved

Preheat oven to 350°. Cut chicken into bite size pieces and roll in bread crumbs. In a large skillet heat oil and sauté garlic. Add chicken and lightly brown both sides. (Be careful not to burn the garlic. If it turns brown, remove it and add a new clove.) Add more oil if necessary while browning chicken.

Place chicken in large baking dish. Season, add vinegar and sprinkle with parsley.

Bake for 30 minutes. Add artichokes and bake 10 more minutes.

6 SERVINGS

Bill's Favorite Barbecued Chicken

1   cup ketchup
½   cup white vinegar
¼   cup Worcestershire sauce
1   cup brown sugar
2   tablespoons dry mustard
2   teaspoons chili powder
1   teaspoon ground ginger
4   medium garlic cloves, crushed
3   tablespoons butter
4   slices lemon
2   broilers, cut in eighths

Combine all ingredients except chicken in saucepan. Stir with whisk over moderate heat until smooth.

Brush chicken with sauce. Broil with rack low in oven, skin side down first. Turn every 10 to 15 minutes, brushing with sauce the first few times and then as needed. Cook about 40 minutes.

8 SERVINGS

Can be barbecued in covered grill. Cooking time might be shorter.
Nice with rice and the extra sauce on the side.

Baked Chicken Breasts
with Gruyère Cheese and Mushrooms

2-3 boneless chicken breast halves
4 eggs, beaten
 salt to taste
1 cup fine bread crumbs
½ cup butter
½ pound fresh mushrooms
4 ounces Gruyère cheese, shredded
1 cup chicken stock
 juice of 1 lemon

Cut the chicken into strips. Combine the eggs and salt in a large bowl and mix well. Add the chicken. Cover and marinate in the refrigerator for 1 hour.

Preheat oven to 350°.

Remove the chicken from the marinade, discarding the remaining marinade. Coat the chicken with the bread crumbs. Cook the chicken in the butter in a small skillet until lightly browned. Remove to a 1½ quart casserole.

Slice the mushrooms over the chicken. Sprinkle with the cheese. Pour the chicken stock over the chicken. Bake for 30 minutes or until the chicken is cooked through. Spoon the lemon juice over the chicken before serving.

2 TO 3 SERVINGS

Chicken Breasts Veronique

12	double saltine crackers
½	teaspoon salt
¼	teaspoon pepper
¼	teaspoon tarragon, crushed
6	boneless chicken breast halves
½	cup butter or margarine, divided
¼	cup minced onion
½	cup chicken stock, or bouillon cube and water
½	cup dry white wine
½	pound mushrooms, sliced
2	cups seedless green grapes

Preheat oven to 375°. Crush crackers into very fine crumbs. (There should be about ¾ cup.) Mix well with seasonings.

Dampen chicken breasts with a few drops of water and coat with crumb mixture. Let stand for about 15 minutes

Brown chicken on all sides in half the butter. Place in shallow ovenproof dish in a single layer.

Sauté onion in butter in skillet until golden. Add chicken stock and wine. Bring to boil, then pour around chicken. Bake uncovered for 35 minutes.

Meanwhile, add remaining butter to skillet and sauté mushrooms until tender. Add grapes. Add to chicken. Bake about 10 minutes longer.

6 SERVINGS

Cranberry Chicken

4	tablespoons soy sauce
4	tablespoons lemon juice
½	teaspoon garlic powder
½	cup margarine
1	(16 ounce) can whole cranberry sauce
6	split chicken breasts

Preheat oven to 425°. Combine first 5 ingredients in saucepan and bring to boil.

Place chicken in baking pan, skin side down. Cover with sauce and bake for 30 minutes.

Turn chicken and bake 30 minutes more, basting about 4 times.

6 SERVINGS

Chicken in Champagne

1	ounce dried mushrooms
½	cup butter or margarine, divided
6	boneless chicken breasts, split
¼	cup brandy
¼	cup finely chopped onion
½	teaspoon finely chopped garlic
6	tablespoons flour
2	teaspoons ketchup
4	chicken bouillon cubes
⅛	teaspoon cayenne
2	cups canned condensed chicken broth, divided
1	cup heavy cream, divided
1½	teaspoons dried tarragon leaves
4	fresh mushrooms, thinly sliced
2	tablespoons tarragon vinegar
1½	cups champagne
	additional wine or broth

Soak dried mushrooms as package directs. Drain and chop fine.

Melt 2 tablespoons butter in Dutch oven. Brown chicken, a few pieces at a time, on all sides, adding butter as needed and removing chicken as it is browned. Return chicken to pot.

Heat brandy slightly in small saucepan. Ignite and pour over chicken. When flame dies down, remove chicken.

Add half of dried mushrooms, onion and garlic to pot and cook a few minutes over low heat. Remove from heat. Stir flour, ketchup, bouillon cubes and cayenne into pot and blend thoroughly. Gradually stir 1 cup chicken broth and ⅓ cup cream into pot. Bring to boil, stirring.

Return chicken to pot. Divide and add tarragon and sliced mushrooms. Simmer, covered for 40-45 minutes, or until chicken is tender. Remove chicken to heated platter.

Combine sauce (5 cups in all) in one pot. Stir in remaining cream, vinegar and champagne and simmer until thickened, about 5 minutes. Pour over chicken and serve.

6 TO 8 SERVINGS

Chicken and sauce may be cooled completely and frozen. To serve from frozen state, sprinkle with additional wine or broth, cover with foil and heat through, about 40 minutes.

Chicken Curry

8   boneless chicken breast halves
       (3 pounds)
¼   cup butter or margarine
2   (10½ ounce) cans condensed chicken
       broth

CURRY SAUCE

¼   cup butter or margarine
1   clove garlic, crushed
1   cup chopped onion
2-3 teaspoons curry powder
¼   cup unsifted flour
1   teaspoon ginger
½   teaspoon salt
½   teaspoon pepper
2   tablespoons grated lime
2   tablespoons lime juice
¼   cup chopped chutney
1   cup chopped tart apple
¼   teaspoon ground cardamom

Wash chicken and dry well on paper towel. In ¼ cup hot butter in large skillet, over medium heat, brown chicken 4 pieces at a time, 5 minutes per side.

Remove chicken as it is browned. Return chicken to pan, add 1 can condensed chicken broth. Reduce heat, cover and simmer for 20 minutes or just until tender. Remove chicken pieces. Keep warm. Measure liquid in skillet. Add remaining can of chicken broth and enough water to make 3 cups. Reserve.

In ¼ cup hot butter sauté garlic, onion, curry powder and apple until onion is tender about 5 minutes. Remove from heat. Stir in flour, cardamom, ginger, salt and pepper; mix well. Gradually stir in reserved 3 cups liquid, lime peel, and lime juice. Bring to boil, stirring. Reduce heat, simmer covered for 20 minutes, stirring occasionally. Stir in chutney, add chicken. Cover and heat just to gentle boil.

Serve with rice.

8 SERVINGS

Chicken Divan

6	boneless chicken breast halves
2	(10 ounce) packages frozen broccoli
4	tablespoons butter
4	tablespoon flour
1½	teaspoons salt
¼	teaspoon pepper
2	cups chicken broth
½	cup light cream
1	cup diced Cheddar cheese
¼	cup dry white wine
3	tablespoons lemon juice
¼	cup grated Parmesan cheese
	paprika

Preheat oven to 425°. Boil chicken breasts until almost tender.

Parboil broccoli, drain well, and place in buttered casserole.

Melt butter in saucepan. Blend in flour, salt, pepper and broth, stirring to boiling point. Stir in cream, cheese, wine and lemon juice and cook 5 minutes.

Place chicken over broccoli and add sauce. Sprinkle with cheese and paprika. Bake for 15-20 minutes.

6 SERVINGS

Ginger Chicken Breasts

4	boneless chicken breast halves, slightly beaten with wooden mallet
⅓	cup regular or low sodium soy sauce
1	tablespoon olive oil
3	tablespoons white wine
2	tablespoons Asian sesame oil
2	cloves garlic, minced
1	piece of fresh gingerroot, about 2 inches, peeled and minced
1	bunch bok choy, coarsely chopped
1	cup peapods
1	cup sliced mushrooms

Preheat oven to 350°. Mix soy sauce, olive oil, white wine, sesame oil, garlic, and ginger in medium size bowl. Add chicken mixture and set aside.

Place bok choy, mushrooms, and peapods in a 9 x 12 inch Pyrex dish.

Place chicken on top of vegetables, pour soy sauce mixture over the top of chicken and vegetables. Bake in oven for 1 hour or until done.

Serve with couscous or rice.

4 SERVINGS

Chicken Jalfrezi

3	tablespoons vegetable oil
1½	pounds chicken thighs, boneless, skinless, cut in half
1	green pepper, chopped
1	red pepper, chopped
1	(14½ ounce) can tomatoes, peeled and diced
2	cloves of garlic, grated
2	tablespoons grated fresh gingerroot
3	teaspoons turmeric
1	teaspoon red chili powder
3	teaspoons ground cumin
3	teaspoons ground coriander
	salt to taste
½	cup fresh cilantro/coriander leaves, chopped, for garnish

Heat the oil in a large deep skillet over medium-high heat. Add onions, garlic, ginger and cook for about 2 minutes. Add the turmeric, cumin, coriander, chili powder and salt. Fry gently, scraping the bottom of the pan frequently. Add the chicken and coat in the spice mixture. Pour in the tomatoes with their juice, cover the pan, and simmer over medium heat for 20 minutes. Uncover, and simmer for another 10 minutes to let the excess liquid evaporate. Add the cilantro leaves; simmer for another 5-7 minutes. Serve the chicken pieces with sauce spooned over the top.

Grilled Marinated Chicken Breast

6	boneless chicken breast halves
½	cup brown sugar
⅓	cup olive oil
¼	cup cider vinegar
3	cloves garlic, crushed
3	tablespoons coarse grain mustard
1½	tablespoons lemon juice
1½	tablespoons lime juice
1½	teaspoons salt
¼	teaspoon pepper

Mix marinade ingredients together. Marinate chicken at least 2 hours. Grill 8 minutes per side over low heat.

6 SERVINGS

Chicken Marsala with Portabella Mushrooms

4	large chicken cutlets (pound to ¼ inches thick)
1	cup flour
⅛	teaspoon salt
⅛	teaspoon pepper
2	eggs, slightly beaten
3	teaspoons olive oil
½	cup butter
2	large portabella mushrooms, sliced
3	scallions, chopped
1	shallot, diced
5	cloves garlic, peeled, left whole
1	lemon
1	cup Marsala wine
2	cups chicken broth
	gravy thickener

Dredge chicken in flour, then dip the chicken in the egg. In a large frying pan, sauté the chicken in the oil and butter until golden brown. Remove the chicken. Add the next four ingredients to the pan and sauté until just tender.

Remove ingredients. Add next 3 ingredients and heat to a slow boil for 2 minutes. Thicken gravy slightly.

Combine all ingredients together, cover and simmer on low for 30 minutes. Just before serving, mash garlic cloves and stir well. Garnish with fresh chopped parsley.

Serve over rice or egg noodles.

4 SERVINGS

133

Nutty Chicken in a Bowl

1	onion, sliced in rings
2	green peppers, sliced in rings
2	tablespoons oil
1	(6 ounce) can tomato paste
¾	cup peanut butter
3	cups chicken broth
1½	teaspoons salt
1	teaspoon sugar
¼	teaspoon nutmeg
4	cups diced cooked chicken
6	cups hot cooked rice

Stir-fry onions and peppers in oil until barely tender. Remove oil.

Blend tomato paste and peanut butter in bowl. Add chicken broth and seasonings. Add this mixture to skillet and heat, stirring. Add chicken. Add more broth if necessary. Pour over rice in individual bowls.

Accompany with small bowls of shredded coconut, chopped peanuts, chopped onion, tomato, green pepper or pineapple cubes for garnish.

8 SERVINGS

Opulent Chicken

4	whole boneless chicken breasts
½	cup margarine or butter, divided
1½	teaspoons salt
½	teaspoon pepper
1	tablespoon paprika
2	(6 ounce) jars marinated artichoke hearts and bottoms
1½	pounds fresh mushrooms, sliced
1	teaspoon tarragon, dry
1½	cups chicken broth
3	tablespoons flour
⅓	cup sherry

Preheat oven to 375°. In skillet, brown breasts in ¼ cup butter. Season them on all sides to taste. Remove. Drain artichokes and arrange with chicken in shallow casserole.

In same skillet, using remaining butter, sauté mushrooms slightly with tarragon. Add broth. Stir in flour and sherry and simmer 3-5 minutes.

Add mushroom mixture to chicken and bake covered for 45 minutes.

4 SERVINGS

Can be assembled 3 days in advance. Bring to room temperature before baking.

Parmesan Encrusted Chicken with Bercy Sauce and Sautéed Swiss Chard

Chef Rich Kunsch at Ledgemont Country Club in Seekonk, Massachusetts.

4   (4 ounce) boneless and skinless chicken breasts
1   cup all-purpose flour
    salt and pepper
4   eggs
¼   cup milk
8   ounces grated Parmesan cheese
1   tablespoon fresh chopped parsley
½   cup oil blended with 2 tablespoons butter (or margarine)
1½ cups Bercy sauce (recipe follows)
2   cups sautéed Swiss chard (recipe follows)

Season flour with salt and ground pepper to taste in a small bowl or pie plate. Combine eggs with milk in a bowl and whisk. Combine Parmesan cheese, chopped parsley and 2 tablespoons of flour mixture. Following a standard breading procedure, dredge chicken in flour, shake off excess, coat thoroughly with egg batter and then press into the Parmesan mixture. Place on a platter or sheet pan until completed.

Preheat oven to 400°. Heat a large sauté pan over medium high heat, add oil and heat. Add butter and melt. Place chicken in pan and sauté 2-3 minutes (on each side) until lightly browned (this can be done in stages depending on the size of the pieces). Remove chicken to a nonstick sheet pan and continue with remaining chicken. Chicken can be prepared ahead of time to this point and finished in an oven when ready to serve. Place chicken in oven and bake 5-8 minutes until cooked through. Serve with sautéed Swiss chard and Bercy sauce.

This dish can be completed with rice pilaf, garlic mashed potatoes or pasta.

continued

BERCY SAUCE

2	tablespoons olive oil
4	tablespoons unsalted butter
1	tablespoon minced garlic
½	cup dry white wine
3	tablespoons lemon juice
1	cup chicken velouté
1	tablespoon fresh chopped parsley
1	tablespoon fresh basil, very thinly sliced
1	tablespoon sliced scallion
2	tablespoons small diced tomatoes
	salt and pepper to taste

Heat a sauté pan over medium high heat. Add oil and garlic and sauté quickly to release flavor. Deglaze with white wine. Bring to a boil and reduce by half.

Add velouté and lemon juice and return to a boil. Reduce heat to low. Incorporate butter with a whisk or by swirling the pan 1 tablespoon at a time, do not allow it to come to a boil.

Remove from heat and finish the sauce with fresh herbs and tomatoes. Serve immediately.

Note: To make chicken velouté: Melt 1½ tablespoons butter over low heat. Add flour and mix well. Turn heat up to medium and cook flour and butter for 2 minutes, stirring constantly. Slowly add 1 cup warm chicken stock into butter and flour mixture, whisking constantly. Cook for about 5 minutes until the sauce slightly thickens.

GARLIC SCENTED SWISS CHARD

2	pounds Swiss chard, separate leaves from stems
	Kosher salt
	pinch baking soda
3	tablespoons extra virgin olive oil
1	large garlic clove, peeled and sliced
	freshly ground black pepper
	aged balsamic vinegar

Clean and trim the chard in cold water. Cut the stems into 1 inch pieces. Bring a large pot of water to a boil with a pinch of salt and baking soda. Adding a pinch of baking soda to the water brings out a brighter color when blanching green vegetables. Blanch leaves, stir to submerge and boil quickly, for 30 seconds, to release color, remove with a slotted spoon and place in an ice bath to cool immediate.

Return pot to a boil and cook the stems for approximately 3 minutes until al dente. Refresh immediately in an ice bath. Pat the leaves dry and slice into 1 inch slices, drain and dry the stems and combine the chard. This dish can be prepared to this point ahead of time and finished when serving.

Combine oil and garlic in a large skillet and heat over medium heat. When garlic begins to color, add chard and warm thoroughly. Season to taste with salt and pepper. Drizzle with balsamic vinegar and serve immediately.

Chicken Cutlets Parmigiana

8	boneless chicken breasts halves
1	egg, beaten
	seasoned bread crumbs
	oil
2	cups spaghetti sauce
8	slices mozzarella cheese
2	tablespoons Parmesan cheese

Preheat oven to 350°. Flatten chicken breasts between sheets of wax paper. Dip in egg, then in crumbs. Sauté in oil until lightly brown on both sides. Remove to ovenproof platter. Spread with spaghetti sauce and top each cutlet with slice of mozzarella and sprinkling of Parmesan cheese. Bake for 20 minutes.

8 SERVINGS

Chicken Scaloppini

4	boneless chicken breast halves
2	teaspoons fresh lemon juice
¼	teaspoon salt
¼	teaspoon black pepper
⅓	cup Italian seasoned bread crumbs (can add Parmesan cheese)
½	cup chicken broth
¼	cup dry white wine
2	cloves garlic
4	teaspoons capers
1	tablespoon butter

Place each chicken breast half between 2 sheets of wax paper and pound thin. Brush chicken with juice and sprinkle with salt and pepper. Dredge chicken in bread crumbs.

In a large skillet, use either cooking spray or oil, heat the pan and add chicken. Cook until each side is done, about 3 minutes per side. Remove from pan.

Add broth and wine to pan stirring constantly for about 30 seconds. Remove from heat and stir in capers and butter. Pour over chicken and serve.

4 SERVINGS

Add Parmesan cheese to bread crumbs if desired.

Mushroom Baked Chicken

4   chicken breasts, halved
2   (10½ ounce) cans cream of
        mushroom soup
2   cups sour cream
1   cup sherry
½   pound fresh mushrooms, sliced

Preheat oven to 350°. Place chicken breasts, skin side up, in large baking dish.

In saucepan heat (not boil) the remaining ingredients, stirring until smooth. Add mushrooms. Pour over chicken breasts. Bake for one hour.

Serve with rice tossed with toasted almonds.

6 SERVINGS

This recipe may be prepared in advance and refrigerated until final cooking.

Chicken with Lemon

2   small chickens, cut up
3   tablespoons butter
¼   cup finely chopped shallots
½   cup dry white wine
10   thin lemon slices
        salt and freshly ground pepper

Separate legs from thighs. Split whole breast in half. Remove bone from breast halves, leaving wings attached.

Season chicken with salt and pepper to taste. Melt butter in skillet and brown chicken skin side down. When golden, turn and brown other side.

Sprinkle chicken with shallots and arrange lemon slices on top. Cover, cooking 5 minutes. Pour off fat and add wine. Cover and cook 15 minutes or until tender.

6 SERVINGS

Serve with pan gravy and rice.

Balsamic Honey Chicken

1	whole chicken, quartered
5	tablespoons Dijon mustard
½	cup balsamic vinegar
1	large sweet onion, sliced
	Kosher salt
	pepper
	honey

Wash and dry chicken, place chicken in a large Pyrex dish. Cover with sliced onions. Sprinkle with salt and pepper. Rub mustard on chicken and onions, drizzle honey on chicken and onions. Pour vinegar on top.

Let marinate for 1 hour in refrigerator. Preheat oven to 350°. Roast for 1 hour, maybe more, depending on size. Serve with rice.

Chicken Cacciatore

4	chicken legs
6	split chicken breasts
	flour
	oil for frying
	butter
2	garlic cloves, chopped
2	onion, chopped
1	small can chicken broth
1	(28 ounce) can crushed tomatoes
	sliced mushrooms, green peppers, black olives
½	teaspoon sugar
¼	teaspoon oregano
¼	teaspoon thyme
¼	teaspoon parsley
1	bay leaf
¼	cup Marsala wine
	salt and pepper to taste

Preheat oven to 325°. Dredge chicken pieces in flour. Fry chicken in oil until brown and crispy. Remove chicken from frying pan. Clean pan. Sauté garlic and onions in butter. Add tomatoes, chicken broth, sugar, salt and pepper. Bring to boil. Add oregano, thyme parsley, bay leaf.

Place chicken in deep oven dish. Pour tomato sauce over chicken until chicken is covered. Cover chicken and bake for 30-45 minutes. Uncover and add Marsala wine, peppers, mushrooms and olives. Cook uncovered for 10-15 minutes.

Remove chicken from casserole dish and spoon sauce over chicken. Serve with pasta and extra sauce.

Chicken Chasseur

1	frying chicken (2½-3 pounds)
½	cup flour
½	teaspoon thyme
2	teaspoons salt
½	teaspoon pepper
2	teaspoons paprika
2	tablespoons butter
2	tablespoons oil
3	green onions, chopped
2	tomatoes, peeled and chopped
¼	cup lemon juice
¼	cup fresh mushrooms
1	cup white table wine
½	teaspoon salt
½	cup chicken bouillon
2	teaspoons chopped parsley
½	teaspoon dried tarragon for garnish

Cut chicken into serving pieces. Combine flour and seasonings in zip top bag. Add chicken, a few pieces at a time, and shake to coat each piece. Brown in heated butter and oil.

Add green onions and tomatoes to chicken. Add remaining ingredients and cook, covered, on low heat for about 1 hour. Garnish with fresh tarragon. Serve with hot rice if desired.

4 SERVINGS

Crispy Chicken

1	fryer, cut in serving pieces
	vegetable oil
	salt
	freshly ground pepper
	garlic powder
1	cup bread crumbs

Preheat oven to 350°. Brush chicken lightly with oil. Season and roll in crumbs.

Arrange in shallow baking pan or cookie sheet with space between pieces so they will crisp. Bake for about 1 hour or until golden brown. (It is not necessary to turn chicken.)

4 SERVINGS

Also great served cold.

# Coq Au Vin

1	chicken (3-4 pounds) skinless, boneless and cut into 2 x 2 inch pieces
6	tablespoons flour
⅓	cup butter or oil
2-3	onions, diced
4	cloves garlic, diced fine
3	carrots, diced
3	stalks celery, diced
2	ounces brandy
2	cups dry red wine
2	cups beef stock or bouillon
½	tablespoon tomato paste
6	mushrooms, sliced
	salt and pepper
3	bay leaves
1	teaspoon thyme

Roll chicken pieces in flour, saving excess and brown in butter or oil. Remove chicken and sauté diced vegetables.

Return chicken to vegetable mixture, reduce heat, sprinkle with flour and stir well. Add brandy and cook 3 minutes. Add wine, stirring until mixture boils. Add beef stock, mushrooms and remaining ingredients. Cover and simmer gently for 30 minutes.

Serve with rice pilaf and green vegetables.

4 SERVINGS

Chicken Fricassee

2	chickens, quartered
4-6	onions, chopped
1	(1 pound) package carrots, peeled and cut into 1 inch slices
2	red peppers, cut into chunks
2	green peppers, cur into chunks
4	stalks celery, chopped
1	handful flat Italian parsley, chopped
2	pounds ripe tomatoes, chopped
	garlic powder to taste
	pepper to taste
	paprika to taste

Put vegetables in big pot, mix up and season. Put chicken on top of vegetables and season. Start out cooking on high, watch and stir. When the juice begins to cook, lower heat and cook on low for about 1 hour until done. Serve with brown rice.

Glazed Chicken and Sweet Potatoes

1   **chicken cut into serving pieces, skinned if you wish**

½   **cup corn flakes**

½   **cup apricot jelly**

2-3   **large cooked sweet potatoes, cubed**

       curry powder

       garlic powder

       rosemary leaves

       pepper

       paprika

Preheat oven to 350°. Oil baking pan lightly. Pour corn flakes in a brown paper bag and crush to make coarse crumbs. Drop chicken pieces into bag and shake to cover with corn flakes and place into pan. Sprinkle with the seasonings and cover pan. Bake for 1 hour.

When almost done, uncover and place boiled sweet potatoes in and around chicken. With fork, break up apricot jelly and drop over both chicken and potatoes. Bake uncovered for 15-20 minutes until nicely glazed.

4 SERVINGS

Hawaiian Chicken

2   **chickens, cut in eighths or 8 small chicken breasts**

¼   **cup brown sugar**

2   **tablespoons sugar**

2   **tablespoons Worcestershire sauce**

1   **tablespoon prepared mustard**

¼   **cup vinegar**

½   **cup ketchup**

¼   **teaspoon salt**

¼   **cup butter**

¼   **teaspoon pepper**

1   **teaspoon paprika**

1   **(20 ounce) can crushed pineapple**

Preheat oven to 350°. Bring all ingredients except crushed pineapple and chicken to boil. Add pineapple.

Bake chicken dry, covered with foil for about 30 minutes. Remove foil and baste with ½ the sauce. Bake another 30 minutes, uncovered. Add remaining sauce and bake 20 minutes more, uncovered.

8 SERVINGS

Lemon Thyme Chicken

A great holiday dish.

3   chickens, cut up
¾   cup fresh lemon juice
½   large onion, minced
1   tablespoon salt
½   tablespoon pepper
½   tablespoon thyme dried or
      2 tablespoons fresh
½   clove garlic, crushed
      green and red grapes for garnish

Preheat oven to 375°. Combine lemon juice, onion, salt, pepper, thyme and garlic. Arrange chicken skin side up. Pour lemon mixture over chicken, marinate overnight.

Bake for 1-1½ hours.

Middle Eastern Chicken

12   ounces brown rice, soak in water
      2-3 hours, drain
1   chicken, cut up
3   tablespoons oil
      salt and pepper to taste
      garlic salt to taste
2   teaspoons ground cumin
3   large onions, chopped
3½   cups water
4   carrots, peeled and cut into
      matchstick pieces
1   cup raisins
2   tablespoons butter

Soak brown rice. Sauté chicken in oil, browning on all sides. Season and when browned, put chicken in oven proof Dutch oven. Sauté onions in same pan, stirring frequently. When onions are browned, pour entire contents of pan onto chicken. Add rice, 3½ cups water and 2 teaspoons salt to chicken. Cover and boil 12-15 minutes.

Preheat oven to 300°. Meanwhile, sauté carrots and raisins in butter. Add to chicken and rice. Cover, cook in oven for 30 minutes or until water is absorbed and chicken is cooked.

Roasted Orange and Garlic Chicken

This recipe is very simple and easy to prepare — always a crowd pleaser. Good for a hearty winter dinner.

1	(2½-3 pound) whole chicken
1	orange
2	sweet onions
2	teaspoons minced garlic
2	tablespoons kosher salt or enough to rub over chicken
	paprika to cover chicken
4	potatoes, peeled and quartered
1	(1 pound) package carrots, peeled and quartered
	salt
	thyme
	olive oil

Cut orange into 4 sections. Squeeze juice over chicken and rub. Stuff peels into cavity.

Cut onions into eighths. Place half under chicken and half into cavity. Place chicken in roasting pan. Arrange potatoes and carrots around chicken. Season with salt, thyme and olive oil

Rub garlic then salt over chicken. Sprinkle with paprika. Set aside to marinate for at least 1 hour.

Preheat oven to 450°. Roast for 1-1¼ hours.

4 SERVINGS

Chicken Piquant

3	pounds chicken parts
¾	cup white or rosé wine
¼	cup soy sauce
¼	cup olive oil
1	cup chicken broth
2	tablespoons grated fresh ginger or 2 teaspoons powdered ginger
1	tablespoon brown sugar
¼	teaspoon oregano

Preheat oven to 375°. Arrange chicken in one tight-fitting layer in a casserole.

In bowl, combine wine with remaining ingredients and pour over chicken. Cover with lid or foil.

Bake for 45 minutes. Turn chicken, then bake 45 minutes longer.

Delicious served with rice.

6 SERVINGS

Pineapple Chicken

⅓   cup cornstarch

3   tablespoons paprika

      salt to taste

5-6   pound chicken, cut into eighths

¼   cup oil

1   cup diced celery

1   cup diced green pepper

1   (20 ounce) can pineapple chunks,
        drained, reserving ¼ cup of juice

2   tablespoons cornstarch

¼   cup pineapple juice

¼   teaspoon paprika

3   tablespoons soy sauce

1   table Worcestershire sauce

2   tablespoons brown sugar

Mix first 3 ingredients and coat chicken with mixture. Fry in hot oil until golden brown. Lower heat, cover and cook 15 minutes. Drain all oil. Add vegetables and drained pineapple and steam 10 minutes.

Dissolve cornstarch in pineapple juice and blend in remaining ingredients. Pour over chicken and stir gently. Cover and steam 10-20 minutes more, or until tender.

Serve on hot fluffy rice.

6 SERVINGS

Chicken Ragu

6-8   chicken thighs

½   cup raisins

½   cup sherry

¼   cup flour

¼   cup butter

1   onion, chopped

1   celery stalk, chopped

1   garlic clove, minced

2   teaspoons curry

1   (24 ounce) jar spaghetti sauce

Preheat oven to 350°. Soak raisins in sherry for 2 hours. Dredge chicken in flour. Brown in butter. Remove from pan. Sauté vegetables, garlic and curry for 3-4 minutes. Place chicken into Pyrex dish. Add spaghetti sauce, sherry and raisins. Bake 1 hour.

4 SERVINGS

 **Yakitori**

¾ cup Japanese soy sauce

¼ cup sugar

½ sake or dry sherry

1 chicken (2½-3 pounds) cut into 16 (1½ inch) pieces, with bone

10-12 scallions, cut into 2 inch pieces
    sesame seeds

Mix soy sauce, sugar and sake. Line bottom of broiling pan with mixture, add chicken in one layer, add remaining sauce and sprinkle with scallions. Marinate about 2 hours, turning and basting occasionally.

Preheat broiler. With bone side up, broil chicken close to top of broiler for 2 minutes. Then move to bottom and broil 5 minutes, basting occasionally. Turn and repeat. Sprinkle generously with sesame seeds. Broil, basting occasionally, until chicken is tender and sesame seeds are delicately brown.

4 SERVINGS

To give chicken a Chinese flavor, use Chinese soy sauce, brown sugar, sherry, and add 3 or 4 slices fresh ginger.

Buttery Cornish Hens

6   Cornish hens, 1 pound each
     salt and pepper to taste
¾   cup softened butter
3   tablespoons chopped chives
¼   teaspoon crushed rosemary
3   tablespoons lemon juice
½   cup warmed apricot jam

Preheat oven to 350°. Wash and pat hens dry, inside and out. Sprinkle skin and cavities lightly with salt and pepper.

Blend butter with chives, rosemary and lemon juice and place about 1 tablespoon in large cavity of bird. Tie legs together.

Place breast side up in shallow roaster at 350° for 1-1½ hours. Melt remaining butter herb mixture and baste occasionally.

When birds are almost done, brush with jam to glaze to a golden brown.

6 SERVINGS

Amaretto Turkey

Gives a very nutty flavor to turkey.

1   (15 pound) turkey
8   garlic cloves, divided
     pepper to taste
1   pint amaretto liqueur
1   cup orange juice
1   apple or 1 orange
1   large sweet onion
2   bay leaves

Preheat oven to 325°. Clean turkey. Place apple or orange inside cavity along with 3 garlic cloves (cracked slightly), bay leaf and pepper.

Rub 2 cloves of garlic on skin of bird and pepper to taste.

Pour orange juice and 1 cup amaretto liqueur over bird. Put 3 garlic cloves, bay leaf and onion in pan.

Cover. Roast for 20 minutes per pound, basting often and adding more liqueur as necessary. Uncover for last 30 minutes.

8 TO 10 SERVINGS

Canard á l'Orange

An elegant entrée for your most important dinner guests.

1   (5 pound) duck seasoned with salt, pepper, garlic powder
½   cup currant jelly
4   tablespoons sugar
1   bay leaf
2-3 whole peppercorns
1½   cups beef bouillon
2   oranges, juice and rind
1   lemon, juice and rind
¾   cup preserved kumquats
     garlic powder to taste
     salt and freshly ground pepper to taste
     about 1 cup dry red wine
     about ½ cup Grand Marnier™

Preheat oven to 450°. Season duck inside and out. Cook, uncovered, on rack in shallow baking pan for about 2 hours. (The high heat drains the fat away and crisps skin.)

Combine remaining ingredients, except wines, and simmer slowly, uncovered, while duck cooks. After 30 minutes, pour a little sauce on duck (not too much, or skin will get rubbery), and add 2-3 tablespoons drippings to sauce. Repeat about every 30 minutes.

Half an hour before serving, add wine to sauce. About 10-15 minutes before serving, add Grand Marnier™.

Serve on well-and tree platter surrounded by sauce. Fruit skins are delicious eating!

Serve with rice, salad and simple vegetable.

2 TO 4 SERVINGS

Simply *More* Fish

The women of the Miriam Hospital Association formed a sewing group to sew draperies, slip covers, dresser scarves, and tray cloths, surgical dressings and baby gowns. Linen showers were held to purchase bed linens.

Accommodations For A Patient

Accommodations include private wards, semi-private rooms, private rooms, and general wards. The same standard of service, the highest possible, is provided for all. The furnishing of the rooms has been carried out with the idea of giving convenience and comfort to the patient, physician and nurse. The conventional hospital furnishings have been avoided and the rooms have the most homelike appearance. The usual hospital monotone of glaring white or apple green is missing. Every modern convenience and facility is employed.

Every patient feels at home at the Miriam.

FIRST ANNIVERSARY ISSUE OF THE MIRIAM HOSPITAL 1927

Simply More Fish

Spicy Beer Battered Fish Bites

1   pound white fish such as cod,
       tilapia, or flounder
1-2 bottles of beer
1   tablespoon lemon pepper
1   tablespoon black pepper
2   tablespoons cayenne pepper
2   cups flour
2   cups cornmeal
       oil for frying

Mix all dry ingredients, then add beer to thicken batter consistency. Cut fish into marshmallow size pieces. Lightly dust fish in flour and then dip into batter before deep frying until golden brown.

2 TO 3 SERVINGS

Mexican Fish

2   pounds cod fillets
1½ cups salsa
1½ cups shredded sharp Cheddar
       cheese
¾   cup coarsely crushed corn chips
2   avocados, sliced
¼   cup sour cream
       olive oil
       salt and pepper

Preheat oven to 400°. Lightly grease one 9 x 13 inch baking dish. Rinse fish fillets under cold water and pat dry with paper towels. Brush both sides with olive oil. Add salt and pepper to taste. Lay fillets in a single layer in prepared baking dish.

Pour the salsa evenly over the top, sprinkle with the shredded cheese. Top with the crushed corn chips. Bake, uncovered, in the preheated oven for 15 minutes or until fish flakes with a fork. Place sliced avocado over the top of the fish. Serve with sour cream.

4 TO 6 SERVINGS

Italian Style Baked Cod

2   cod fillets
1   (14½ ounce) can diced tomatoes
¼   cup bread crumbs
     oregano
     pepper
     olive oil

Preheat oven to 400°. Lay cod in baking dish and fold about 2 inches of the thin end under the fish. Spoon the tomatoes over each fillet. Sprinkle bread crumbs on top of the tomatoes. Add a generous amount of oregano. Pepper to taste. Drizzle the olive oil sparingly.

Bake for 20-30 minutes depending on your desired moistness.

2 SERVINGS

Flounder Pie

12   double unsalted saltines
¼   teaspoon dried dill
½   teaspoon salt
3   teaspoons minced onion
3   tablespoons butter
2   tablespoons lemon juice
¼   cup slivered almonds
1   pound flounder fillets
2   tablespoons melted butter
4   tablespoons dry white wine

Preheat oven to 375°. Break crackers into coarse crumbs. It should make about 1 cup. Mix with dill and salt. Set aside. Sauté onion in 3 tablespoons butter until tender. Stir in crumb mixture, almonds and lemon juice.

Line the bottom of a 9 inch pie plate with ½ the flounder. Cover with a layer of about ¾ of the crumb mixture. Cover with remaining flounder. Mix melted butter with wine and brush top of the fish with the mixture. Place remaining crumb mixture around the edge. Bake approximately 15 minutes.

4 SERVINGS

Gefilte Fish Redone!

12	pieces gefilte fish with jelly
6	carrots, sliced
2	onions, sliced
2	tablespoons Hungarian paprika

Boil 10 cups of water mixed with jelly from the fish. Add carrots and onions. Boil for 15 minutes and reduce to a simmer for another 20 minutes. Add fish, sprinkle generously with paprika and cook for 30 minutes. Remove fish and cool. Refrigerate and serve cold.

12 SERVINGS

Best if prepared 1-2 days ahead.

Baked Haddock

1½	pounds of haddock fillets, skinless
1	sleeve low sodium Ritz crackers
2	tablespoons mayonnaise
5-6	slices white American cheese, thinly sliced
1	lemon

Preheat oven to 350°. In a baking dish, lay the haddock fillets side by side. Spread the mayonnaise over the fillets evenly. Lay the cheese slices over the mayonnaise to cover the fish. Crumble the Ritz crackers over the cheese, covering the surface. Squeeze ½ the lemon juice over the cracker topping. Bake for about 30-35 minutes or until the cheese starts to bubble. Cut the other ½ of the lemon for individual juice on each serving.

4 SERVINGS

Marinated Fish Steak Kabobs

2	pounds halibut or swordfish steaks
¼	cup olive oil
½	cup dry white wine
2	tablespoons lemon juice
1	tablespoon minced garlic
1	teaspoon salt
⅛	teaspoon pepper
½	teaspoon oregano
12	cherry tomatoes
6	fresh mushrooms

Cut fish steaks into chunks, removing any bones and skin. Combine oil and spices and marinate fish several hours, or overnight. Place fish and vegetables on skewers and grill 5 minutes per side.

4 TO 6 SERVINGS

This entire dish can be baked, uncovered, at 375° for approximately 10-15 minutes.

Halibut Kabobs

¼	cup soy sauce
¼	cup olive oil
¼	cup lemon juice
¼	cup snipped parsley
½	teaspoon salt
	pepper
1	pound halibut, cubed
	large stuffed green olives
	lemon wedges

Combine first 6 ingredients for basting sauce. Let stand 1 hour at room temperature, stirring now and then.

On skewers, alternate fish, olives, and lemon. Broil over hot coals, turning and brushing frequently with sauce. Do not overcook.

2 TO 3 SERVINGS

Pan Seared Halibut with Escarole and Chickpeas

Red Stripe Restaurant in Providence, Rhode Island

4	**fresh halibut steaks, trimmed**
2	**large lemons**
2	**heads fresh escarole**
1	**can cooked chickpeas**
2	**tablespoons vegetable or canola oil**
	olive oil for drizzling
	salt
	pepper
	crushed red pepper flakes

Trim escarole heads by cutting in half and removing the core. Escarole tends to be one of the more "dirt absorbing" leafy greens so after cutting into roughly 3 x 3 inch pieces, "float" the lettuce in a large amount of cold water to remove any stubborn particles. Strain and thoroughly pat dry with paper towel.

Place a skillet over medium high heat for about 6 minutes until it is very hot. Add about 2 tablespoons vegetable oil (olive oil will just smoke away under this heat) and let the oil heat. Season the fish with salt and black pepper just before placing gently in the hot pan. Lower heat to medium. Resist all urges to touch the fish at this point. Let the fish brown itself without movement for about 4 minutes in the pan. The pan should not be smoking hot at this point since the fish lowered the temperature of the pan. Add a good dollop of butter into the pan and lower the heat to low. Work the butter around the pan and then tilt the pan so that the butter forms a small pool near the handle. With a small soup spoon baste the fish with the now brown butter to explode the flavor.

After basting, the fish should now be pliable and able to be flipped gently without much resistance. Flip the fish over and continue to cook over low heat for about six more minutes. Heat another skillet with extra virgin olive oil and when hot, add the escarole. This will cook down considerably within 1 minute, so don't be afraid to load up the pan. Season liberally with salt, pepper and red pepper flakes and when almost cooked through add chickpeas.

To serve, place escarole and chickpeas on plate and top with halibut. Cut a lemon in half and drizzle some fresh squeezed lemon juice on top of the fish. Add a splash of extra virgin olive oil on top.

4 SERVINGS

Baked Halibut with Tomatoes, Garlic and Olive Sauce

4   halibuts fillets (about 6 ounces each)
5   tablespoons olive oil
2   medium size tomatoes, sliced
       ½ inches thick
1   can (6 ounces) pitted ripe olives
1   clove garlic
     salt and pepper to taste

Preheat oven to 375°. Place fillets in a shallow baking pan. Brush with 1 tablespoon oil. Salt and pepper to taste. Arrange tomatoes over the top. Bake until the fish is opaque in the thickest part, 15-20 minutes.

Place garlic and olives in blender and whirl until finely minced. Add remaining 4 tablespoons of oil in a thin steady stream. Whirl until the mixture forms a paste.

To serve, spoon mixture evenly over each fillet.

4 SERVINGS

Salmon over Couscous

1   pound shredded carrots
1   cup uncooked couscous
½   cup sliced almonds
½   cup raisins
¼   cup chopped fresh mint
1   tablespoon olive oil
1   teaspoon salt
½   teaspoon pepper
1½   cups water
4   skinless salmon fillets
       (6 to 8 ounces each)

Preheat oven to 450°. In a 9 x 13 inch baking pan, mix together carrots, couscous, almonds, raisins, mint, oil water, salt and pepper. Place the salmon fillets on top of the couscous mixture. Season with additional salt and pepper. Cover pan with foil and bake 35 minutes.

2 TO 3 SERVINGS

Italian Salmon

1   **pound salmon fillet**
½   **cup soy sauce**
¾   **cup Italian dressing**

Preheat oven to 350°. Marinate salmon fillet in the soy sauce and Italian dressing mixture for at least 30 minutes. Bake or grill until light pink throughout.

2 TO 3 SERVINGS

Pesto Salmon in Crushed Tomatoes

2   **pounds salmon, skin removed**
1   **(6 ounce) package pesto, divided**
2   **(28 ounce) cans crushed tomatoes**
¾   **cup bread crumbs**
½   **teaspoon kosher salt**
¼   **teaspoon pepper**
1   **teaspoon garlic powder**
     olive oil

Rub front and back of salmon with olive oil. Rub approximately 2 ounces of pesto all over salmon, slightly more on the top. Marinate for 20 minutes.

Mix bread crumbs and 4 tablespoons of pesto, firmly cover the top of the salmon with the mixture. Broil on top shelf on high for 3-5 minutes. Reduce heat to 450° and move fish to the bottom oven rack for 17 minutes or to taste.

SAUCE
Cook crushed tomatoes in a saucepan on medium heat and add 4 tablespoons of pesto, ½ teaspoon kosher salt, ¼ teaspoon pepper and 1 teaspoon garlic powder. Simmer until ready to serve.

Serve salmon over warm tomato sauce.

4 TO 6 SERVINGS

Salmon Casserole

1	package frozen chopped spinach
8	slices wheat bread
1	cup grated Swiss cheese, divided
½	cup chopped green onions
1	pound salmon fillet
3	eggs
3	egg whites
2½	cups milk
2	teaspoons dried dill
1	teaspoon dried mustard
1	teaspoon dried basil
	salt and pepper to taste
2	tablespoons grated Parmesan cheese

Preheat oven to 350°. Cook spinach and press out extra water. Trim crust off bread and cut into cubes. Spray a casserole with cooking spray and spread bread cubes on the bottom.

Layer ½ Swiss cheese over the bread. Layer spinach and onions and then salmon. Layer the rest of the Swiss cheese on top. In a bowl beat eggs, milk, dill, mustard, basil, salt and pepper. Pour over layers and refrigerate for 2 hours. Top with Parmesan and bake for 1 hour.

2 TO 3 SERVINGS

Soy Ginger Salmon

1	pound salmon fillet
⅓	cup chopped scallions

MARINADE

1	tablespoons sesame oil
1-2	tablespoons rice wine vinegar
1	teaspoon fresh garlic
1	teaspoon fresh ginger

Preheat oven to 400°. Whisk marinade ingredients in a casserole. Marinate fish for 10 minutes on each side. Bake 20 minutes. Sprinkle scallions over cooked salmon.

2 TO 3 SERVINGS

Baked Salmon with Spinach

Makes a great presentation!

1	pound salmon fillet
1	lemon
1	teaspoon garlic powder with parsley flakes
	pepper to taste
½	teaspoon dill
1	package spinach or 1 pound fresh spinach, cooked
2	pounds ripe plum tomatoes
2	Yukon gold potatoes or yams, quartered
¼	cup Vermouth or white wine
	olive oil

Preheat oven to 350°. Wash salmon and pat dry. Squeeze lemon over salmon. Sprinkle with pepper, garlic powder and dill and set a side.

Put spinach on the bottom of a casserole. Put the salmon on top of the spinach. Chop tomatoes and put on the top of the fish. Cook the potatoes in the microwave for 4 minutes and then place around the salmon. Pour Vermouth or white wine on top of the dish and drizzle a bit of olive oil over the dish as well.

Bake 30 minutes covered with aluminum foil. Uncover the dish and then bake another 20-25 minutes. When it flakes, it is done.

2 SERVINGS

Mustard Glazed Salmon

2	tablespoons fresh lemon juice
2	tablespoons Dijon mustard
2	tablespoons brown sugar
1	teaspoon ground cumin
4	(6 ounce) salmon fillets
	salt
	pepper

Preheat oven to 400°. Combine the first 4 ingredients together in a baking dish. Salt and pepper both sides of the fish. Place fish in the dish and marinate for 10 minutes on each side. Cook for 15-20 minutes on the bottom rack.

4 TO 6 SERVINGS

Salmon in Black Bean Sauce

1   pound salmon
1   can black beans, drained and rinsed
      salt
      pepper

MARINADE
⅓   cup toasted sesame oil
⅓   cup teriyaki
¼   cup maple syrup
1   teaspoon Dijon mustard

Preheat oven to 425°. Mix all ingredients of marinade together (can be done 2-3 days ahead). Rub salmon generously with sesame oil, put marinade in large casserole dish, add black beans and mix. Place salmon upside down in the dish and marinate for 20 minutes. Flip salmon over, spoon several tablespoons of marinade over fish before cooking.

Change oven to broil and cook fish on top rack for 5 minutes, or until brown. Move fish to bottom rack and change oven back to 425°. Cook for approximately 15 minutes or desired temperature. May be served right from the pan.

2 TO 3 SERVINGS

Pecan Crusted Salmon

8   salmon fillets (4-5 ounces each)
2   cups pecans
1   tablespoon garlic minced
½   teaspoon salt
¼   teaspoon cayenne pepper
½   cup extra virgin olive oil

Preheat oven to 450°. Coarsely grind pecans, add garlic, salt, cayenne pepper. Generously cover each salmon fillet in olive oil and then roll in pecan mixture.

Heat a large fry pan on medium/high. Lightly sauté each piece of salmon, on one side, transferring it to a baking pan. Crumb side up. Bake fish 7 minutes or to taste.

8 SERVINGS

Jay's Pan Seared Salmon
with Bleu Cheese, Nectarine and Arugula Salad

Whole Foods Market

SALAD
- arugula
- endive
- radicchio
- hearts of palm
- halved grape tomatoes
- nectarine
- mountain Gorgonzola

LEMON VINAIGRETTE
2	whole lemons
1	cup Greek olive oil
1	teaspoon apple cider vinegar
	salt
	pepper

PAN SEARED SALMON
¾	pound Atlantic salmon, skinned

Chop endives and radicchio. Mix with arugula. Dice the hearts of palm. Halve the grape tomatoes. Thinly slice the nectarines and crumble the bleu cheese.

Toss together the ingredients and top with lemon vinaigrette and salmon slices.

VINAIGRETTE

Squeeze lemons. Mix juice with other ingredients.

SALMON PREPARATION

Season salmon with garlic powder salt and pepper to taste. Sear on high for 2 minutes, per side. Slice into ½ inch slices for your salad.

2 SERVINGS

Sesame Seed Crusted Salmon

4	salmon fillets (6 ounces each)
	salt
	pepper
2	tablespoons sesame seeds
2	tablespoons black sesame seeds
2	tablespoons olive oil

Rub both sides of salmon with olive oil, salt and pepper to taste. Mix both sesame seeds together in a large bowl. Dip salmon skin side down in the seeds. Heat oil in a large skillet over medium high heat. Sear the salmon seed side down in the pan and cook until golden brown. Turn the fillets over and continue cooking for 4-5 minutes or to taste

4 SERVINGS

Macadamia Nut Encrusted Salmon with Orange Honey Glaze

Redlefsen's Rotisserie and Grill in Bristol, Rhode Island.

4   salmon fillets, pin bones removed

BREADING
¼   loaf sourdough bread
1   teaspoon fresh sage
1   teaspoon fresh thyme
½   ounce melted butter
      salt
      pepper
1½   ounces Macadamia nuts

ORANGE HONEY GLAZE
1   cup fresh squeezed orange juice
¼   cup honey
½   ounce fresh gingerroot, minced
¼   ounce brown sugar
      cornstarch

Tear sourdough bread into small pieces and pulse in a food processor until you reach a medium course texture. Transfer the bread crumbs to a mixing bowl and add the sage, thyme, butter, salt and pepper.

Grind the macadamia nuts in the food processor and add to the bread crumb mixture. Toss. Transfer to a sheet pan and toast on a low heat in the oven until a light golden brown.

Preheat oven to 350°. Coat a saucepan with melted butter and sauté the gingerroot until soft and the aromas release. Add the orange juice, honey and brown sugar and bring to a boil. Lower the heat and thicken the sauce until it is a glaze consistency with a cornstarch slurry. Make this by mixing equal parts cornstarch and cold water.

Brush the glaze on top of the salmon fillets and top with the Macadamia nut breading. Cook the salmon fillets in oven until medium rare about 8-10 minutes or longer for desired doneness. Spoon the remaining glaze on four plates, top with the salmon and serve with jasmine rice and seasonal vegetables.

4 SERVINGS

Easiest Salmon Ever

1   pound salmon fillet
2   tablespoons (reduced sodium) soy
    sauce
2   tablespoons mango sauce
2   tablespoons hoisin sauce

Pour sauces over fish. Let marinate for 10 minutes. Grill or bake until done.

2 TO 3 SERVINGS

Light Salmon Loaf

1   (14 ounce) can red salmon
3   slices whole wheat bread
1   cup 1 percent milk
½   pound sliced fresh mushroom
1   large diced onion
2   eggs
1   egg white
½   pint reduced fat sour cream

Preheat oven to 400°. Tear bread into small pieces. Soak the bread in the milk. Let it stand a few minutes so the bread absorbs all the milk. Sauté the onions and mushrooms in a pan that has been coated with vegetable cooking spray. Drain and crumble the salmon in a bowl. Beat together the whole eggs and the egg white. Add the eggs, mushrooms, onion and soured cream together and mix well. Bake in a pan coated with non stick spray for 40-45 minutes. Let loaf sit in a pan for 10-15 minutes before serving.

6 SERVINGS

 Fourth of July Poached Salmon

2	tablespoons butter
1	medium onion, chopped
1	carrot, chopped
2	stalks celery, chopped
1	quart water
½	cup dry white wine
	salt
	peppercorns
1	fresh salmon (5-7 pounds) cleaned

GARNISH

paper thin slices of lemon, twisted

1-2 cucumbers, scored, slice thin and twisted (marinate in vinegar and sugar)

fresh parsley

black olive and radish flowers on chive stems

capers

Melt butter in fish poacher or roasting pan and add vegetables. Cook 5 minutes. Add water, wine and seasoning. Simmer 5 minutes more. Wrap salmon in cheesecloth and lower into boiling liquid. Reduce heat. Simmer, covered about 1 hour or 8 minutes to the pound.

Carefully remove salmon, unwrap and remove the skin. Transfer to serving platter and chill. (May be made for fewer people with salmon steaks.)

Garnish and decorate platter as desired. Serve with cucumber sauce.

10 TO 12 SERVINGS

Cucumber Sauce

Keeps practically forever!

¾-1	pint mayonnaise
1	pint sour cream
2	tablespoons capers
1	cucumber, chopped fine
¼	medium onion, grated
2	tablespoons fresh dill weed, snipped fine or 1 tablespoon dried dill weed
	fresh lemon juice to taste
	freshly ground pepper
	white horseradish to taste

Combine all ingredients and refrigerate. (May be used with poached salmon or other cold fish dishes.)

ABOUT 1 QUART

Baked Scrod with Crumbs and Tomatoes

2   pounds of scrod (cod)
2   large tomatoes, sliced
½   cup bread crumbs
2   tablespoons butter
1   teaspoon oregano
    salt
    pepper
    lemon

Preheat oven to 350°. Spray a glass baking dish with cooking spray. Salt and pepper fish and place in the dish. In a small saucepan, melt butter and add bread crumbs and oregano. Mix well and cover fish with the mixture.

Layer sliced tomatoes on top of the fish. Dot with extra butter. Bake for 20-25 minutes. Squirt lemon juice over cooked fish before serving

4 TO 6 SERVINGS

Grapefruit and Miso Glazed Red Snapper

Melissa Petitto-Chef to the Stars

4-6   ounces red snapper fillets
2   tablespoons grapefruit zest
1   grapefruit
2   tablespoons packed light brown sugar
2   tablespoons with miso paste
    sea salt
    pepper

Preheat oven to 425°. In a small bowl, whisk together zest, juice, sugar and miso paste. On a sheet pan, arrange fillets, skin side down and season with salt and pepper. Spoon miso mixture over each fillet. Bake for 15 minutes, basting occasionally. Serve immediately.

4 SERVINGS

Basil Sole

1   pound sole
2   tablespoons pesto
     garlic powder
     salt
     pepper
½   cup fresh basil cut in small strips
1   cup cherry tomatoes, sliced in half

Preheat oven to 425°. Rub sole with pesto. Lightly sprinkle with garlic powder, salt and pepper. Sprinkle basil and tomatoes on top of sole. Bake on bottom shelf for 15 minutes. Serve over salad greens or spinach.

2 TO 3 SERVINGS

Swordfish with Avocado Butter

2   pounds swordfish

MARINADE
½   cup canola oil
⅓   cup soy sauce
¼   cup fresh lemon juice
1   teaspoon lemon peel
1   clove garlic, minced

AVOCADO BUTTER
½   cup butter (room temperature)
½   cup mashed avocado
       (approximately 2 avocados)
5   tablespoons fresh lemon juice
2   tablespoons minced parsley
2   garlic cloves, minced
     salt
     pepper

Mix all ingredients for marinade. (Can be done the day before.)

Preheat oven to 425°. Marinade swordfish for 20 minutes in baking dish. Prepare avocado butter by mixing all ingredients together. Spread avocado butter evenly on top of fish. Salt and pepper to taste. Bake on the bottom rack for 15 minutes or to desired tenderness.

4 TO 6 SERVINGS

Swordfish in Tomato Sauce

1   **pound swordfish, rubbed with olive oil**

     salt

     pepper

SAUCE

1   **can crushed tomatoes**

1   **teaspoon basil**

1   **teaspoon oregano**

1   **teaspoon garlic powder**

1   **teaspoon onion powder**

     salt

     pepper

Optional addition to sauce: 1/3 cup sliced spicy banana peppers

Preheat oven to 425°. Mix all sauce ingredients. Marinate fish for 20 minutes. Cook on bottom shelf for 20 minutes or desired tenderness.

2 TO 3 SERVINGS

Grilled Swordfish with Parsley and Caper Sauce

1   **pound swordfish**

¼   **teaspoon salt**

¼   **teaspoon pepper**

SAUCE

2   **scallions, chopped, white and green parts separated**

¾   **cup parsley**

⅓   **cup water**

3   **tablespoons rice vinegar**

1   **teaspoon Dijon mustard**

2   **tablespoons capers, drained**

Make sauce in food processor by combining white part of scallions, parsley, water, rice vinegar, oil and mustard. Blend until slightly chunky. Stir in capers and green parts of scallions.

Preheat grill to medium/high. Salt and pepper swordfish. Coat lightly with olive oil. Grill about 7 minutes each side.

Transfer ⅓ of sauce to serving platter. Place cooked fish on top, drizzle generously with remaining sauce over fish.

2 TO 3 SERVINGS

 # Swordfish on Skewers

2 pounds swordfish, cut in 1½ inch cubes
5 tablespoons oil
1 tablespoon lemon juice
2 teaspoons onion juice
½ teaspoon paprika
  salt to taste
1 thickly sliced onion
  bay leaves
  lemon juice
  fresh parsley
  sliced tomatoes

Wash and dry fish. Mix next 5 ingredients in bowl. Add fish and marinate 20 minutes.

Place fish on skewers, alternating with thick slices of onion and bay leaves.

Broil over medium hot coals or under broiler, turning frequently, for 6-10 minutes.

Sprinkle with lemon juice and garnish with parsley and sliced tomatoes.

4 SERVINGS

 # Bill's Famous Vineyard Swordfish

3 pound piece fresh swordfish, cut uniformly 1½ inches thick
  salt
  freshly ground pepper
  light sprinkling garlic powder
  lemon juice
¼ pound butter
  chopped parsley for garnish
  lemon wedges for garnish

Build a very hot fire in a covered charcoal grill. Set grate close to coals.

Season fish and sprinkle both sides with lemon juice. Put fish on grill and butter top side. When bottom is seared, turn carefully. Repeat 3 or 4 times until golden brown.

Butter top, cover and cook about 8 minutes. Turn and repeat. Turn, butter top and cook, uncovered, another 8 minutes. (Total cooking time is 22-24 minutes.) Fish is done when it turns from pink to white inside and flakes easily.

Serve garnished with fresh parsley and lemon wedges.

6 TO 9 SERVINGS

Steamed Tilapia with Ginger and Scallion

4	Tilapia fillets
½	cup thinly sliced scallion
¼	cup thinly sliced ginger
2	tablespoons canola oil
1	tablespoon soy sauce
1	tablespoon sugar
1	tablespoon rice cooking wine

Place tilapia in a steam basket and steam for 8-10 minutes. During the last two minutes of the steam time, heat the canola oil in a separate small saucepan. Add soy sauce, sugar and rice wine when the oil is hot and bring to a boil. Add scallion and ginger and cook for 1½ minutes. Pour the ginger and scallion sauce over the steamed fillet. Serve immediately.

4 SERVINGS

Spicy and Nutty Tilapia

1	pound tilapia fillets
½	cup low fat mayonnaise
¼	cup brown mustard
½	cup pecans, finely chopped
	salt
	pepper

Preheat oven to 350°. Lightly butter or coat with vegetable cooking spray a large shallow baking pan. Combine mayonnaise and mustard in a small bowl.

Pat fish dry with paper towels. Place fish in baking dish and spread the mayonnaise mixture over each fillet. Sprinkle each fillet with pecans, pressing nuts gently into the fish. Add salt and pepper to taste.

Bake for 15-17 minutes.

2 TO 3 SERVINGS

Mediterranean Trout

2   pounds trout
1   teaspoon garlic powder
1   teaspoon parsley
½   teaspoon oregano
2   teaspoons olive oil
       salt
       pepper
¾   cup black olives, chopped
¾   cup tomatoes, chopped
¾   cup green pepper, chopped
¼   onion, chopped

Preheat oven to 425°. Place fish in a baking pan sprayed with cooking spray. Lightly cover fish with olive oil. Salt and pepper. Mix olives, tomatoes, green peppers and onions together. Add 2 teaspoons of olive oil. Add garlic powder, parsley and oregano and mix well. Pour over fish and cook for 15 minutes.

4 TO 6 SERVINGS

Grilled Tuna Steaks with Tangerine Salsa

       cooking spray
4   tuna steaks (6 ounces each)
       salt
       pepper

SALSA
1½   cups tangerine sections (fresh or
          canned), chopped
1   cup roasted peppers, chopped
2   tablespoons red onion, finely
          chopped
2   tablespoons fresh cilantro, chopped
1   tablespoon fresh lime juice
½   ground cumin
¼   teaspoon garlic powder

Coat grill with cooking spray and preheat to medium/high. Lightly coat both sides of fish with olive oil. Salt and pepper. Cook 5 minutes each side.

SALSA

Combine tangerines, peppers, onion, cilantro, lime juice, cumin and garlic powder.

Salt and pepper to taste. Serve salsa over cooked tuna.

4 SERVINGS

Dijon Seared Tuna

1   pound tuna steak
1   tablespoon mayonnaise
1   tablespoons Dijon mustard
     flour
     hot red pepper relish
     salt
     pepper
2   tablespoons sesame oil

Mix mayonnaise and mustard. Spread this mixture over both side of the tuna steak. Salt and pepper to taste. Place flour on a flat plate and then dust both sides of the tuna with flour.

Heat sesame oil in sauté pan over medium/high heat. Cook tuna 5 minutes on each side, covered. Serve with hot pepper relish.

2 TO 3 SERVINGS

Seared Sesame Encrusted Tuna

This dish is great cut into slices and dipped in soy sauce!

1   pound Sushi grade tuna
½   cup sesame seeds
1   teaspoon kosher salt
1   teaspoon fresh ground pepper
⅛   teaspoon sesame oil

On a plate, mix sesame seed, salt and pepper. Rinse tuna and coat all sides with sesame mixture. Heat pan with sesame oil. Place the tuna in a pan until the bottom is light colored and the center is still red. Flip and repeat on all sides.

2 TO 3 SERVINGS

Spicy Tuna Fish Sandwich

1   can tuna fish, rinsed and drained
1   tablespoon low fat mayonnaise
1   tablespoon Dijon mustard
1   teaspoon hot red pepper relish
     salt
     pepper

Mix all above ingredients. Toast French bread and serve tuna on top with lettuce and tomato.

2 SERVINGS

Simply *More* Vegetarian Entrées

The original Outpatient Clinic.

The Miriam Hospital provided services to those who could not afford to pay. In fact, 6,789 free treatments were given in a single year during the 1930's.

The women remained committed to raising funds for The Miriam Hospital. Special events, such as balls, concerts and the Strawberry Festival in 1939, pictured above, allowed the association to provide services to the hospital and the community.

In the muted atmosphere of World War II, galas and balls were out of the question. The women's focus shifted, but they continued to raise record sums of money for the hospital. The number of indigents who needed their help fell. The labor shortage encouraged the women to volunteer within the hospital to alleviate some of those needs.

During this time, it became apparent that the Parade Street facility could no longer meet the needs of a modern general hospital, so a search began for a suitable site. In March of 1944, an agreement was signed to purchase the former Jewish Orphanage of Rhode Island at 164 Summit Avenue. The fund drive was interrupted by the war and building materials were in short supply. Renovations and construction had to wait until the end of World War II.

Cheese and Bean Quesadillas

1½   cups refried beans
1   cup corn kernels
½   cup salsa
6   (8-inch) whole wheat tortillas
2   cups grated Cheddar cheese
1   teaspoon chili powder
3   tomatoes, chopped
1   ripe avocado, peeled and cubed
1   teaspoon ground cumin
      juice of 1 lime
      salt and freshly ground black
        pepper to taste

Combine beans, corn kernels, and salsa in a saucepan. Heat over medium heat until hot, stirring constantly. Lay tortillas on a flat surface and sprinkle with ⅓ cup cheese. Spread about ½ cup of bean mixture on one half of tortilla and fold over. Repeat until all 6 quesadillas are ready for cooking.

Spray a large nonstick skillet with vegetable cooking spray. Cook quesadilla on medium heat, turning 2-3 times, until tortillas are brown on both sides and cheese melts. Respray pan and repeat until all quesadillas are cooked.

While quesadillas are cooking, mix chili powder, tomatoes, avocado and cumin. Sprinkle mixture with lime juice and season with salt and pepper. Serve this mixture over cooked quesadillas.

6 SERVINGS

Black Bean Nachos

1   (15 ounce) can black beans, drained
      and rinsed
1   (15 ounce) jar salsa
1   (12 ounce) can whole kernel corn,
      drained
1   bunch scallions, diced
1   bag restaurant style tortilla chips
1   cup shredded Cheddar cheese
1   tomato, chopped

Preheat oven to 375°. Combine black beans, corn, salsa and scallions.

Place tortilla chips on baking sheet. Spoon 2 tablespoons mixture over each chip and sprinkle with cheese. Bake for 3-5 minutes or until cheese melts. Garnish with chopped tomatoes and serve immediately.

4 SERVINGS

Chickpea Dal

3   tablespoons oil
1   (15 ounce) can chickpeas, drained
1   medium onion, chopped
1   tablespoon minced or grated fresh ginger
1   tablespoon minced garlic
1   tablespoon ground cumin
½   teaspoon ground turmeric
1   tablespoon ground coriander
½   teaspoon red pepper powder (cayenne) or to taste
2   large tomatoes, peeled and chopped
½   teaspoon salt or to taste
2   tablespoons fresh lemon or lime juice
¼   cup chopped cilantro leaves

Heat a nonstick saucepan over moderate heat. Add oil, when hot, add onion, ginger and garlic. Stir until onion is translucent. Add cumin, turmeric, coriander and red pepper. Cook stirring, for about 20 seconds, being careful not to burn. Add tomatoes. Bring to a boil, reduce heat and simmer for 1 minute. Add chickpeas. Cook, stirring often, for 10 minutes to allow flavors to blend and to reduce liquid. Add salt to taste. Add in the chopped cilantro leaves. Remove from heat.

Serve with rice and pita bread.

5 SERVINGS

Potatoes can also be added.

Black Beans and Rice

1   pound black beans
3   bouillon cubes
3   onions, chopped
1   tablespoon olive oil
2   teaspoons crushed garlic
½   teaspoon Tabasco sauce
4   cups cooked white or brown rice

Wash beans in colander. Do not soak them. Place beans in large pot. Cover with water to a height 2-3 inches above the level of the beans. Add bouillon. Bring to a boil and simmer, covered, for 2 hours until the water is mostly absorbed (or to level of beans).

Chop onions and sauté in olive oil for 10-15 minutes until caramelized. Add onions to beans. Add garlic and hot sauce. Serve with cooked rice.

6 SERVINGS

Crunchy Vegetable Burrito Banditos

½ cup shredded carrots

½ cup chopped broccoli

½ cup chopped cauliflower

2 green onions, thinly sliced

4 ounces shredded low-fat Cheddar cheese

½ cup nonfat Ranch dressing

½ teaspoon chili powder

4 (7 inch) flour tortillas

1 cup torn iceberg lettuce, bite size pieces

In a large mixing bowl, combine carrots, broccoli, cauliflower, onions, cheese, dressing and chili powder. Mix well. Lay tortillas on a flat surface and spoon about ½ cup vegetable mixture and ¼ cup lettuce down the center. Wrap each tortilla around the vegetable mixture.

4 SERVINGS

Sweet Potato Quesadilla

A recipe from the University of Rhode Island SNAP-ED Family Nutrition Program

1 medium sweet potato, cooked, peeled and mashed or 1 (15 ounce) can sweet potatoes, drained and mashed

½ cup black beans, rinsed and drained

2 whole wheat tortillas, 6 to 8 inches

2 tablespoons tomato salsa

2 tablespoons shredded Cheddar cheese

vegetable cooking spray

In a medium size bowl, mix mashed sweet potato and black beans. Coat a medium sized skillet with cooking spray or lightly rub with oil. Turn the pan to medium heat.

Place one tortilla in pan. Spread the sweet potato and black bean mixture onto the tortilla. Top with salsa and shredded cheese. Cover with other tortilla. Cook for 2-3 minutes until bottom tortilla begins to crisp. With a wide spatula, turn the quesadilla over and cook for another 2-3 minutes until crisp. Remove from pan to a cutting board and cut into quarters.

2 SERVINGS

Crespelle

3 tablespoons unsalted butter

2 eggs

⅓ cup flour

⅔ cup milk

2 teaspoons grappa or brandy

FILLING

8 ounces spinach, blanched, squeezed of all excess water and chopped

1½ cups fresh ricotta

nutmeg to taste

salt to taste

pepper to taste

BÉCHAMEL

1¼ cups milk

2 tablespoons unsalted butter

2 tablespoons flour

nutmeg to taste

salt to taste

pepper to taste, optional

10-12 ounces tomato purée, divided

5 ounces chicken stock

grated mozzarella cheese

grated Pecorino Romano cheese

freshly grated Parmigiano-Reggiano

chopped fresh rosemary, thyme, sage and parsley for garnish

CLARIFY BUTTER

Cut butter into small pieces and melt over low heat without stirring and without allowing butter to sizzle. Let simmer for 10-15 minutes. The solids will rise to the top. Scoop off or strain through a fine strainer to obtain the clear, yellow liquid.

CRÊPES

Place eggs, flour, milk and grappa in a bowl and stir until all flour is absorbed and the mixture is well combined. Strain if necessary. Cover and refrigerate 1 hour.

Brush crêpe pan or other 7 inch nonstick skillet with clarified butter and place over medium heat. Lift the pan off the heat and pour about 3 tablespoons batter onto the center of the pan, tilting and rotating the pan to form a thin layer that coats the entire bottom of the crêpe pan. Return to heat and cook until the crêpe settles and starts to bubble. With a thin metal spatula, flip the crêpe over in the pan. The bottom should be golden brown. Cook the other side until you start to get some speckles of color, but not as much as you achieved on the first side.

Stack the finished crêpe onto a piece of wax paper and repeat with remaining batter. Stack the finished crêpes with a piece of wax paper between each crêpe. Makes 8 crêpes.

SPINACH RICOTTA FILLING

Combine cheese and spinach in a food processor and pulse until well mixed. Season with nutmeg, salt and pepper.

BÉCHAMEL

Melt butter in a medium to heavy saucepan over low heat. Stir in flour to make a roux. Stir the roux over medium heat for 2-3 minutes until fragrant. Slowly add the milk, a little at a time, while stirring to avoid getting lumps. Once all the milk has been added, bring the sauce to a simmer over low heat and continue stirring, without boiling, until the sauce reaches the consistency of cream soup. Season with nutmeg, salt and pepper.

Preheat oven to 450°. Fill 8 crêpes by placing ¼ cup filling in the center of each crêpe and folding the outer flaps toward the center to create a purse.

Place 8 ounces tomato purée and 5 ounces chicken broth in a baking dish. Place the crêpes in the sauce, overlapping slightly. Top with a touch more tomato purée and spoon béchamel over the top. Sprinkle some grated mozzarella and Pecorino Romano over the béchamel. Bake for 12-15 minutes until the center of the filling is hot. Grate Parmigiano-Reggiano over the top and garnish with chopped fresh herbs.

4 TO 6 SERVINGS

Eggplant Rollatini

2　large eggplants
3　large eggs, divided
2　cups plain or seasoned bread crumbs
½　cup olive or vegetable oil
2　pounds ricotta cheese
1　tablespoon chopped parsley
¾　cup Parmigiano-Reggiano cheese
　　salt and pepper to taste
¾　cup shredded mozzarella cheese
1　(24 ounce) jar tomato or marinara sauce

Slice eggplants lengthwise very thin. Beat 2 eggs in shallow dish. Dip eggplants in beaten egg and then in bread crumbs. Heat olive oil in large frying pan and cook breaded eggplant slices until golden on both sides. Place eggplant on pan lined in paper towel to absorb oil. In mixing bowl, combine ricotta cheese, parsley, Parmigiano cheese, 1 egg and salt and pepper, mixing well. In deep baking dish, put tomato sauce on bottom of dish to coat the pan.

Preheat oven to 375°. Take a slice of eggplant and place a tablespoon of ricotta cheese mixture on one end and roll eggplant into a log shape. Place in baking dish and continue stuffing and rolling until all eggplant is done. Pour additional sauce on top of finished eggplant rollatini and top with mozzarella cheese. Bake for 40 minutes or until bubbling.

4 TO 6 SERVINGS

Serve with favorite pasta and sauce.

Eggplant Mozzarella Melts

½ cup flour

½ teaspoon salt

¼ teaspoon freshly ground black pepper

1 cup low-fat milk

1 large egg

½ teaspoon garlic powder

1 cup seasoned bread crumbs

1 large eggplant, peeled and cut crosswise into ¼ inch thick slices

1 tablespoon olive oil

1 cup shredded part-skim mozzarella cheese

2 tablespoons grated Parmesan cheese

1 (24 ounce) jar marinara or pasta sauce

Preheat oven to 400°. Coat a large baking dish with cooking spray. Combine flour, salt and pepper in a shallow dish. Whisk together milk, egg and garlic powder in a separate shallow dish. Place the bread crumbs on a large plate.

Dip the eggplant slices one at a time into the flour mixture, turning to coat both sides. Next, the milk mixture, again coating both sides, and then the bread crumbs. Set the slices on a platter.

Heat the oil in a large skillet over medium-high heat. Add the eggplant slices several at a time and cook until golden brown, about 2 minutes per side. Drain on paper towels.

Transfer the eggplant to the prepared baking pan, arranging the slices in a single layer, and evenly sprinkle the mozzarella and Parmesan cheeses over the eggplant. Bake until cheese is golden and bubbly, about 10 minutes. Let rest a few minutes before serving. Serve with your favorite pasta sauce.

4 SERVINGS

Spinach Lasagna

1   **(10 ounce) package lasagna noodles**
1   **pound fresh spinach**
2   **cloves garlic, chopped**
3   **tablespoons parsley, divided**
1   **tablespoon basil**
1   **teaspoon oregano**
1   **cup bread crumbs**
1   **(16 ounce) can tomatoes**
1   **(6 ounce) can tomato paste**
1   **pound ricotta cheese**
2   **teaspoons salt**
     few pinches pepper
½   **cup grated Parmesan cheese**
½   **pound mozzarella cheese, thinly sliced**
1   **cup tomato sauce**

Preheat oven to 375°. Boil lasagna noodles according to package directions. Cook and drain spinach.

Chop spinach and mix with garlic, 1 tablespoon parsley, basil and oregano. Mix in bread crumbs, tomatoes and tomato paste.

Mix together ricotta, salt, pepper and remaining parsley.

In a greased 9 x 13 inch pan, layer ingredients as follows: lasagna, spinach, ricotta, Parmesan and mozzarella. Repeat layers until ingredients are used up, ending with a layer of spinach and a little mozzarella. Pour tomato sauce on top. Bake for 30 minutes.

6 TO 8 SERVINGS

Baked Pasta with Kalamata Olives and Cheese

1   **pound penne pasta**
¼   **cup olive oil**
2   **(25 ounce) jars thick and chunky tomato sauce with roasted red peppers**
1   **(35 ounce) can peeled tomatoes**
2½   **cups grated Havarti cheese**
⅓   **cup sliced pitted kalamata olives**
⅓   **cup grated Parmesan cheese**
¼   **cup chopped fresh basil**

Preheat oven to 375°. Cook pasta according to package directions. Drain and return to pot. Coat with a little olive oil. Add tomato sauce and tomatoes. Mix well and transfer to a 13 x 9 inch glass baking dish. Mix in Havarti cheese. Sprinkle olives and then Parmesan cheese on top. Bake for 30 minutes. Garnish with fresh basil and serve.

4 SERVINGS

Southwest Lasagna

Mary M. Flynn, PhD, RD, LDN is a research dietician at The Miriam Hospital and Brown University.

8   tablespoons olive oil
2   cups chopped red onion
1   (15 ounce) can black beans, rinsed and drained
1   cup salsa
1   cup canned crushed tomatoes
4   ounces shredded Cheddar or Mexican blend cheese
1½   cups part-skim ricotta cheese
1   egg
1   teaspoon dried oregano
6-8   cooked lasagna noodles

Preheat oven to 350°. Heat olive oil in a skillet on medium heat. Add chopped onions. Stir to coat with oil and sauté until soft, about 15 minutes. Stir in black beans and cook and additional 3-5 minutes. Add the salsa and tomatoes and cook for about 5 minutes. Scramble the egg and add to the ricotta cheese. Mix in dried oregano.

Pour three cups of the tomato vegetable mixture in a baking dish. Cover with a layer of cooked noodles. Top with ricotta cheese mixture. Cover with another layer of noodles. Add the rest of the tomato vegetable mixture and then sprinkle the shredded cheese evenly on top. Cover with aluminum foil and bake for 30 minutes. Let stand 10-15 minutes before serving.

8 SERVINGS

Vegetarian Lasagna

1   cup minced onion

2   tablespoons olive oil

1   pound fresh spinach, cleaned, stemmed and chopped

½   cup grated Parmesan cheese, divided

1   cup pesto

2   cups ricotta

½   cup toasted sunflower seeds

2   ounces sun-dried tomatoes, divided

½   pound grated mozzarella cheese, divided

24   lasagna noodles, cooked

Sauté onion in olive oil until soft. Remove from heat. Stir in raw spinach. Add ¼ cup Parmesan cheese. Stir in pesto, ricotta, sunflower seeds and some salt and pepper. Combine.

If using sun-dried tomatoes not packed in olive oil, soak them in hot water for 20 minutes while preparing filling and then drain. Slice or chop tomatoes.

Preheat oven to 350°. Grease 9 x 13 inch baking dish. Place layer of noodles on bottom. Spread ⅓ of filling on noodles. Add a layer of sun-dried tomato slices. Repeat layers — noodles, filling, sun-dried tomatoes 2 more times. Add a final layer of noodles and then top with mozzarella and Parmesan cheese. Drizzle a little olive oil over the top. Cover with foil and bake 40 minutes.

6-8 SERVINGS

Moroccan Casserole

2	tablespoons olive oil
1	(15 ounce) can chickpeas or black beans, rinsed and drained
¼	teaspoon salt
1	(14 ounce) can broth
1	(14 ounce) can chopped tomatoes
1	package cubed butternut squash
½	cup raisins
2	teaspoons cumin
1	teaspoon cinnamon
1	teaspoon paprika
1	cup couscous
1	cup frozen peas

Heat oil and cook chickpeas or black beans for 3-5 minutes. Add broth, tomatoes, squash, raisins, and spices. Bring to a boil. Cover, reduce heat, and cook for 15 minutes. Stir in couscous and peas. Remove from heat and allow to stand 5 minutes.

3 TO 4 SERVINGS

Black Pepper Fettuccine à la Vodka

1	(12 ounce) package black pepper fettuccine, or substitute your favorite flavor
¼	cup butter
½	cup vodka
¼	teaspoon red pepper flakes
¼	teaspoon Worcestershire sauce
1	cup thick tomato sauce
½	cup half and half
	salt and pepper to taste
¾	cup freshly grated Parmesan cheese

Bring water to a boil and cook pasta according to package directions.

While cooking pasta, melt butter in a large skillet. Add vodka, pepper flakes and Worcestershire sauce. Stir and cook on medium high heat for 5 minutes until alcohol is cooked off. Stir in tomato sauce and half and half. Let simmer for 5 minutes over medium heat. Sauce will start to thicken. Add salt and pepper to taste.

Add drained pasta and toss. Reduce heat and stir in cheese. Serve immediately.

2 TO 3 SERVINGS

Cavatelli with Spicy Autumn Squash

From Chef Terranova at Johnson and Wales University College of Culinary Arts

¼   cup olive oil

6   garlic cloves

1   red onion, thinly sliced

1   teaspoon crushed red pepper

1½   pounds fresh baby pumpkin, peeled and diced

1   tablespoon fresh thyme

1   pound cavatelli, cooked

1   cup chicken broth

¼   cup grated Romano cheese

¼   cup grated Parmesan cheese

3   tablespoons butter

1   tablespoon chopped fresh parsley

Heat oil until hot. Add the garlic and sauté until lightly browned. Remove garlic and discard. Add the onions and red pepper and sauté until wilted. Add the pumpkin and thyme and continue to sauté until the pumpkin is barely firm. Add the pasta and heat until hot. Add the broth and heat again until very hot.

Remove from heat and add cheeses, butter and parsley and toss to coat. Serve at once.

4 SERVINGS

Cavatappi with Spinach, Beans and Asiago Cheese

A great vegetarian addition to a party buffet.

1   pound cavatappi or gemelli pasta

1   (10 ounce) package fresh spinach, cleaned and coarsely chopped

4   garlic cloves, crushed

6   ounces shredded Asiago cheese

1   teaspoon salt

½   teaspoon pepper

6   tablespoons olive oil

2   (15 ounce) cans cannellini beans, rinsed and drained

½   cup sun-dried tomatoes, soaked or in oil, thinly sliced

Cook pasta according to package directions. While pasta is cooking, combine spinach, garlic, cheese, salt and pepper in a large bowl. Add olive oil, beans and sun-dried tomatoes. Toss. Drain pasta and add to other ingredients. Toss well. Sprinkle with freshly ground black pepper and more cheese, if desired.

4 TO 6 SERVINGS

Great reheated the next day too.

Asian Pasta

1	pound udon noodles
1	teaspoon sugar
1	tablespoon white vinegar
3	tablespoons soy sauce
3	tablespoons creamy peanut butter
3	tablespoons sesame oil
¼-1	teaspoon oriental chili paste with garlic
½	cup coconut milk, heated, or ½ cup hot pasta water
	chopped scallions for garnish
	steamed peapods, julienned, for garnish
	crispy chow mein noodles for garnish

Cook pasta according to package directions. Combine remaining ingredients to make a sauce, mix well with a whisk. Mix sauce with cooked pasta.

If not serving right away, let food cool to room temperature, mixing often to allow sauce to be absorbed. Refrigerate and serve cold. To serve, garnish with your choice of scallions, peapods and crispy noodles.

6 TO 8 SERVINGS

Pasta Margherita

Melissa Petitto is a registered dietician and Chef to the Stars.

¼	cup olive oil
1	small sweet onion, diced
4-6	cloves garlic, minced
4	large ugly tomatoes, chopped
1	ball fresh mozzarella, diced
½	cup basil, chiffonade
	sea salt
	pepper
1	pound linguine

Cook linguine according to package directions, reserving about 1 cup cooking liquid.

In a large sauté pan, heat oil over medium heat. Add onion and sauté for 5 minutes or until translucent. Add garlic and sauté until fragrant, about 30 seconds. Add tomatoes and toss with onions and garlic.

Turn off heat and add mozzarella and basil. Season with salt and pepper. Toss with pasta and add cooking liquid if too dry.

6 SERVINGS

Orecchiette with Cool Chickpeas

From Al Forno Restaurant in Providence, Rhode Island

1   **heaping tablespoon finely chopped red onion**

4   **tablespoons extra virgin olive oil**

1   **teaspoon or more finely chopped fresh hot pepper**

1   **cup cooked chickpeas**

1   **tablespoon finely chopped fresh flat-leaf parsley**

1½   **tablespoons freshly squeezed lemon juice**

5   **large fresh mint leaves**

8   **ounces dried orecchiette or pasta shells**

    lemon wedges, optional

In a large bowl, combine the onion, olive oil, hot pepper, chickpeas, parsley and lemon juice. Slice the mint into a fine chiffonade and stir into the chickpeas. Allow to marinate at room temperature for at least 20 minutes and up to an hour.

Bring a large pot of water to a boil. Add a generous amount of salt and drop in the pasta. Cook, stirring often, until al dente.

Drain the pasta and toss in the bowl with the chickpeas. Set aside for 5 minutes to allow the pasta to absorb the flavors. Serve with a crusty loaf of bread to dip into the sauce and lemon wedges to spritz each serving, if you like.

2 TO 4 SERVINGS

Reprinted with permission from *On Top of Spaghetti* by Johanne Killeen and George Germon, published by William Morrow, an Imprint of Harper Collins Publishers.

Pasta with Tomatoes, Basil and Brie

4	large ripe tomatoes, cubed
1	pound Brie, remove rind and pull into irregular pieces
1	cup fresh basil, cut into strips
3	cloves garlic, minced
1	cup olive oil
2½	teaspoons salt
½	teaspoon pepper
1	pound penne or fusilli pasta
	freshly ground black pepper for garnish
	grated Parmagiano-Reggiano cheese for garnish

Combine first 5 ingredients. Let them fuse together at room temperature for at least 2 hours.

Prepare pasta according to package directions. Drain most of the water from the pasta, leaving just enough to coat the bottom of the pan. Pour tomato mixture over hot pasta. Garnish and serve.

6 TO 8 SERVINGS

Can be served hot or at room temperature.

Zucchini, Corn and Basil Fusilli

1	pound fusilli
3	ears corn, kernels cut from cob
1½	pounds zucchini, coarsely chopped into ½ inch pieces
1	(5-7 ounce) container basil pesto
	grated Parmigiano-Reggiano for garnish

Cook fusilli in a boiling salted water until al dente. Drain, reserving 1 cup pasta cooking water and set aside. Add ½ cup pasta water and vegetables to pot. Cook partially covered for 2 minutes. Add pesto and cooked pasta to the veggies and mix well. If needed, slowly add additional pasta water to moisten. Sprinkle with cheese and serve.

6 SERVINGS

You can substitute yellow squash for all or part of the zucchini.

Stromboli

1 (10 ounce) package frozen chopped
 spinach
2 tablespoons olive oil
1 (8 ounce) package sliced fresh
 mushrooms
1 small onion, chopped or sliced
1 (16 ounce) package fresh pizza
 dough
2 teaspoons flour
1 (8 ounce) package shredded
 Cheddar cheese
½-1 cup sliced black olives

Preheat oven to 350°. Defrost spinach and drain well. Sauté mushrooms and onions in olive oil.

Dust your hands and a cutting board with flour. Stretch out pizza dough into a 10-12 inch diameter circle. Spread spinach, mushrooms, onions and olives evenly over dough, leaving about 1 inch bare around the edges. Sprinkle cheese on top of ingredients.

Roll or fold over the dough, with the fillings inside, a couple of times. The stromboli will resemble a jelly-roll. Place stromboli on a greased cookie sheet with fold facing down. Tuck the ends of the dough under to seal the ingredients inside. Glaze top of and sides of stromboli with oil. Bake 30-40 minutes until golden brown. Cool, cut into slices and serve.

Grilled Tofu

1 package tofu, soft or firm
3 tablespoons teriyaki marinade

Slice tofu into 8 pieces, about ⅓ inch thick. Dip tofu pieces in marinade and allow them to sit in the marinade for one hour, turning over halfway during marinade time.

Remove from marinade and spray with vegetable cooking spray to prevent them from sticking to the grill. Grill on medium high heat for 2-3 minutes per side.

2 TO 4 SERVINGS

Risotto Primavera

2   tablespoons olive oil
1½   cups sliced fresh mushrooms
½   cup diced carrots
½   cup chopped onions
2   cloves garlic, minced
1   cup Arborio rice
3   cups stock
½   cup sherry or white cooking wine
1   cup shredded fontina cheese
¼   cup grated Parmesan cheese
       chopped fresh parsley for garnish
       diced tomatoes for garnish

In a large saucepan, sauté first 4 ingredients in olive oil until tender. Add uncooked rice. Stir over medium heat for 3-5 minutes until rice is golden brown. In a separate saucepan, heat stock and wine to a boil. Slowly add 1 cup of broth mixture to the rice, stirring constantly until broth is absorbed. Add ½ cup broth mixture at a time, repeating the cook and stir method until all of the broth has been added and absorbed. Rice mixture should appear creamy. Add fontina and Parmesan cheeses and blend well. Garnish with fresh parsley and chopped tomatoes.

4 SERVINGS

1 tablespoon bouillon granules and 3 cups water can be substituted for stock.

Garden Style Sloppy Joes

2   teaspoons olive oil
1   cup chopped onion
1   cup chopped celery
½   cup diced carrots
1   (8 ounce) package tempeh or tofu, crumbled
2   cups canned, crushed tomatoes, do not drain
¼   cup water
¼   cup hot and spicy barbecue sauce
2   teaspoons chili powder
½   teaspoon dried oregano
       salt and pepper to taste
       hamburger buns

Heat oil in non-stick skillet over medium heat. Sauté onion, celery, carrot and tempeh for about 5 minutes. Stir in tomatoes and next 6 ingredients. Bring to a boil. Cover, reduce heat, and simmer for 10 minutes, stirring occasionally. Uncover and continue cooking until mixture thickens. Serve on toasted hamburger buns.

8 SERVINGS

Asian Baked Tofu

1	package firm tofu
⅓	cup low sodium soy sauce
1	teaspoon mustard
¼	cup mirin or Japanese sweet wine
¼	cup brown rice vinegar
1	tablespoon sesame oil
	pinch white pepper

Rinse tofu. Place on cutting board and cover with paper towel. Place a few cans on top of tofu to press out the water. Allow to drain for 15 minutes to a few hours, pouring off water occasionally. As more moisture is removed, the texture of the cooked tofu becomes firmer.

In a large bowl or deep dish plate, whisk together the rest of the ingredients to form a marinade. Slice tofu block first in half lengthwise and then 3 times width wise to make squares. Place tofu blocks in marinade and allow to sit at least 1 hour, or even overnight, in the refrigerator.

Preheat oven to 350°. Using a slotted spoon, drain marinade and place tofu on an oiled baking sheet, reserving the marinade. Bake for 15 minutes, baste the tofu with the reserved marinade and turn the tofu over. Bake another 15-20 minutes basting with marinade as needed.

2 TO 4 SERVINGS

Serve tossed with stir-fry vegetables and rice noodles or in a sandwich on multi-grain bread.

Tofu, Broccoli and Garlic Sauce

1   **pound firm or extra firm tofu, cut into chunks**

4   **tablespoons soy sauce, divided**

2   **tablespoons rice vinegar**

3   **tablespoons sugar**

1   **teaspoon cornstarch dissolved in 1 tablespoon water**

    cayenne pepper to taste

1   **teaspoon dark sesame oil**

    few drops hot pepper sauce

1   **tablespoon canola oil**

3   **tablespoons minced garlic**

1   **bunch broccoli, chopped**

1   **red pepper, chopped**

    cooked brown rice

Marinate tofu chunks in 2 tablespoons soy sauce for at least 30 minutes

Mix together 2 tablespoons soy sauce, rice vinegar, sugar, cornstarch slurry, cayenne pepper, sesame oil and hot pepper sauce. Set sauce aside.

Stir-fry garlic in oil. Add tofu and stir-fry a few more minutes. Add broccoli and stir-fry until it turns bright green, usually about 5 minutes. Add sauce and mix well to coat broccoli and tofu and to allow sauce to thicken. Serve over cooked brown rice.

4 SERVINGS

Tofu Chop Suey

1 package extra firm tofu, well drained and cubed

3 tablespoons soy sauce, divided

⅓ cup cold water

2 tablespoons cornstarch

1 teaspoon sugar

2 tablespoons canola oil

½ cup chopped scallions

2 cups chopped celery

1 cup hot water

¼ teaspoon black pepper

2 cups fresh bean sprouts

1 green pepper, thinly sliced

3 cups cooked brown rice

chow mein noodles for garnish

Marinate cubed tofu in 2 tablespoons soy sauce for 30 minutes. In a small bowl, prepare thickening sauce by mixing ⅓ cup cold water, cornstarch, 1 tablespoon soy sauce and 1 teaspoon sugar. Set aside.

Heat oil in a skillet or wok on medium high heat. Add scallions and stir-fry. Add celery, hot water and black pepper and continue cooking. Add marinated tofu and continue stir-frying. Cover and cook 2 additional minutes. Add sprouts and green peppers. Mix well. Pour in thickening sauce and briefly toss all ingredients together.

Serve hot over brown rice and garnish with chow mein noodles.

4 SERVINGS

Simply *More* Kugels, Grains & Pasta

Laying the cornerstone for The Miriam Hospital on Summit Avenue.

**The Miriam Hospital Women's Association made
its own contribution to the cornerstone box. Included were
the charter of the Association and a copy of its history.**

The Association, now known as the Miriam Hospital Women's Association, contributed financially to this new hospital, raising $100,000 between 1950 and 1955. They used creative methods of fund-raising. The 1950 annual meeting attracted 500 women to a program called "Cavalcade of Brides" in which members of the association modeled bridal gowns ranging from a 1905 wedding to a then modern 1949 creation.

The new 150-bed Miriam Hospital opened on Summit Avenue in 1952. It was truly a gift of the Jewish community to all the people of Rhode Island.

Faye's Apple Kugel

1	(12 ounce) package medium egg noodles
12	Cortland apples
½	cup vegetable oil
1	cup sugar
1	teaspoon salt
4	eggs
	cinnamon to taste

Cook noodles and drain. Preheat oven to 350°.

Peel, core and thinly slice or coarsely chop apples. Stir eggs. Gently mix together noodles, apples, eggs, oil, sugar, salt and cinnamon. Pour all ingredients into a greased 2 quart rectangular baking dish. Bake for 30 minutes. Increase heat to 400° and bake for an additional 30 minutes until brown.

6 TO 8 SERVINGS

Easy Noodle Kugel

8	ounces elbow macaroni or other noodles
3	eggs
½	cup, or less, sugar
2	teaspoons vanilla extract
1	cup light sour cream
3-4	ounces whipped cream cheese
¼	cup raisins
1	(8 ounce) can crushed pineapple, drained, optional
	brown sugar
	cinnamon
	sliced almonds

Cook macaroni according to package directions. Drain.

Preheat oven to 350°. Beat eggs very well. Add sugar and beat again. Add vanilla extract, sour cream, and cream cheese. Beat again. Stir in noodles, raisins and pineapple. Pour into a buttered 9 inch square casserole. Cover lightly with a mixture of brown sugar, cinnamon and almonds. Bake for 50-60 minutes.

Can be frozen for up to 2 months.

6 SERVINGS

Esther's Noodle Pudding

1	pound broad noodles
7-8	eggs, beaten
1	(16 ounce) can peaches, drained and diced
1	(15 ounce) can crushed pineapple, drained
3	apples, peeled and diced
1	cup yellow raisins
1	cup sugar
2	teaspoons cinnamon
2	teaspoons vanilla extract
	juice of ½ lemon
	juice of ½ orange
¾	cup shortening, melted

Preheat oven to 350°. Cook noodles according to package directions. Drain. Mix with eggs and stir in remaining ingredients.

Pour into greased 10 x 13 inch pan. Bake for 45 minutes.

16 OR MORE SERVINGS

Mother's Noodle Pudding

½	pound wide noodles
3	eggs, beaten
½	cup sugar
½	pint sour cream
½	pound creamed cottage cheese
1	cup milk
½	cup white raisins
¼	cup butter, melted
1	teaspoon vanilla extract
	sugar
	cinnamon

Boil noodles according to package directions and drain. Mix all ingredients and bake for 45-60 minutes in greased 9 x 12 inch casserole. Sprinkle with sugar and cinnamon.

6 TO 8 SERVINGS

Potato Kugel

A family favorite for generations.

6	potatoes
2	onions
2	eggs yolks, beaten
4	tablespoons matzo meal
1	teaspoon baking powder
1½	teaspoons salt
¼	teaspoon freshly ground pepper
4	tablespoons vegetable oil, divided
2	egg whites, stiffly beaten

Preheat oven to 375°. Peel potatoes, cut into eighths. Cut onions into quarters. In a food processor, with metal blade, combine several chunks of potato with one or two of onion and grate in batches. The onion keeps the mixture from turning color. Don't grind too finely; it should not look like mush. Place potato onion mixture into a colander to drain well. Combine in a bowl with egg yolks, matzo meal, baking powder, salt, pepper, and 2 tablespoons of oil. Mix well. Fold in egg whites carefully, but thoroughly. Pour mixture into a greased 1 ½ quart rectangular glass baking dish. Drizzle remaining oil on top. Bake for 1 hour or until browned on top.

10 TO 12 SERVINGS

If you want to prepare ahead of time and freeze, underbake it until very lightly browned. To serve, thaw and put a little oil on top and bake again until hot and very brown on top.

Potato-Apple Bake

⅓	envelope onion soup mix
4	tablespoons margarine
3	large potatoes
½	cup applesauce

Preheat oven to 400°. Boil potatoes until soft. Mash. Melt margarine and mix together margarine, onion soup mix, mashed potatoes and applesauce. Place in 1 quart baking dish. Bake 30 minutes or until lightly browned.

6 SERVINGS

Matzo Charlotte

2	cups matzo farfel
3	egg yolks
3	egg whites, beaten
⅔	cup sugar
¼	cup red wine or orange juice
½	teaspoon salt
2	teaspoons grated orange rind
3	tablespoons melted shortening

Preheat oven to 350°. Soak farfel in cold water for a few minutes. Drain and crush to a paste. Beat egg yolks and sugar together until thick. Stir in wine, orange juice, salt, orange rind and 2 tablespoons shortening. Add farfel and mix well. Fold in egg whites.

Pour into a greased 2 quart baking dish. Bake for 30 minutes until browned and set.

6 SERVINGS

Circle of Barley

4	cups chicken broth
1¼	cups pearl barley
1	teaspoon salt
½	cup diced fresh mushrooms
⅓	cup chopped onions
¼	cup chopped green pepper
2	tablespoons butter
2	eggs, beaten
½	cup grated sharp cheese

Bring broth to a boil. Add barley and salt. Simmer one hour, stirring occasionally. Add water as needed.

Preheat oven to 350°. Sauté mushrooms, onions and green peppers in butter. Drain barley and mix all ingredients together. Pour into greased 1 quart ring mold. Place mold in pan of hot water and bake for 30 minutes, or until firm to the touch.

Unmold and serve. For a finishing touch fill center with vegetables.

6 SERVINGS

Bulgur Pilaf

¾   **cup butter, divided**
3   **cups coarse bulgur**
2   **onions, finely chopped**
6   **cups chicken broth**
2   **teaspoons salt**
1   **teaspoon pepper**
1   **teaspoon curry powder**
1   **cup pine nuts**

Preheat oven to 375°. Melt ½ cup butter, add bulgur and sauté well. In another pan, sauté onion in ¼ cup butter until golden. Add onion to bulgur. Add remaining ingredients and stir well. Place in greased 2 quart casserole and bake, uncovered, for 30 minutes. Adjust seasonings and stir. Bake 10 minutes more.

12 SERVINGS

Bulgur Pilaf II

May be used as a stuffing for roast lamb or chicken.

3   **cups broth**
4   **bay leaves**
½   **teaspoon allspice**
4   **whole cardamom seeds**
¼   **teaspoon ground ginger**
¼   **teaspoon ground cinnamon**
¼   **teaspoon dried thyme**
¼   **cup olive oil**
2   **medium onions**
2   **cups bulgur**
⅓   **cup currants**
¼   **cup pine nuts or pecans, toasted**

Place broth, bay leaves and spices in large covered saucepan. Bring to a boil and simmer for five minutes. Strain and bring back to a simmer.

In a skillet, sauté onions in olive oil until golden. Add bulgur and cook 3-4 minutes until mixture is dry. Add to broth, cover and cook over very low heat for 25 minutes. Add currants and let stand, covered for 2 minutes. Stir in nuts and serve.

8 SERVINGS

Brown Lentils Simmered with Onion and Garlic

A recipe from Ira Brandstein, Director of Food and Nutrition at The Miriam Hospital.

5	cups hot water
1	cube low sodium vegetable bouillon
1	teaspoon olive oil
⅓	cup diced yellow onions
2	tablespoons minced garlic
1	(10 ounce) package dried lentils

Combine hot water and bouillon. Stir well to dissolve completely. Set aside.

In saucepan, heat oil and sauté onion for 3-4 minutes until lightly caramelized and translucent. Add garlic. Sweat for 2 minutes. Add lentils and stir evenly to coat with oil. Add broth and bring to a boil. Reduce heat and simmer for 30 minutes until lentils are very tender, but not falling apart.

8 SERVINGS

Grandma Lena's Majedra

1-2	tablespoons olive oil
1	cup lentils, soaked in 2 cups of water, cleaned, rinsed and drained
1	large onion, chopped
1	cup long grain white rice
½	teaspoon salt, divided
	water

Heat olive oil in large heavy frying pan. Add chopped onion and ¼ teaspoon salt. Cook about 10 minutes until soft and lightly golden. Remove ⅓ of onions and set aside.

Add lentils and rice to onions and stir. Add 3 cups of water and another ¼ teaspoon salt. Bring to a boil, cover and reduce heat. Simmer for 10 minutes. Add another cup of boiling water, stir and cook another 10 minutes until lentils and rice are soft. If further cooking is needed, more water may need to be added. Gently stir in reserved onions. Salt to taste.

Serve with a chopped salad or sour cream.

Couscous with Currants and Pine Nuts

¼ **cup chopped onion**

4 **tablespoons olive oil**

2 **cups broth or water**

2 **cups couscous**

⅓ **cup currants**

½ **cup toasted pine nuts**

¼ **cup minced fresh basil**

Sauté onion in olive oil. Add broth. Bring to a boil.

Remove from heat. Stir in couscous. Let stand, covered, for 5 minutes. Fluff with a fork. Add currants, pine nuts and basil. Stir gently. Season with salt and pepper to taste.

8 SERVINGS

Herbed Basmati Rice

2 **teaspoons margarine or butter**

1 **garlic clove, minced**

½ **cup raw basmati rice**

1 **cup water**

¼ **teaspoon salt**

2 **tablespoons thinly sliced green onion tops**

2 **teaspoons minced fresh basil**

1 **teaspoon minced fresh thyme thyme springs for garnish**

Melt margarine in saucepan over medium heat. Add garlic and sauté one minute. Add rice and stir well. Add water and salt and bring to a boil. Cover, reduce heat, and simmer 20 minutes or until liquid is absorbed. Stir in green onions, basil and thyme. Garnish with thyme sprigs and serve.

2 TO 3 SERVINGS

Brown Rice with Pine Nuts and Cranberries

½   cup pine nuts
1   teaspoon olive oil
2   tablespoons unsalted butter
2   medium shallots, minced
1   cup long grain brown rice
3   cups low sodium chicken broth
4   turns freshly ground white pepper
½   cup dried cranberries
¼   cup finely minced Italian parsley

Preheat oven to 325°. Place pine nuts and olive oil in small oven pan. Let them brown for about 5-10 minutes. Watch carefully and remove when they are a caramel color. Cool and set aside.

Place butter in a stovetop, ovenproof casserole. Sauté shallots lightly in butter over low to medium heat. Add rice and stir to coat each kernel. Pour in the broth and pepper and stir over heat for 5 minutes.

Cover and place casserole for 45 minutes, or until liquid is absorbed. Remove from oven and add pine nuts and cranberries and mix well. Return to oven for 5 minutes.

Top with finely minced parsley and serve.

4 SERVINGS

This is low sodium and you may salt to taste.

Fried Brown Rice

2-3   tablespoons oil
1   small onion
2   scallions
¼   fresh red pepper
¼   cup coarsely shredded cabbage, optional
2   cups cooked brown rice
2   teaspoons soy sauce
1-2   teaspoons toasted sesame seeds or sunflower seeds, divided

Dice all vegetables. Heat oil in a large heavy skillet. Sauté onions until golden. Add remaining vegetables and sauté until limp. Add rice. Mix and turn. Add soy sauce and cook for a few minutes, stirring continuously. Serve immediately, sprinkling ½ teaspoon sesame or sunflower seeds on each serving.

2 TO 3 SERVINGS

Brown and Wild Rice with Wheat and Rye Berries

1   tablespoon oil
1   medium onion, chopped
1½   cups Texmati brown and wild rice
        blend with wheat and rye berries
2   (14½ ounce) cans chicken broth
1½   teaspoons poultry seasoning
¼   teaspoon allspice
¼   teaspoon salt
1   (7 ounce) package dried fruit blend
        cut into small pieces
¼   cup chopped parsley

Sauté onion in oil. Stir in rice, broth and seasonings. Cook according to package directions, for about 45 minutes. Stir in fruit and parsley. Cover and let stand 5 minutes.

6 SERVINGS

Green Rice

1   cup rice
2   cups broth
1   teaspoon salt
2   teaspoons butter or olive oil
¼   cup sliced green onion
¼   diced green pepper
¼   cup slivered almonds
½   cup chopped parsley
        diced pimiento, optional

Combine rice, broth and salt in saucepan. Bring to a boil, cover and simmer for 15 minutes or until tender.

Sauté onions, green pepper and almonds in butter for 3-5 minutes. Fold in freshly cooked rice along with parsley. Diced pimiento can be added for additional color.

6 SERVINGS

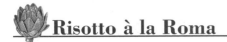

Risotto à la Roma

3½	cups chicken broth
½	cup Marsala wine
4	tablespoons butter
1	large onion, diced
2	cups rice
¼	teaspoon saffron
2	tablespoons hot water
½	cup grated Parmesan cheese

Heat broth and wine in saucepan. In skillet, melt butter and sauté onion until golden. Add rice and brown lightly, stirring constantly.

Pour rice into broth. Cover and cook 20 minutes or until liquid is absorbed. Dissolve saffron in hot water. Add saffron and cheese to rice.

Ideal with poultry or fish.

8 TO 10 SERVINGS

Pecan Wild Rice Pilaf

Great with lamb and chicken.

1	cup wild rice, well rinsed
4	cups chicken broth
1	cup coarsely chopped pecans
1	cup dried currants
1	bunch scallions, sliced
½	cup chopped parsley
½	cup chopped fresh mint or 1 tablespoon dry mint
	grated rind of 2 oranges
2	tablespoons olive oil
1	tablespoon orange juice
	salt and pepper to taste

Bring broth to a boil. Add wild rice. Cover and cook 50 minutes over low heat. Pour into large bowl. Add remaining ingredients and toss. Serve at room temperature.

8 TO 10 SERVINGS

Yummy Noodle Rice

¾ cup butter or margarine
½ pound extra fine noodles
2 cups uncooked rice
2 (10½ ounce) cans chicken broth
2 (10½ ounce) cans French onion soup
1 can water
1 (8 ounce) can sliced water chestnuts

Preheat oven to 350°. Melt butter in a deep pan. Pour in noodles and stir until browned. Stir in rice. Pour in chicken broth and French onion soup. This may sizzle. Pour in one cup water and then add water chestnuts. Mix well. Pour into 9 x 13 inch baking dish. Cook for 45 minutes.

8 TO 12 SERVINGS

Mushroom Orzo

I cup dry orzo
1 small yellow onion, finely chopped
1 teaspoon olive oil
½ pound shiitake mushrooms, stemmed and sliced
   salt and pepper to taste
2 tablespoons coarsely chopped parsley
1 tablespoon grated Parmesan cheese

Cook orzo according to package directions. Drain and rinse under cold water. Sauté onions slowly in oil, covered tightly except while stirring, until translucent. Add mushrooms and sauté until wilted. Season with salt, pepper and parsley. Add orzo. Stir to reheat. Toss in Parmesan cheese.

4 SERVINGS

Orzo with Parmesan Cheese

A delicious summer side dish.

1½   **cups dry orzo**

3   **cups broth**

¼   **cup olive oil**

2-3   **large tomatoes, seeded and coarsely chopped**

1   **cup basil leaves, coarsely chopped**

¼-½ **cup grated Parmesan cheese**

    salt and pepper to taste

Cook orzo. Drain and place in serving bowl. Add remaining ingredients. Toss. Season with salt and pepper. Gently toss and serve.

6 SERVINGS

Pasta with Mom's Secret Sauce

1   **pound ziti**

¼   **cup olive oil**

2   **tablespoons sesame oil**

1   **clove garlic, crushed**

4   **tablespoons soy sauce**

    small dash red pepper flakes

3   **tablespoons toasted sesame seeds**

Cook pasta according to directions on the box. Drain.

In microwave safe bowl, mix olive oil, sesame oil, garlic, soy sauce and red pepper flakes. Microwave for 20-30 seconds until hot. Pour sauce over pasta and mix. Sprinkle toasted sesame seeds over top and serve.

6 SERVINGS

Linguini with Olive Oil and Pepper Flakes

1   **pound linguini**

⅓   **cup olive oil**

    salt and pepper to taste

¼   **teaspoon red pepper flakes**

Cook linguini according to package directions. Drain. Coat with olive oil. Add salt and pepper to taste. Add pepper flakes and mix thoroughly.

6 SERVINGS

Baked Polenta

6½   cups water

2   teaspoons salt

2   cups dry polenta

6   tablespoons unsalted butter, divided

1   cup freshly grated Parmesan cheese

Bring water to a boil. Add salt, and then while stirring, add polenta. Reduce heat until mixture is barely bubbling and continue cooking while stirring for 20-25 minutes, until thickened and smooth. The polenta will start to come away from the pan. If using more finely ground quick cooking polenta, the cooking time is only three minutes. Check package instructions.

Remove polenta from heat. Stir in 4 tablespoons butter and ½ cup freshly grated Parmesan cheese. Spread out evenly into 13 x 9 inch square baking dish to a thickness of ½ inch. Allow to cool.

Preheat oven to 375°. Butter an ovenproof baking dish. Cut polenta into 2 inch squares and arrange overlapping in baking dish. Melt 2 tablespoons butter and drizzle over polenta. Sprinkle generously with freshly grated Parmesan cheese. Bake for 15 minutes until golden and bubbly. Serve immediately.

8 TO 10 SERVINGS

Squares of cooked and chilled polenta can be fried and topped with tomato sauce.

Pasta Puttanesca

1   (28 ounce) cans Italian plum
     tomatoes
2   cloves garlic, crushed
½   cup chopped parsley
1   teaspoon oregano
1   red pepper, chopped
1   (2 ounce) can anchovies, drained
     and sliced
¼   cup olives
2-4 tablespoons capers
1   pound pasta

Combine all ingredients. Cook for 10-15 minutes. Serve over your favorite hot pasta.

6 SERVINGS

Indian Potatoes

2   pounds small new potatoes
1¾   teaspoons salt, divided
2½   tablespoons vegetable oil
1   teaspoon cumin seeds
1   teaspoon ground cumin
½   teaspoon Garam Masala
⅛   teaspoon cayenne pepper
2   tablespoons cilantro

Wash potatoes and place them in a saucepan. Add 1 teaspoon salt and cover with water. Bring to a boil and cook until potatoes are cooked, but still firm. Drain.

Heat oil in large frying pan over medium-high heat. When oil is hot, cook cumin seeds for approximately 2 minutes. Add potatoes, turn the heat down to medium, and brown the potatoes lightly on all sides. Turn the heat to low, add ¾ teaspoon salt, ground cumin, Garam Masala (a spice mixture used in Indian cooking), and cayenne pepper. Stir and cook for one minute. Add cilantro just before serving and toss to mix.

4 TO 6 SERVINGS

Just before cooking time ends, 1 can of chickpeas, rinsed and drained, may be added.

Potato Pancakes

1   large onion, cut up
6   large potatoes, peeled and cut up
2   eggs
2   tablespoons flour or matzo meal
1   teaspoon salt
¼   teaspoon pepper
    vegetable oil
    applesauce
    sour cream

Grate onion or chop in blender. Grate potatoes. If using blender, add a little water to each batch and drain with strainer. Add potatoes to onion and mix. This keeps potatoes white. Add eggs, flour, and seasonings, and mix well. Heat oil in skillet. Add a spoonful of batter for each pancake and fry to deep brown on each side.

Serve with sour cream or applesauce.

6 TO 8 SERVINGS

Rosemary Roasted Potatoes

10   medium red potatoes, cut into quarters
6   cloves garlic, minced
1½   tablespoons chopped fresh rosemary or 2 teaspoons dry
1   teaspoon chopped fresh thyme or ½ teaspoon dry
    salt and pepper to taste
¼   cup olive oil

Preheat oven to 400°. Place potatoes in a baking dish. Sprinkle with herbs and seasonings. Pour olive oil over all and toss to coat well. Bake for 45 minutes or until potatoes are tender and crusty, stirring occasionally.

6 SERVINGS

Can also use fingerling potatoes, cut in half, or substitute half of red potatoes with blue potatoes.

Twice Baked Potatoes

4   medium baking potatoes
1   cup sour cream
½   cup milk
1   medium onion, chopped
1   tablespoon chopped chives
    salt and pepper to taste
2   tablespoons shredded Cheddar
    cheese

Preheat oven to 350°. Bake potatoes until soft. Allow to cool slightly and cut in half lengthwise. Scoop potato from the shells, reserving the shells.

Mash potato filling with sour cream and milk. Mix in onion, chives and seasonings. Fill shells and place on cookie sheet. Sprinkle cheese on top. Bake 30 minutes.

4 SERVINGS

Can be made in advance and reheated.

Sweet Potato Pancakes

A recipe from Ira Brandstein, Director of Food and Nutrition at The Miriam Hospital.

1   pound sweet potatoes, peeled and
    shredded
½   cup eggs, beaten
3   tablespoons flour
1   tablespoon light brown sugar
¼   teaspoon ground cinnamon
⅛   teaspoon ground nutmeg
3   tablespoons finely sliced green
    onions
⅓   cup vegetable oil
    peach chutney, optional

Combine sweet potato, egg, flour, brown sugar, cinnamon, nutmeg and green onion. Toss gently to distribute evenly.

Pour oil in a skillet to ¼ inch deep. Heat over medium heat to 350°. Using a wooden spoon, portion batter into skillet, flattening each slightly to a diameter of 4 inches. Cook for 2-3 minutes or until edges start to brown. Turn carefully. Cook 1-2 minutes more or until edges brown. Drain well. Keep hot until serving. Top with peach chutney if desired.

6 SERVINGS

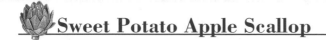

Sweet Potato Apple Scallop

2   **cups boiled sweet potatoes, peeled and thinly sliced**
1½   **cups tart apples, peeled, cored and thinly sliced**
½   **cup brown sugar**
1   **teaspoon salt**
¼   **cup butter**

Preheat oven to 350°. Layer a greased casserole with half of all ingredients. Dot with butter. Repeat.

Bake covered for 30 minutes. Uncover and bake until apples are soft and top is brown.

6 SERVINGS

Sweet Potatoes and Apricots

A favorite.

3   **large sweet potatoes**
1½   **cups dark brown sugar**
4   **teaspoons cornstarch**
1   **orange, juice and rind**
½   **teaspoon salt**
1   **(17 ounce) can apricot halves in syrup**
3   **tablespoons butter**

Boil sweet potatoes in their jackets for 30 minutes, or until tender. Remove jackets and halve potatoes lengthwise. Arrange cut side down in greased 8 inch square baking dish.

Preheat oven to 375°. In saucepan, combine sugar, cornstarch, rind and juice of orange, salt and syrup from apricots. Heat gently until sauce thickens and then add butter.

Place apricots, cut side down, over potatoes. Pour sauce over all. Bake for 25 minutes.

6 SERVINGS

Sweet Potato Casserole with Praline Topping

Almost good enough to be dessert.

6	sweet potatoes, approximately 3 pounds
½	cup butter
1	(8 ounce) can crushed pineapple in juice
1	teaspoon cinnamon
2	teaspoons brown sugar

PRALINE TOPPING

1	cup brown sugar
⅓	cup butter, softened
½	cup flour
1	cup chopped pecans

Boil potatoes until tender. Drain, peel and mash. Add remaining ingredients and place in greased 9 x 13 inch baking dish.

Preheat oven to 350°. Mix topping ingredients together and sprinkle over sweet potato mixture. Bake for 25 minutes.

8 TO 10 SERVINGS

Omit praline topping and replace with 2 cups miniature marshmallows during last 5 minutes of baking.

Southern Sweet Potato Stuffing

Johnson and Wales University gives us this delightfully different dressing for your bird.

6   boiled sweet potatoes or yams,
    about 4 cups
2   tablespoons butter
½   teaspoon salt
2   teaspoons brown sugar
    sherry to taste
1   orange, grated
½   teaspoon nutmeg
    dash cinnamon
½   cup chopped onion
1   cup chopped celery
2   cups bread crumbs
5   tablespoons chopped parsley

Mash potatoes with butter, salt, brown sugar, sherry and spices. Sauté onion and celery for about 3 minutes. Combine with potatoes and all other ingredients and mix well.

Zucchini Potato Latkes

A new version from Whole Foods Market.

1   large onion
6   small tender zucchini, trimmed
3   large yellow potatoes, scrubbed but unpeeled
3   large eggs
1   teaspoon safflower oil
2   teaspoons salt
¼   teaspoon black pepper
½-¾ cup matzo meal or potato flour
    high heat safflower oil for frying

Grate onion in food processor and remove to a large bowl. Grate zucchini in the food processor and add to the onion. Grate potatoes in the processor and add to the onion and zucchini. The juice of the onions prevents the potatoes from turning black. (Alternatively, finely dice the onions and grate the zucchini and potatoes with a box grater.)

Using your fingers, pick up small handfuls of the zucchini-potato mixture and squeeze out as much moisture as possible, reserving the liquid. Put pressed mixture in a clean bowl. Allow reserved liquid to settle in a bowl for a few minutes. Carefully pour off the watery part of the reserved liquid but do not discard the thick starchy sediment at the bottom of the bowl. Scrape that into the potato mixture.

In a small bowl, mix the eggs, oil, salt and pepper and combine with the potato mixture. Add the matzo meal to the batter, starting with ½ cup and adding more if necessary until the potato mixture has enough body to form pancakes.

Heat a ½ inch depth of oil in a heavy skillet, preferably cast iron. Drop potato mixture into hot oil to form pancakes of approximately 3 inches in diameter. Take care not to crowd pancakes. Fry, turning once, until golden on both sides for a total of approximately 6 minutes. Drain on clean paper bags. Keep pancakes warm while the rest are frying by placing cooked, drained pancakes in a preheated 400° oven.

6 SERVINGS

Simply *More* Vegetables

The Gift Shop in 1953.

The Miriam Hospitality Shop

In January 1953, The Gift and Coffee Shops opened in a prime location just off the lobby of the new Miriam Hospital. Although established as a convenience for patients and visitors, the gift shop soon evolved into a shop with inventory that appealed to hospital personnel and the public as well. The Gift Shop stocked gifts for everyone, from jewelry, stationery, and home decorating items to stuffed animals, books and toys for children.

Started in 1953, the shops, which were funded with $1000 in "seed money" borrowed from the Women's Association, reported a net profit of $14,000 in just two years. Since then the shops have been recognized for donating hundreds of thousands of dollars to The Miriam Hospital.

The Coffee Shop was very small. It consisted of a counter, a soda fountain and a couple of tables. The kitchen facilities were merely coffee and tea pots and a small refrigerator. Because of a lack of storage, staff ordered supplies daily, and served only sandwiches. They did, however, do a big "take out" business.

Asparagus with Creamy Lemon Sauce

1	pound fresh asparagus, trimmed
3	tablespoons butter, divided
2	tablespoons flour
¼	cup fresh lemon juice
1	cup boiling water
¼	teaspoon salt
	dash Tabasco sauce
½	cup sour cream

Melt 2 tablespoons butter in saucepan. Stir in flour and cook 2 minutes, stirring constantly. Add water and lemon juice. Cook, stirring constantly, until thickened and smooth. Simmer 5 minutes. Add salt and Tabasco. Just before serving, add sour cream and remaining butter. While simmering, steam or microwave asparagus, until tender, but crisp. Spoon sauce over and serve.

6 SERVINGS

Cold Asparagus with Mustard Vinaigrette

This dressing is excellent on green beans and other salads.

2½-3	pounds asparagus, trimmed
½	cup rice wine vinegar
½	cup Dijon mustard
¾	cup olive oil
¾	cup canola oil
2-3	tablespoons honey
2	shallots, finely minced
	salt and pepper to taste

Cook asparagus until just tender. Immediately rinse with cold water until cool. Dry thoroughly and chill.

Whisk vinegar and mustard together. Add oils, whisking vigorously. Add remaining ingredients and mix. This dressing can be made in a food processor.

Arrange asparagus spears on individual plates or a platter. Drizzle with dressing.

8 SERVINGS

Grilled Asparagus

1 pound fresh asparagus, trimmed
2 tablespoons olive oil
   Kosher salt
   freshly ground black pepper

Preheat grill on high heat. Lightly coat asparagus with olive oil. Season with salt and pepper to taste. Grill over high heat for 2-3 minutes or to desired tenderness.

6 SERVINGS

Three Bean Casserole

1 (10 ounce) package frozen lima beans
½ pound frankfurters, optional
2 tablespoons butter or olive oil
1 onion, chopped
1 garlic clove, minced
1 (16 ounce) can kidney beans, drained
2 (16 ounce) cans baked beans
1 teaspoon prepared mustard
1 tablespoon brown sugar
½ cup ketchup
½ cup dry red wine
½ teaspoon salt
   dash pepper

Preheat oven to 350°. Cook lima beans as directed and drain. Slice frankfurters and sauté in butter with onions and garlic until tender. Stir in lima beans and remaining ingredients. Place in 2 quart casserole and bake for 30 minutes.

8 SERVINGS

Cannellini Beans and Spinach

1   **(15 ounce) can cannellini beans**
1   **pound fresh spinach, cleaned**
3-4   **cloves garlic, chopped**
2-3   **tablespoons olive oil**
      salt and pepper to taste

Sauté garlic in olive oil. Add cannellini beans and cook together with garlic for about 5 minutes. Add spinach to mixture and continue stirring until spinach is thoroughly wilted and all ingredients are hot. Add salt and pepper to taste.

SERVES 4

String Beans à la Betsy

An unusual way to serve beans, A good party dish, as it can be prepared early in the day and heated before serving.

2   **pounds string beans**
2   **medium onions, chopped**
¼-½ **pound fresh mushrooms, chopped**
      oil for sautéing
1   **cup bread crumbs**
1   **cup Italian dressing**

Preheat oven to 350°. Cook string beans in boiling salted water until tender but crisp.

Sauté onions and mushrooms in oil. When onions are golden, add bread crumbs and sauté until golden brown. Place beans, onions, mushrooms and crumbs in casserole. Add Italian dressing and mix thoroughly. Heat in oven and serve.

 Beets Orange

½ cup orange juice
2 tablespoons lemon juice
1 tablespoon vinegar
½ teaspoon salt
  dash pepper
1 tablespoon sugar
1 tablespoon cornstarch
1 tablespoon water
1 (16 ounce) can whole beets, drained
2 tablespoons butter

In double boiler, combine orange juice, lemon juice, vinegar, salt, pepper and sugar. Dissolve cornstarch in water and add. Cook until clear, stirring constantly.

Add beets and heat through. Add butter and blend.

4 SERVINGS

Broccoli with Caramelized Onions and Pine Nuts

3 tablespoons pine nuts, or chopped slivered almonds, toasted
2 tablespoons olive oil
1 cup chopped onion
¼ teaspoon salt or to taste
4 cups broccoli florets
2 teaspoons balsamic vinegar
  freshly ground pepper to taste

Heat oil in pan over medium heat. Add onions and salt. Cook for 15-20 minutes, stirring often, until soft and golden brown.

While onions are cooking, steam broccoli until just tender, 4-6 minutes. Transfer to serving bowl. Add onions, pine nuts and pepper. Toss to coat and serve.

4 SERVINGS

Roasted Brussels Sprouts

1½ pounds fresh brussels sprouts
4   tablespoons extra virgin olive oil
    kosher salt
    freshly ground black pepper

Preheat oven to 400°. Wash brussels sprouts, trim ends and cut larger brussels sprouts in half (from the stem end). Place in shallow baking pan or cookie sheet. Toss with olive oil, salt and pepper.

Roast 30-40 minutes, stirring or shaking occasionally until fork tender and crisp on the outside.

4 SERVINGS

Red Cabbage Lorraine

Great with duck.

2   pounds red cabbage, coarsely
        shredded
4   tablespoons butter
2   medium onions, thinly sliced
4   large tart apples, peeled, cored and
        quartered
2   cloves garlic, minced
¼   teaspoon allspice
¼   teaspoon caraway seed
    salt and freshly ground pepper
    sprinkling of sugar
2   tablespoons wine vinegar
2   cups dry red wine
¼   cup water

Preheat oven to 375°. In Dutch oven, cook cabbage with butter over medium heat for 5 minutes, stirring occasionally. Remove from pot.

In same pot, make layers of cabbage, onions, apples and spices. Top with a sprinkling of water. Mix vinegar, wine and water. Add to pot. Bake for 50-60 minutes.

8 SERVINGS

Honey Buttered Carrots

1	pound fresh carrots, cleaned
¼	cup butter
¼	cup pecan halves
3	tablespoons honey
2	tablespoons golden raisins
¼	teaspoon grated orange rind
	salt and pepper to taste

Cut carrots into 1 inch rounds. Cook in boiling, salted water to cover until tender. Drain.

Stir in remaining ingredients and bring to a boil. Cook until liquid is absorbed and carrots are glazed, about 10-15 minutes.

6 SERVINGS

Carrot Soufflé

Everyone loves this Thanksgiving staple. With a change of flour to cake meal or potato starch, it works well for Passover too.

1	pound carrots
3	eggs
⅓	cup sugar
2	tablespoons flour
1	teaspoon baking powder
1	teaspoon vanilla extract
½	cup butter, melted
	dash nutmeg
	dash cinnamon

TOPPING

¼	cup cornflakes, crushed
3	tablespoons light brown sugar
2	tablespoons butter
¼	cup chopped walnuts

Preheat oven to 350°. Steam carrots until very soft. Purée in food processor. Add eggs and blend. Add sugar, flour, baking powder, vanilla extract, butter, nutmeg and cinnamon and blend. Pour into deep soufflé dish or casserole.

Combine topping ingredients and sprinkle over casserole. Bake for 1 hour. Test for doneness with a knife that comes out clean.

4 TO 6 SERVINGS

Marinated Carrots

2   **pounds carrots, pared, quartered and sliced into 1 inch lengths**
1   **teaspoon salt**
¼   **teaspoon pepper**
½   **teaspoon prepared yellow mustard**
¾   **cup sugar**
¾   **cup cider vinegar**
½   **cup oil, divided**
1   **(10½ ounce) can tomato soup**
1   **cup chopped green pepper**
1   **cup chopped onion**

Cover carrots with water in a covered pan. Bring to a boil and simmer 5 minutes until carrots are slightly soft. Drain and cool.

Mix salt, pepper and mustard in a little oil. Add remaining dry and liquid seasonings. Combine well with a whisk. Add vegetables, cover and chill.

Cauliflower Marietta

Good and easy.

1   **small head cauliflower**
1   **clove garlic, split**
¼-½ **cup olive oil**
1   **(14 ounce) can tomatoes, chopped**
    salt
    freshly ground pepper

Cut core from cauliflower and separate flowerets slightly.

Sauté garlic in oil in heavy skillet. Remove and put cauliflower in pan. Cover with tomatoes and their liquid. Add salt to taste and lots of black pepper. Steam until cauliflower is tender, about 20 minutes.

6 SERVINGS

227

Baked Cauliflower Purée

Lower in calories and carbohydrates than mashed potatoes which it resembles.

1   large cauliflower, separated into flowerets
1   medium onion, chopped
½   cup buttermilk
3   tablespoons butter
    salt and pepper to taste
    chopped parsley for garnish

Preheat oven to 350°. Cook cauliflower and onion in saucepan, with water to cover, until tender. Place mixture in a food processor and purée until smooth, slowly adding buttermilk. Add cooking water if more liquid is needed. Add butter, salt and pepper and pulse a few seconds more. Place in a 1 quart baking dish and bake until heated through.

6 SERVINGS

This dish can be made ahead and reheated.

Eggplant Casserole

2   large eggplants, divided
1   teaspoon salt
¼   cup olive oil
1   cup herb stuffing mix, divided
1   medium onion, chopped
½   green pepper, chopped
3   fresh tomatoes, or 1 (16 ounce) can tomatoes, drained and chopped
1   (8 ounce) package shredded mozzarella cheese, divided
½   cup grated Parmesan cheese

Preheat oven to 350°. Peel and cube eggplant. Place in saucepan with salt and water to cover. Boil 10 minutes or until tender. Drain.

Grease casserole with olive oil. Sprinkle ½ cup stuffing mix on bottom. Place ½ of cooked eggplant on top of stuffing. Spread onions, green pepper and tomatoes over eggplant. Sprinkle ½ mozzarella over tomatoes. Repeat layering remaining eggplant, mozzarella, stuffing mix and top with Parmesan cheese.

Bake for 30 minutes until hot and bubbly.

6 TO 8 SERVINGS

Escarole with Olives, Raisins and Pine Nuts

1	garlic clove, sliced
2	tablespoons olive oil
1	pound escarole, rinsed well and dried, trimmed and cut into bite size pieces
1	tablespoon sliced kalamata olives
2	teaspoons golden raisins
	salt and pepper to taste
2	teaspoons pine nuts, lightly toasted

In a large skillet, sauté garlic in olive oil over moderately high heat. Discard the garlic once it is golden. Add escarole, olives, raisins, salt and pepper to skillet. Stir and sauté mixture for 1 minute. Then reduce heat, cover and cook mixture for another 4 minutes until escarole is tender. Stir in pine nuts and cook for 1 more minute or until all liquid is evaporated.

2 SERVINGS

Ratatouille

4	large onions, chopped
4	large potatoes, chopped
2	large zucchini, chopped
5	small yellow squash, chopped
2	large tomatoes, chopped
½	cup butter
	dill
	mixed herbs
	salt and pepper to taste

In a large nonstick fry pan, melt butter over high heat. Sauté all vegetables in order shown. Continue to cook, stirring often, until liquid is reduced to a sauce. Add a couple of pinches dill and mixed herbs. Season with salt and pepper to taste, adjusting flavor as desired. Use immediately or freeze. When ready to serve, bring to room temperature and heat at 325° for 15 minutes.

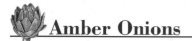 # Amber Onions

6	large onions, peeled and halved
1	tablespoon butter, melted
2	tablespoons tomato juice
2	tablespoons honey
1	teaspoon salt
¼	teaspoon paprika

Preheat oven to 350°. Place onions in single layer in 13 x 9 inch casserole.

Combine remaining ingredients and pour over onions. Bake, covered, for 1 hour.

8 SERVINGS

Fall Vegetable Medley

1	large red pepper, cut into 2 inch squares
1	large yellow pepper, cut into 2 inch squares
1	medium carrot, cut into 2 inch chunks
1	small red onion, cut into wedges
2	beets, peeled, cut into 2 inch squares
6	garlic cloves with skins
2	tablespoons olive oil
¼	cup balsamic vinegar

Preheat oven to 400°. Combine the vegetables. Toss with olive oil and balsamic vinegar and place in a single layer on a baking sheet. Roast vegetables uncovered for 25 minutes or until soft.

6 SERVINGS

Spinach Casserole

Everyone's favorite.

2   (10 ounce) packages frozen chopped
     spinach
½   pound plain or chive cream cheese,
     softened
¼   pound butter, divided
1   cup bread crumbs
     salt and pepper to taste

Preheat oven to 350°. Cook spinach according to package directions. Drain well. Mix with cheese and half the butter. Season and place mixture in 1½ quart casserole.

Melt remaining butter and toss with crumbs. Sprinkle crumbs over spinach mixture. Bake 20-30 minutes or until bubbly and lightly browned.

6 SERVINGS

Creamed Spinach

1   cup diced onions
2   tablespoons butter
⅓   cup licorice flavored liqueur,
     optional
1   cup heavy cream
     salt and pepper to taste
1   (10 ounce) bag fresh spinach
2   tablespoons olive oil
1   teaspoon chopped garlic

Sweat onions in butter by heating in heavy pan, covered, over low heat until tender but not brown. Add liqueur, if desired, and simmer until liquid is reduced by half. Add cream, salt and pepper. Simmer 10 minutes.

Wash spinach and remove ribs. Tear into bite size pieces or coarsely chop. In separate pan, heat oil with garlic until garlic is golden. Add spinach and simmer, uncovered, for 5 minutes. Add cream mixture. Season to taste.

4 SERVINGS

Baby spinach works well.

Butternut Squash Casserole

2	pounds butternut squash, peeled and seeded, and cut into 3 x 2 inch pieces
3	gingersnaps, crushed
4	tablespoons butter
¼	cup brown sugar
½	cup maple syrup
½	(3 ounce) can French fried onion rings

Parboil squash about 20 minutes. Drain well and mash.

Preheat oven to 300°. Combine with all ingredients except onion rings and place in ungreased 2½ quart casserole. Bake for about 2 hours. Sprinkle with onion rings during last half hour of cooking.

8 SERVINGS

Sweet Pea Stuffed Acorn Squash

4	small acorn squash, cut in half and seeded
½	cup water
1	tablespoon olive oil
⅓	cup orange juice
½	cup diced celery
½	cup diced onion
1	(10 ounce) package frozen baby sweet peas
1	tablespoon cornstarch
½	cup chicken broth
2	teaspoons honey
⅓	cup dried, sweetened cranberries
	salt and black pepper to taste

Preheat oven to 350°. In an oven proof glass baking dish, place squash upside down, add water and bake for 25 minutes or until tender. Remove from baking dish, but keep warm while preparing sweet pea mixture.

Meanwhile, in a medium saucepan, heat olive oil. Add celery and onion and cook for 5 minutes until tender. Add orange juice and frozen peas. Cook for another 5 minutes stirring frequently. Whisk together cornstarch and chicken broth and add this to the pea mixture. Remove mixture from heat and stir in honey, cranberries and salt and pepper to taste.

Divide sweet pea mixture into acorn squash cavities and serve.

8 SERVINGS

Acorn Squash with Apple Stuffing

2   acorn squash

     salt

2   medium cooking apples, peeled,
     cored and sliced

¼   cup sugar

¼   teaspoon cinnamon

     butter or margarine

Preheat oven to 350°. Halve squash lengthwise. Remove seeds and fibers and dust lightly with salt.

Add sugar and cinnamon to apples and fill squash cavities with mixture. Dot with butter. Bake for 1 hour.

4 SERVINGS

Summer Squash Casserole

1   pound yellow squash

1   medium onion, chopped

     salt and pepper to taste

2   tablespoons butter

1-2 eggs, beaten

½   cup shredded Cheddar cheese

1   tablespoon parsley flakes

1   cup bread crumbs

¼   teaspoon baking powder

Preheat oven to 350°.Cook squash, onions, salt and pepper in a small amount of water until tender, allowing most of the liquid to evaporate. Drain and mash. Add butter. Stir in eggs. Add remaining ingredients. Pour into greased 2 quart casserole and bake 40 minutes.

6 SERVINGS

Succotash

2	pounds fresh lima beans
½	cup butter
2	pounds fresh okra, sliced
4	fresh ripe tomatoes, chopped
5	ears corn, cut from cob
	salt and pepper to taste

Cook lima beans 15 minutes in boiling salted water. Drain. In large skillet, melt butter. Add corn and okra and cook 15 minutes. Add tomatoes, salt and pepper, stir and cook a few more minutes. Add corn and cook an additional 7 minutes, stirring often.

8 SERVINGS

Frozen vegetables work well too.

Sautéed Cherry Tomatoes with Pine Nuts

A recipe from Ira Brandstein, Director of Food and Nutrition at The Miriam Hospital.

¼	cup olive oil
1	tablespoon minced garlic
4	pints cherry tomatoes, washed and stems removed
⅓	cup pine nuts, toasted
¾	ounce fresh basil leaves, minced (about ½ cup)
⅓	cup red wine vinegar
½	teaspoon salt
⅜	teaspoon ground black pepper

Heat oil in skillet. Add garlic and sauté until softened. Add tomatoes and sauté for 5-7 minutes. Do not overcook or tomatoes will burst. Stir in pine nuts, basil, vinegar, salt and pepper. Sauté for 2 minutes. Serve hot.

8 SERVINGS

Tomatoes Florentine

4   tomatoes, halved
1   (10 ounce) package frozen chopped
        spinach, defrosted and drained
1   tablespoon chopped onion
1   tablespoon butter
     salt and pepper to taste
     Parmesan cheese

Preheat oven to 325°. Place tomatoes in buttered casserole and bake for 10 minutes.

Meanwhile, mix spinach with onion, butter, salt and pepper in saucepan and cook 10 minutes.

Pile spinach mixture on tomatoes, sprinkle cheese and bake until heated through, about 10 minutes.

4 TO 8 SERVINGS

Tsimmes

5   large carrots
5   white potatoes
3   sweet potatoes
¾   pound prunes
¾   pound dried apricots
¼   cup honey
½   teaspoons cinnamon
     dash nutmeg
     juice of 1 lemon

Preheat oven to 350°. Peel potatoes and carrots. Cut the potatoes and carrots into quarters. Put them in a casserole and cover with water. Add the prunes, apricots, brown sugar, nutmeg and lemon juice. Stir until coated and mixed together.

Bake covered for 1 hour.

8 SERVINGS

# Vegetable Kebabs

1   (16 ounce) can small whole white
    potatoes
½   pound mushrooms
2   tomatoes, cut into eighths
1   green pepper, cubed
1   onion, cubed
    butter
    Parmesan cheese

Preheat broiler. Alternate vegetables on skewers. Brush with butter and sprinkle with cheese. Place on broiler rack. Broil 4 minutes on each side.

4 SERVINGS

Zucchini Casserole

3   cups sliced, unpeeled zucchini,
    divided
1   medium onion, chopped, divided
1   (24 ounce) jar favorite marinara
    sauce, divided
2   tablespoons bread crumbs, divided
2-4 ounces, sliced provolone cheese,
    divided
    grated Parmesan cheese

Preheat oven to 350°. Pour some tomato sauce on the bottom of a shallow baking dish. Spread half the zucchini slices on top of the sauce, then half of the onion, half the cheese and then half of the bread crumbs. Repeat the second layer and end with marinara sauce on top. Sprinkle with Parmesan cheese. Bake for 1 hour.

Roasted Zucchini

A recipe from Ira Brandstein, Director of Food and Nutrition at The Miriam Hospital.

2   pounds fresh zucchini, sliced ⅝ inch
     thick

¾   cup Balsamic and Basil Vinaigrette
     on page 72
     oil

Brush prepared vegetables with vinaigrette until well-coated. Arrange vegetables in single layer on baking sheets. Hold for 30 minutes. If excess liquid accumulates, drain and discard before cooking.

Preheat oven to 475°. Place marinated, drained zucchini in a single layer on baking sheets that have been lightly oiled or lined with parchment paper. Place in oven and cook 10-20 minutes or until vegetables are just tender and lightly caramelized (lightly browned). Turn or stir only if needed to promote even cooking.

Serve immediately or cool on clean, chilled sheets in a single layer, handling carefully to prevent breakage.

8 SERVINGS

This is also delicious cold or warm the next day.

Triple Vegetable Casserole

2	Spanish onions, sliced
2	tablespoons olive oil
¼	teaspoon dry thyme
2	garlic cloves, minced
4	large tomatoes
2	medium eggplant
2	medium zucchini

Preheat oven to 325°. Sauté onions, thyme and garlic in olive oil until tender. Spread in bottom of casserole. Thinly slice tomatoes, eggplant and zucchini. Place on top of onions in a repeating, slightly overlapping pattern — tomatoes, eggplant, zucchini, to fill the casserole.

Drizzle olive oil and thyme on top. Bake uncovered for 30 minutes. Turn oven up to 350° and cook another 10 minutes.

Simply *More* Desserts

The Soda Fountain in the Coffee Shop was a favorite of staff and visitors.

The Soda Fountain

When the new Miriam Hospital opened on Summit Avenue, the Coffee Shop featured a sparkling new soda fountain that was completely run and staffed by volunteers from the Women's Association. These women reported that "it was fun, but also hard work as they had to be on their feet so much."

A story is told about how the volunteers learned to make ice cream sodas. They were taught the mechanics of good soda preparation at the Hood's ice cream plant in Providence. During the first week or two of operation, the women misjudged the quantity of ingredients to use, resulting in a surfeit of fizz which overflowed the counters. They spent considerable time cleaning up, but everything was always spotless.

When the hospital was remodeled in 1966 and again in 1978, both the Gift and Coffee Shops were enlarged and remodeled. The Coffee Shop was able to expand its selection and served delicious sandwiches, salads, coffees and desserts, including wonderful bakery items.

 Apple Cake

1	cup oil
2	cups sugar
4	eggs
2	cups flour, sifted
3	teaspoons baking powder
⅓	cup orange juice
3	teaspoons vanilla extract
2	large apples, peeled, cored and sliced thin
1	teaspoon cinnamon mixed with 4 teaspoons sugar

Preheat oven to 350°. Put first 7 ingredients in mixer and beat 10 minutes. Mix apples with cinnamon-sugar mixture. Pour ⅓ of batter into greased 10 inch tube pan. Top with ⅓ of apple mixture. Repeat twice, ending with layer of apples. Bake for 1½ hours. Cool in pan 30 minutes, then remove carefully.

8 SERVINGS

Apple Nut Cake

1½	cups oil
2	cups sugar
2	eggs
1	teaspoon vanilla extract
3	cups chopped, peeled raw apples
1	cup chopped nuts
3	cups flour
1	teaspoon baking soda
1	teaspoon salt
1	teaspoon cinnamon
½	cup confectioners' sugar
1	tablespoon milk

Preheat oven to 350°. Beat oil, sugar, eggs and vanilla extract for 4 minutes with electric mixer. Fold in the next 2 ingredients. Mix flour, baking soda, salt and cinnamon together and add to mixture. Dough will be stiff.

Bake in ungreased 10 inch tube pan for 1 hour 30 minutes. Cool in pan 10 minutes and remove.

Sift confectioners' sugar and mix with enough milk to pouring consistency. Drizzle over cake.

 # Banana Cake

½   **cup butter**

1¼   **cups sugar**

2   **eggs, lightly beaten**

1   **teaspoon baking soda**

4   **tablespoons sour cream or yogurt**

1   **cup ripe bananas, mashed**

1½   **cups cake flour**

¼   **teaspoon salt**

1   **teaspoon vanilla extract**

Add 1 cup chocolate chips

Preheat oven to 350°. Cream butter and sugar. Add eggs. Dissolve baking soda in sour cream. Add to mixture and beat well. Add bananas, flour, salt and vanilla extract. Mix well.

Pour into greased and floured 8 inch square pan. Bake for 30-35 minutes.

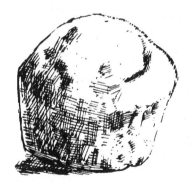

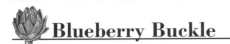 Blueberry Buckle

¾ cup sugar

¼ cup soft shortening

1 egg

½ cup milk

2 cups flour

2 teaspoons baking powder

½ teaspoon salt

2 cups blueberries

  whipped cream or ice cream, optional

TOPPING

½ cup sugar

⅓ cup flour

½ teaspoon cinnamon

¼ cup soft butter

Preheat oven to 375°. Mix sugar, shortening and egg. Stir in milk. Sift dry ingredients together and fold in. Fold in blueberries and spread batter evenly in greased 9 inch square pan.

Combine topping ingredients and sprinkle on top. Bake for 45-50 minutes. Serve warm, topped with whipped cream or ice cream, if desired.

9 SERVINGS

Carrot Cake

1½ cups vegetable oil

2 cups sugar

4 eggs

2 cups flour

2 teaspoons baking soda

2 teaspoons baking powder

2 teaspoons cinnamon

½ teaspoon salt

¼ teaspoon nutmeg

1 cup chopped pecans

3 cups grated carrots

1 cup golden raisins

1 teaspoon vanilla extract

Preheat oven at 350°. Blend oil and sugar. Add eggs, one at a time, and blend.

Sift together dry ingredients. Add to mixture and blend well. Fold in remaining ingredients. Pour into greased and floured 10 inch springform pan and bake for 35-45 minutes.

10 SERVINGS

Karen's Carrot Cake

4	jumbo eggs
2	cups sugar
1½	cups oil
2½	cups flour
2	teaspoons baking powder
1½	teaspoons baking soda
1	teaspoon salt
1	teaspoon cinnamon
2	(4 ounce) jars carrot baby food
1	(8 ½ ounce) can crushed pineapple, including juice
½	cup chopped walnuts
½	cup shredded coconut

CREAM CHEESE BUTTER FROSTING

1	(4 ounce) package cream cheese
¼	cup butter
½	pound confectioners' sugar
1½	teaspoons vanilla extract
	chopped walnuts, optional

These cakes freeze well.

Preheat oven to 350°. Butter and flour lasagna pan. Beat eggs, sugar and oil. Add remaining cake ingredients and blend well with spoon. Pour into lasagna pan. Bake 45 minutes. Allow to cool.

Mix frosting ingredients together. Cut cake into thirds and frost each cake individually. Top with walnuts, if desired.

Arthur's Favorite Cheesecake

CRUST

½   cup butter, softened

1   cup sifted flour

    pinch salt

¼   cup sugar

1   egg yolk

FILLING

2½   pounds cream cheese, softened

1¾   cups sugar

6   eggs

2   tablespoons flour

¼   teaspoon salt

1   teaspoon vanilla extract

½   cup heavy cream

CRUST

Blend butter, flour, salt and sugar. Add egg yolk and blend well. Wrap dough in plastic bag and refrigerate 1 hour. Preheat oven to 400°. Roll out ⅓ of dough on floured surface, forming 9 inch circle. Place on bottom of 9 inch springform pan and bake for 10 minutes. Remove from oven. Grease sides of pan. Roll out remaining dough in strips to fit sides and press in place, joining bottom edges.

FILLING

Turn oven up to 475°. Beat cheese until light and fluffy. Add sugar, eggs, flour, salt, and vanilla extract, beating well after each addition. Add cream. Blend well. Pour into prepared pan. Bake for 10 minutes. Reduce heat to 225° and bake for 1 hour longer. Turn off oven and open door. Allow to cool in oven for 10 minutes. Cool away from drafts. Cake cools in 4 hours. When cool, loosen cake with knife and remove sides of pan.

12 SERVINGS

Chocolate Swirl Cheesecake

1   (6 ounce) package semisweet
      chocolate bits
1   cup flour, divided
1   cup plus 2 tablespoons sugar,
      divided
¼   teaspoon salt
¼   cup butter
3   (8 ounce) packages cream cheese,
      softened
2   teaspoons vanilla extract
6   eggs, separated
1   cup sour cream

Preheat oven to 400°. Melt chocolate bits in double boiler, over hot water. Combine ¾ cup flour with 2 tablespoons sugar and salt. Cut in butter till fine particles form. Stir in 2 tablespoons chocolate. Press into bottom of 9 inch springform pan. Bake for 10 minutes. Combine sugar and cream cheese in bowl. Blend in ¼ cup flour and vanilla extract. Add egg yolks, beat well. Blend in sour cream. Beat egg whites into soft peaks. Fold in cheese mixture. Set aside 1¾ cups of cheese mixture, add melted chocolate. Pour half of plain mixture into prepared pan. Top with chocolate mixture and cover with remaining plain mixture. Cut through mixture to marbleize. Place in oven. Immediately reduce heat to 300°. Bake 1 hour. Turn off oven. Leave cake in closed oven 1 hour. Remove from oven and cool 3 hours. Chill 6 hours before serving. Decorate with shaved chocolate curls if desired.

16 SERVINGS

Tofu "Cheesecake"

1 cup whole wheat graham cracker
   crumbs
¼ cup Grape Nuts cereal
¼ cup melted butter or margarine
1 (12 ounce) package soft tofu
½ cup sugar
¾ cup refrigerated egg substitute
   juice of ½ lemon
1¼ teaspoons vanilla extract
1 tablespoon arrowroot flour
1 pint strawberries, cleaned and
   halved

TOPPING

½ cup low fat sour cream
½ teaspoon vanilla extract
1½ tablespoons sugar

Preheat oven to 350°. Mix graham cracker crumbs and cereal in food processor until finely processed. Put crumbs in preheated non-stick skillet coated with vegetable cooking spray. Mix until warm. Gradually add melted butter. Mix well. Spread on bottom and sides of 9 inch pie plate that has been coated with vegetable cooking spray. Press firmly until crust forms. Set aside.

Crumble tofu into bowl. Using an electric mixer, gradually add sugar while scraping down sides of bowl. Mix well for 3 minutes. Add egg substitute, lemon juice, vanilla extract and arrowroot flour. Mix until well blended, approximately 2-3 minutes longer. The mixture will not be completely smooth. Pour into prepared pan and bake 35 minutes. Cool.

Mix topping ingredients together. Spread over pie when it has completely cooled. Chill until topping is set. Garnish with strawberry halves around the edges and serve.

No Bake Cream Cheesecake

2   packages ladyfingers
1   (8 ounce) and 1 (3 ounce) packages cream cheese
¾   cup sugar
1   pint heavy cream
1   teaspoon vanilla extract
1   (21 ounce) can pineapple pie filling

In large bowl, whip cream cheese and sugar and set aside. In another bowl, whip heavy cream with vanilla extract. Then combine the two mixtures. Use an angel food pan, or springform pan or a glass bowl. Place ladyfingers around the pan and on the bottom. Pour in half the cheese mixture and half the pie filling. Place the remaining ladyfingers on top of this. Pour remaining cheese mixture and the rest of the pie filling. Chill 24 hours.

Amazon Chocolate Cake

1½   cups flour
⅓   cup unsweetened cocoa
1   teaspoon baking soda
1   cup sugar
½   teaspoon salt
5   tablespoons vegetable oil
1½   teaspoons vanilla extract
1   tablespoon cider vinegar
1   cup cold water
     confectioners' sugar

Preheat oven to 350°. Whisk together flour, cocoa, baking soda, sugar and salt. In a separate bowl, whisk together oil, vanilla extract, vinegar, and cold water. Whisk dry ingredients into wet, until completely lump free. Pour into greased 9 inch round cake pan. Bake 30-35 minutes until top springs back when gently pressed. Cool thoroughly before removing from pan. Dust with confectioners' sugar.

Andy's Chocolate Cake

1	egg
½	cup cocoa
1½	cups flour
1	teaspoon baking soda
1	cup sugar
½	cup shortening
½	cup milk
1	teaspoon vanilla extract
½	cup hot water
	pinch of salt

NEVER-FAIL ICING

1	cup sugar
½	teaspoon cream of tartar
¼	teaspoon salt
2	egg whites, unbeaten
3	tablespoons water
1	teaspoon vanilla extract
2	tablespoons marshmallow fluff

Preheat oven to 375°. Put all cake ingredients in bowl in order given. Mix only after last ingredient is added. Beat well for 10 minutes. Pour into greased 9 inch square pan. Bake for 40 minutes. Cool cake before frosting.

NEVER-FAIL ICING

Put all ingredients in top of double boiler and stir. When water boils in bottom of double boiler, reduce heat to low, insert top section. Beat mixture with electric mixer at highest speed for 3 minutes. Frost cake immediately.

Chocolate Chip Coffee Cake

2   cups all-purpose flour
1½   cups sugar
1   cup butter, melted
1   cup sour cream
2   eggs
2   tablespoons milk
1   tablespoon vanilla extract
2   teaspoons baking powder
1   teaspoon baking soda
     pinch of salt
1   (6 ounce) package chocolate chips
     cinnamon sugar or confectioners'
        sugar, optional

Preheat oven to 350°. Butter 10-inch tube pan. Combine first 10 ingredients in large bowl of electric mixer and beat on low speed until smooth. Fold in chocolate chips. Turn into pan. Bake until tester inserted in center comes out clean, about 45 minutes. Let cool in pan 10 minutes. Invert onto wire rack and let cool completely. Dust top of cake with cinnamon sugar or confectioners' sugar if desired.

15 TO 20 SERVINGS

Chocolate Mocha Cake

1   (18¼ ounce) box chocolate cake mix
1   (3½ ounce) box instant vanilla
        pudding
16   ounces sour cream
2   eggs
¼   cup oil
¼   cup coffee flavored liqueur
1   cup chocolate chips
     confectioners' sugar

Preheat oven to 350°. Mix cake mix, pudding mix, sour cream, eggs, oil and liqueur together. Beat for 2 minutes. Stir in chocolate chips. Pour into greased Bundt pan. Bake for 1 hour. Cool and sprinkle with confectioners' sugar.

Chocolate Cake Roll

6   **eggs, separated**
½   **teaspoon cream of tartar**
1   **cup sugar, divided**
4   **tablespoons cocoa**
4   **tablespoons flour**
¼   **teaspoon salt**
1   **teaspoon coffee liqueur**
1   **pint whipping cream**
     confectioners' sugar

Preheat oven to 350°. Line jelly-roll pan with well greased wax paper. Beat egg whites and cream of tartar until stiff. Add ½ cup of sugar.

In a separate bowl beat yolks and ½ cup of sugar until thick and lemon colored. Beat cocoa, flour and salt into the yolks. Add coffee liqueur. Fold egg yolk mixture into the whites. Pour mixture into jelly-roll pan. Cook at 350° until springs back, about 15 minutes. Cool.

Put cooled cake onto a dish towel and roll the long way. Put bowl and beaters in refrigerator for 15 minutes. Whip cream in chilled bowl until it reaches whipped cream consistency. Add confectioners' sugar to taste. When ready to fill with whipped cream mixture, undo the roll and put it on a plate, fill and re-roll.

Chocolate Almond Torte

Very rich flourless chocolate cake.

CAKE

6	ounces dark sweet chocolate
¾	cup sweet butter
¾	cup sugar
6	eggs, separated
	pinch of salt
6	ounces almonds, very finely ground

ICING

½	cup heavy cream
1	teaspoon instant coffee
8	ounces dark sweet or semisweet chocolate

Preheat oven to 375°. Melt chocolate over hot water. Remove from heat and cool. Butter 9 inch springform pan and line bottom with wax paper. Butter paper and coat bottom and sides with fine dry bread crumbs.

In small bowl, cream butter and sugar. Beat until light. Add egg yolks, one at a time. Stir in cooled melted chocolate and grated almonds. Transfer mixture to large bowl. Beat egg whites with pinch of salt until stiff but not dry. Fold about ⅓ of beaten whites into chocolate mixture to lighten it, then fold in balance.

Turn into prepared pan. Place on oven rack just below the center of the oven and bake for about 20 minutes. Reduce heat to 350° and bake for 45 minutes. Remove from oven and place on wet towel. Cool before removing from pan.

Place cake upside down on cake plate. Pour icing over cake, using spatula to completely cover top and sides. Smooth icing.

ICING

Heat cream until it just begins to boil. Remove from heat and stir in instant coffee until dissolved. Add chocolate. Stir until melted and smooth. Cool for about 10 minutes.

12 SERVINGS

Coconut Torte

TORTE

1	cup graham cracker crumbs
½	cup flaked coconut
½	cup chopped salted cashew nuts
4	eggs whites
	pinch of salt
1	cup sugar
1	teaspoon vanilla extract

TOPPING

½	cup heavy cream
1	tablespoon confectioners' sugar
1	teaspoon lemon peel
¼	cup flaked coconut

Preheat oven to 325°. Combine graham cracker crumbs, coconut and cashew nuts. Beat egg whites and salt until soft peaks form. Gradually beat in sugar. Continue beating until stiff peaks form. Add vanilla extract. Fold in graham cracker mixture and pour into greased 9 inch square pan. Bake for 45-50 minutes or until top looks dry. Cool. Cover with topping before serving.

TOPPING

Whip the cream. Add confectioners' sugar, lemon peel and coconut.

8 TO 10 SERVINGS

Coconut Coffee Cake

¼	cup butter
¾	cup sugar
1	egg
½	cup milk
1½	cups sifted flour
2	teaspoons baking powder
½	teaspoon salt

COCONUT MIXTURE

½	cup light brown sugar
2	tablespoons flour
2	teaspoons cinnamon
2	tablespoons melted butter
⅔	cup flaked coconut

Preheat oven to 375°. Cream shortening and sugar. Add egg and beat well. Add milk. Sift together dry ingredients and gradually fold into batter. Pour half of batter into greased and floured 8 inch square pan. Combine ingredients for coconut mixture and sprinkle half over batter. Add remaining batter and top with rest of coconut mixture. Bake for 30 minutes.

8 SERVINGS

Cranberry Coffee Cake

½	cup butter
1	cup sugar
2	eggs
1	teaspoon baking powder
1	teaspoon baking soda
2	cups sifted flour
½	teaspoon salt
½	pint sour cream
1	teaspoon almond extract
1	(16 ounce) can whole cranberry sauce
½	cup chopped walnuts or almonds

TOPPING

¾	cup confectioners' sugar
½	teaspoon almond extract
2	tablespoons warm water

Preheat oven to 350°. Cream butter with sugar until light and fluffy. Add eggs one at a time, beating well after each. Add sour cream and almond extract. Sift together dry ingredients and fold in. Spoon half the batter into greased and floured tube pan. Stir cranberry sauce in bowl and spread half over batter. Sprinkle on half of nuts. Repeat with remaining batter, cranberry sauce and nuts. Bake for about 55 minutes. Cool, remove from pan and pour topping over cake.

TOPPING

Place sugar in bowl. Add almond extract and mix. Add water, a few drops at a time, until desired consistency is reached.

10 SERVINGS

Streusel Coffee Cake

1	cup shortening
1	cup sugar
3	eggs
3	teaspoons baking powder
2½	cups flour, sifted
1	teaspoon baking soda
1	cup sour cream
1	teaspoon vanilla extract

Preheat over to 350°. Blend shortening and sugar, add eggs. Alternately add dry ingredients and sour cream. Add vanilla extract. Pour ½ of batter into greased, floured tube springform pan. Sprinkle with one half of topping. Add remaining batter and sprinkle with remaining topping. Bake for 1 hour. Cool on rack.

10 SERVINGS

TOPPING

¾	cup brown sugar
1	cup chopped nuts
1	tablespoon cinnamon

Add ¾ cup chocolate chips to topping.

Fudge Pudding Cake

Forms its own chocolate sauce while it bakes

1	cup flour
¾	cup sugar
2	tablespoons cocoa
2	teaspoons baking powder
¼	teaspoon salt
½	cup milk
2	tablespoons margarine, melted
1	cup chopped nuts
1	cup packed brown sugar
¼	cup cocoa
1¾	cups hot water
	whipped cream or ice cream

Preheat oven to 350°. Mix flour, sugar, cocoa, baking powder and salt. Stir in milk, margarine and nuts. Pour into ungreased 9 inch square pan.

Mix brown sugar and cocoa and sprinkle over batter. Pour hot water over batter. Bake for 45 minutes. While hot, cut into squares. Serve with whipped cream or vanilla ice cream.

8 SERVINGS

Texas Sheet Cake

2	cups sugar
2	cups flour
½	teaspoon salt
1	cup butter
1	cup water
4	tablespoons cocoa
½	cup sour cream
2	eggs
1	teaspoon baking soda

Preheat oven to 375°. Sift together sugar, flour and salt. In saucepan, bring butter, water and cocoa to boil. Add immediately to flour mixture. Mix in sour cream, eggs and soda and mix well. (Batter will be thin.) Bake in greased jelly-roll pan for 20-30 minutes. Prepare Butternut Frosting while cake bakes. Frost as soon as removed from oven.

24 SERVINGS

Butternut Frosting

6	tablespoons evaporated milk or ⅓ cup buttermilk
1	cup margarine
4	tablespoons cocoa
1	cup chopped walnuts
1	(16 ounce) box confectioners' sugar
1	teaspoon vanilla extract

Boil milk, margarine and cocoa in heavy pan until bubbly. Stir in nuts, sugar and vanilla extract. Spread over hot cake.

Honey Cake

This cake is best prepared 2-3 days in advance.

3	eggs
2	cups light brown sugar
1	pound honey
1	cup oil
¼	teaspoon allspice
4	cups flour, sifted
4	teaspoons baking powder
1	teaspoon baking soda
8	ounces strong tea
	juice from 1½ oranges
	grated orange peel from 2 oranges

Preheat oven to 350°. On slow speed, mix eggs, sugar, orange peel, honey, oil and all spice. Mix flour, baking powder and soda together in separate bowl. Add to egg mixture, alternating with tea and orange juice.

Line 2 (9 inch) square pans or 1 large pan with wax paper. Pour in batter. Bake for 30 minutes. Reduce heat to 325° and bake an additional 30 minutes. Cool on rack. Remove paper.

12 TO 15 SERVINGS

Lemon Supreme Cake

1	(18¼ ounce) box lemon supreme cake mix
½	cup sugar
4	eggs
1	cup apricot nectar
½	oil

GLAZE

1-1½ cups confectioners' sugar

¼	cup lemon juice

Preheat oven to 350°. Mix all ingredients well and beat on high for 2 minutes with an electric mixer. Bake in a greased Bundt pan for 45-60 minutes. Allow to cool for 5 minutes.

While cooling, mix confectioners' sugar and lemon juice to form a glaze. Invert cake onto cake plate and poke gently with a fork. Drizzle glaze over top while cake is still hot.

16 SERVINGS

Mocha Sour Cream Cake

3   **cups flour**
3   **teaspoons baking powder**
1   **teaspoon baking soda**
1   **teaspoon salt**
1   **cup butter**
1   **cup sugar**
3   **eggs**
1   **cup sour cream**
1   **teaspoon vanilla extract**

FILLING
1   **(6 ounce) package chocolate bits**
½   **cup packed brown sugar**
2   **tablespoons instant coffee**

GLAZE, OPTIONAL
2   **teaspoons instant coffee**
3   **tablespoons boiling water**
1¾   **cups confectioners' sugar**

Preheat oven to 350°. Combine flour, baking powder, soda and salt and set aside. Cream butter and sugar well. Add eggs, one at a time, beating well after each addition. Add flour mixture alternately with sour cream, dividing into three parts. Add vanilla extract. Combine ingredients for filling. Spoon ⅓ batter into greased 10 inch Bundt pan. Top with half of filling, add ⅓ more batter and balance of filling. Top with remaining batter. Bake for 70 minutes. Turn out on rack and cool completely. Glaze if desired.

GLAZE
Dissolve instant coffee in boiling water. Add confectioners' sugar and stir until smooth.

10 SERVINGS

Linzer Torte

DOUGH

1	cup flour
¾	cup finely chopped almonds, divided
1	cup confectioners' sugar
½	teaspoon cinnamon
⅛	teaspoon ground cloves
1	tablespoon grated lemon rind
1	cup butter
1	egg

TOPPING

½	cup raspberry jelly
1	egg, beaten

Set aside 2 tablespoons almonds. Put dough ingredients in food processor and pulse until well-mixed. It will not form a ball. Turn out into waxed paper. Refrigerate several hours or overnight.

Preheat oven to 375°. Press ⅔ of dough into bottom of ungreased 9 inch springform pan. Spread evenly with jelly. Cut remaining dough into 16 pieces. With lightly floured hands, make each piece into log shapes about 2 inches long. Roll each log on a flat surface with your hand until it reaches desired length and about the thickness of a pencil. You will need 10 (9 inch long) rolls and 4 (6 inch long) rolls. Use the 10 rolls to make crisscross design on top of the jelly. Place the other rolls around the edges. Brush with beaten egg and sprinkle with reserved 2 tablespoons chopped almonds. Bake for 40 minutes until golden brown.

Bavarian Torte

CRUST

½	cup butter softened
⅓	cup sugar
¼	teaspoon vanilla extract
¾	cup flour
⅔	cup finely chopped pecans

FILLING

¼	cup sugar
1	(8 ounce) package cream cheese, softened
1	egg
½	teaspoon cinnamon
1	tablespoon sugar
1	(29 ounce) can peach slices, well drained
½	teaspoon vanilla extract

Preheat oven to 450°. Beat butter, sugar and vanilla extract until well blended. Gradually add flour until well mixed. Stir in pecans. With lightly floured hands, press mixture into bottom one inch up sides of 10 inch springform pan. Set aside.

Beat cream cheese and sugar just until smooth. Beat in egg and vanilla extract just until blended. Pour into crust. Combine cinnamon and sugar, and toss gently with peaches. Arrange on top of cream cheese mixture. Bake 10 minutes. Reduce oven to 400° and bake for another 25 minutes. Cool 20 minutes then carefully remove sides.

Serve warm or cold.

Merle's Mom's Delicious Torte

½	cup margarine
1	teaspoon almond extract
1	cup sugar
1	cup flour
1	teaspoon baking powder
2	eggs
2	(15 ounce) cans apricots and/or plums
	lemon juice
	sugar
	cinnamon

Preheat oven to 350°. Mix margarine, almond extract, sugar, flour, baking powder and eggs together. Put batter in springform or pie pan. Cut plums and apricots in half and arrange on top of batter. Sprinkle generously with lemon juice, sugar and cinnamon. Bake for 1 hour.

Peach Torte

DOUGH

½   cup butter
½   cup low fat cream cheese
½   teaspoon salt
1½   cups flour

FILLING

2   (28 ounce) cans sliced cling peaches, drained and rinsed
1   (8 ounce) package low fat cream cheese
½   teaspoon cinnamon
½   cup sifted confectioners' sugar

Preheat oven to 375°. In food processor, cream butter and cream cheese until well blended. Add salt and flour; mix until blended. Roll dough on floured surface to about ⅓ inch thickness. Pat into greased 11 inch round torte pan, with removable side if possible.

Spread peach slices over crust, completely covering crust. Spread sour cream over peaches. Mix cinnamon and sugar together and sprinkle over sour cream. Bake for 30 minutes.

Poppy Seed Cake

¾   cup butter
1¼   cups sugar
2   eggs, separated
½   cup poppy seeds soaked in ½ cup milk
2   cups flour
2   teaspoons baking powder
1   teaspoon vanilla extract
1   tablespoon water
    confectioners' sugar

Preheat oven to 350°. Cream butter and sugar at medium speed with mixer. Add egg yolks and continue beating. Add poppy seeds and milk alternately with sifted dry ingredients. Add vanilla extract mixed with water. Carefully fold in stiffly beaten egg whites.

Pour batter into a tube pan which has been greased and coated with confectioners' sugar. Bake for 1 hour. Cool. Turn out of pan and sprinkle with confectioners' sugar.

12 TO 16 SERVING

May also be baked in 2 (9 inch) round pans for 45 minutes and frosted with plain or coffee icing.

One Step Pound Cake

2¼   cups sifted flour
2   cups sugar
½   teaspoon salt
½   teaspoon baking soda
1   teaspoon vanilla extract
1   cup butter or margarine, softened
1   cup pineapple or orange yogurt or
      sour cream
3   eggs
1   teaspoon grated lemon peel,
      optional

GLAZE
1   cup confectioners' sugar
1-2   tablespoons lemon juice

Preheat oven to 325°. Combine all ingredients in large bowl and blend at low speed. Beat for 3 minutes at medium speed.

Pour batter into greased 10 inch Bundt or tube pan. Bake for 60-70 minutes. Remove from pan and cool completely. Glaze.

GLAZE
Combine sugar and lemon juice to drizzling consistency.

10 TO 12 SERVINGS

Passover Sponge Cake

2   large lemons
9   eggs, separated
2   cups sugar
¼   cup club soda or seltzer
½   cup potato starch
½   cup cake meal

Preheat oven to 350°. Grate and squeeze lemons for ¼ cup lemon juice and 2 teaspoons lemon zest. Set aside. Beat egg whites until stiff.

Whip egg yolks, sugar, club soda and lemon juice. Add dry ingredients. Beat 3 minutes. Fold in egg whites and lemon zest. Beat for 2 minutes. Pour into tube pan and bake 70 minutes.

Aunt Vivian's Pesach Apple Cake

3	eggs
¾	cup plus ⅓ cup sugar, divided
½	cup oil
¾	cup cake flour
4	apples, peeled and sliced
1	tablespoon cinnamon
½	cup chopped nuts

Preheat oven to 350°. Beat eggs and ¾ cup sugar for 4 minutes at high speed. Add oil and cake flour and mix at low speed. Mix together ⅓ cup sugar and cinnamon. Pour half of batter in greased 8 inch square pan. Add slices apples, nuts and ½ of the cinnamon and sugar mixture. Add rest of batter and sprinkle with remaining cinnamon and sugar. Bake for 40 minutes.

You can double the recipe and bake for a little longer in a 9 x 13 inch pan.

Viennese Nut Cake

6	eggs
1	cup sugar
1½	cups finely ground toasted walnuts
¾	cup flour
¼	teaspoon baking powder
¼	cup butter, melted

FILLING

1½	cups ground toasted nuts
½	cup sugar
⅓	cup milk
2	tablespoons rum

Preheat oven to 325°. Beat eggs, gradually adding sugar, until very light and fluffy. Mix in nuts, flour and baking powder only until blended. Fold in butter. Turn into well greased and lightly floured 9 inch springform. Bake for 40 minutes, or until cake tester comes out clean. Cool.

Make filling by mixing nuts, sugar and milk together in a saucepan. Bring to a boil, stirring occasionally. Stir in rum and let cool.

Remove cake from pan. Cut into two layers and spread filling between layers, May be frosted with your favorite icing or whipped cream.

8 SERVINGS

Lemon Roll

FILLING

3	tablespoons cornstarch
⅓	cup sugar
1	teaspoon lemon zest
⅓	cup fresh lemon juice
¾	cup water
1	jumbo egg yolk
1	tablespoon unsalted butter

CAKE

4	jumbo egg whites
⅛	teaspoon salt
⅛	teaspoon cream of tartar
½	cup sifted superfine sugar
½	cup sifted cake flour
2	teaspoons fresh lemon juice
½	teaspoon vanilla extract
½	teaspoon almond extract
3	tablespoons confectioners' sugar
	lemon zest for garnish

In a small saucepan, combine cornstarch and sugar. Whisk in zest, juice and ¾ cup water. Cook approximately 3 minutes until boiling, thick and smooth. Add a little of the hot mixture into the yolk and mix back into the pan. Cook over low heat, stirring constantly, for 1 minute. Remove from heat and add butter. Cool to room temperature so a skin doesn't form. Cover and refrigerate. Filling can be made a day in advance.

Preheat oven to 300°. Spray 15 ½ x 10 ½ inch jelly-roll pan with vegetable cooking spray. Line with parchment or wax paper and spray again. Beat egg whites with salt and cream of tartar for about 1 minute until small white bubbles appear. Do not overbeat into peaks. With rubber spatula, gently fold in sugar, 2 tablespoons at a time. Sift 2 tablespoons of flour at a time over egg whites and fold gently. Fold in lemon juice, vanilla and almond extract. Evenly spread into pan. Bake 20-25 minutes.

Spread kitchen towel on counter and evenly cover area the size of pan with confectioners' sugar. Invert cake onto towel and peel off paper immediately. Cut off crisp edges with a serrated knife. Roll cake up, from short end, into towel. Let cool for 25 minutes in towel. Unroll, spread with filling leaving ½ inch margins. Roll up again and let stand, covered with the towel, 20 minutes longer. Remove towel and sift any remaining sugar over roll. Ease onto platter, garnish and serve.

Baklava

SYRUP

¾   **cups sugar**

¾   **cup honey**

1   **cup water**

2   **tablespoons lemon juice**

½   **teaspoon cinnamon**

NUT MIXTURE

2   **cups ground walnuts**

½   **cup sugar**

1   **teaspoon cinnamon**

⅓   **teaspoon ground cloves, optional**

1   **pound phyllo leaves, defrosted**

1   **cup butter, melted**

Cook all ingredients for syrup until clear and slightly thickened. Set aside to cool.

Combine nuts, sugar, cinnamon and cloves.

Preheat oven to 350°. Butter a 15 x 10 x 2 inch pan. Place a phyllo leaf in pan and brush with butter, Repeat three more times. Sprinkle with nut mixture. Then add one phyllo leaf at a time, brush with butter and top with nut mixture, until 4 leaves remain. Add these leaves one at a time, brushing each with butter. Using a sharp knife, cutting all the way to the bottom, cut into diamond shaped pieces. Bake for 45 minutes.

Remove from oven and spoon syrup over hot baklava. Allow to cool at least 4 hours before serving.

25 PIECES

Apricot Squares

2 cups flour
1 cup butter
2 egg yolks
1 teaspoon vanilla extract
¾ cup brown sugar

TOPPING
1 (10 ounce) jar apricot preserves
  chopped nuts

Preheat oven to 350°. Combine all ingredients thoroughly. Press dough into jelly-roll pan. Coat with preserves and sprinkle with nuts.

Bake for 30 minutes. Score in squares and return to oven with heat off for 15 minutes.

Fran's Famous Brownies

Children and adults clamor for these!

½ cup butter
4 (1 ounce) squares unsweetened chocolate
1 tablespoon water
4 eggs
2 cups sugar
1 teaspoon vanilla extract
1 cup flour
1 teaspoon baking powder
  pinch of salt
1 cup coarsely chopped walnuts, divided

Melt butter, chocolate and 1 tablespoon water. Stir and cool.

Meanwhile, beat eggs. Gradually add sugar. Mix in butter and chocolate. Add vanilla extract.

Sift together flour, baking powder and salt. Add flour mixture and ¾ cup nuts, alternating the two.

Grease and flour 13 x 9 inch pan. Pour batter into pan and sprinkle remaining nuts on top. Bake on bottom shelf of oven for about 25 minutes, or until tester comes out clean. Leave in oven 2 minutes longer. Cut into squares. Cool for 30 minutes.

1 BROWNIE LOVER!

Cream Cheese Brownies

4	ounces high quality semisweet or bittersweet chocolate
5	tablespoons butter, divided
3	ounces cream cheese
1	cup sugar, divided
3	eggs, divided
½	cup plus 1 tablespoon flour, divided
1 ½	teaspoons vanilla extract, divided
½	teaspoon baking powder
¼	teaspoon salt
½	cup coarsely chopped walnuts
½	teaspoon almond extract

Preheat oven to 350°. Melt chocolate with 3 tablespoons butter over low heat, stirring constantly. Cool.

Cream remaining butter with cream cheese. Gradually add ¼ cup sugar. Continue to cream until light and fluffy. Stir in 1 egg, 1 tablespoon flour and ½ teaspoon vanilla extract. Blend cheese mixture well.

In another bowl, beat 2 eggs until light colored and fluffy. Gradually add ¾ cup sugar, beating until thickened. Fold in baking powder, salt and ½ cup flour. Blend cooled chocolate into this batter. Stir in nuts, 1 teaspoon vanilla extract, and almond extract. Measure 1 cup of batter and set aside.

Spread remaining batter into a greased 9 inch square pan. Pour cheese mixture over batter. Drop remaining chocolate batter from a tablespoon on to cheese mixture. Swirl mixture together to marble. Bake for 35-40 minutes. Cool and cut into squares.

20 BROWNIES

Extra Rich Brownies

Very rich, very good.

1   cup sugar
2   eggs, room temperature
     pinch salt
5   ounces semisweet chocolate
3   (1 ounce) squares unsweetened
       chocolate
½   cup unsalted butter
¼   cup flour
1   teaspoon vanilla extract
1   cup mini chocolate chips

Preheat oven to 375°. Grease 8 inch square pan. In a large bowl, beat the sugar, eggs and salt for 15 minutes. Meanwhile, melt the semisweet and unsweetened chocolates and the butter in a double boiler over a low flame. When mixture is ¾ melted, take off the heat and stir until the chocolates and butter are completely melted and the mixture is smooth. Cool to lukewarm and gently fold into the sugar-egg mixture. Fold in the flour, vanilla extract, and finally the chocolate chips. Batter is very thick. Spread the mixture in the prepared pan and set in the middle of the oven. Bake 20-25 minutes. Cool on rack for 6 hours and cut into squares.

The butter and chocolates can also be melted in the microwave in 30 second increments for approximately 2 minutes.

Passover Fudgies

Originally made for Passover, now a year-round favorite.

4   eggs
2   cups sugar
1   cup margarine, melted
6   tablespoons cake flour
1   cup cocoa
1   cup nuts

Preheat oven to 375°. Beat eggs. Add sugar gradually. Add margarine. Beat well. Sift dry ingredients. Add to mixture. Stir in nuts. Pour into greased 9 x 13 inch pan and bake 25 minutes. It will be slightly moist when done.

Easy Low Fat Brownies

Dense and Fudgy

4	(1 ounce) squares unsweetened chocolate
1	(4 ounce) jar prune baby food
3	large egg whites
1	cup sugar
1	teaspoon salt
1	teaspoon vanilla extract
½	cup flour
¼	cup chopped walnuts, optional

Preheat oven to 350°. Spray 8 inch square pan with vegetable cooking spray. Melt chocolate in microwave. In a separate bowl, combine flour, salt and walnuts.

Beat together egg whites, prunes, sugar and vanilla extract. Mix in melted chocolate. Blend in flour until combined. Pour into prepared pan and bake 25-30 minutes. Cool.

Chocolate Espresso Cookies

4	ounces semisweet chocolate
4	ounces unsweetened chocolate
¾	cup unsalted butter, room temperature
⅔	cup flour
4	eggs
4	teaspoons vanilla extract
2	tablespoons instant coffee
½	teaspoon baking powder
1½	cups sugar
¾	cup semisweet chocolate chips
⅔	cup chopped pecans
	splash orange liqueur or orange juice

Preheat oven to 325°. Line cookie sheets with parchment paper. Melt chocolates and butter; cool slightly. Sift flour, baking powder and set aside. Mix eggs, vanilla extract, coffee, and liqueur in mixing bowl and add sugar and mix well. Then add melted chocolate and stir. Add flour mixture and blend. Fold in chips and nuts. Drop onto cookie sheets by generously rounded tablespoons, 2 inches apart. Bake for 13-14 minutes until cookies rise slightly and form a thin crust. Remove from pan immediately and place on a rack to cool.

Chocolate Chip Oatmeal Cookies

1¼   cups margarine
¾   cup firmly packed brown sugar
½   cup granulated sugar
1   egg
1   teaspoon vanilla extract
1 ½   cups flour
1   teaspoon baking soda
1   teaspoon salt, optional
1   teaspoon cinnamon, optional
¼   teaspoon nutmeg, optional
3   cups rolled oats
1   (12 ounce) package chocolate chips

Preheat oven to 375° Beat the margarine and sugars until fluffy. Add egg and vanilla extract and continue to blend. Mix flour, baking soda and any of the optional ingredients and then slowly add to the other mixture, blending well. Stir in the oatmeal and chocolate chips.

Drop by rounded tablespoonfuls onto ungreased cookie sheets. Bake 8-9 minutes for chewy cookies and 10-11 minutes for crispy ones. Cool briefly on the cookie sheet and then transfer to a wire rack to cool.

4½ DOZEN

Mother's Butter Cookies

1   cup butter
⅔   cup sugar
1   egg
2½   cups flour
½   teaspoon baking powder
⅛   teaspoon salt
1   teaspoon vanilla extract

Preheat oven to 400°. Cream butter and sugar. Add egg and beat. Sift together dry ingredients and add to batter. Add vanilla extract and mix well. Put dough through a cookie press.

Bake on an ungreased cookie sheet for 10-12 minutes. Watch carefully as they burn easily.

Sugar Cookies

½   cup shortening
½   teaspoon salt
½   teaspoon grated lemon rind
½   teaspoon nutmeg
1   cup sugar
2   eggs
2   cups sifted flour
1   teaspoon baking powder
½   teaspoon baking soda
1   tablespoon milk

Preheat oven to 375°. Combine first 6 ingredients and beat until smooth. Sift flour with baking powder and soda, add to shortening mixture and blend. Add milk and mix well.

Measure level tablespoons of dough on greased cookie sheet. Flatten cookies by stamping with a flat bottomed glass covered with a damp cloth. Sprinkle with sugar, or press raisins or chopped nuts into cookies. Bake for 10-12 minutes.

3½ DOZEN COOKIES

For orange sugar cookies, add 2 teaspoons grated orange rind into first mixing step. Omit milk and use 1 tablespoon orange juice instead.

Cheese Tarts

1   pound cream cheese, softened
½   cup sugar
2   eggs
2   teaspoons vanilla extract
15 vanilla wafers
1   (22 ounce) can pineapple, cherry or
    lemon pie filling

Preheat oven to 375°. Mix cream cheese, sugar, eggs and vanilla extract with spoon, then beat at medium speed for 5 minutes.

Put paper liners in cupcake tins. Place vanilla wafer in bottom of each and fill to about ¼ inch from top with cheese mixture. Bake for 18 minutes.

When cool, spoon on pie filling. Refrigerate.

15 SERVINGS

 # Cheese Cake Squares

CRUST

⅓   cup butter

⅓   cup firmly packed brown sugar

1   cup flour

½   cup finely chopped walnuts

FILLING

¼   cup sugar

1   (8 ounce) package cream cheese

1   egg

2   tablespoons milk

1   tablespoon lemon juice

½   teaspoon vanilla extract

Preheat oven to 350°. Cream butter and brown sugar. Add flour and nuts. Mix together until it forms a crumb mixture. Reserve 1 cup of mixture for topping. Press remainder on bottom of 8 inch square pan. Bake for 12-15 minutes until golden brown.

Blend sugar and cream cheese until smooth. Add remaining ingredients and beat well. Spread filling on crust and sprinkle with reserved crumbs. Bake for 25 minutes. Cool. Cut into squares.

16 SQUARES

 # Cherry Nut Squares

1¼   cups flour, divided

3   tablespoons confectioners' sugar

½   cup butter, softened

2   eggs, slightly beaten

1   cup sugar

½   teaspoon salt

½   teaspoon baking powder

1   teaspoon vanilla extract

1   cup chopped nuts

½   cup flaked coconut

1   cup canned, pitted, water packed cherries, well drained

Preheat oven to 350°. Mix 1 cup flour, confectioners' sugar and butter together. Blend well. Spread evenly in 9 inch square pan. Bake for 25 minutes.

Mix remaining ¼ cup flour and rest of ingredients together. Spread on baked mixture and bake 25 minutes longer. Cool. Cut into squares.

25 SQUARES

 **Chewy Date Bars**

CRUST

1¼	cups sifted flour
⅓	cup sugar
½	cup butter, room temperature

BATTER

⅓	cup brown sugar, packed
⅓	cup sugar
2	eggs
1	teaspoon vanilla extract
2	tablespoons flour
1	teaspoon baking powder
½	teaspoon salt
¼	teaspoon nutmeg
1	cup chopped walnuts
1	(8 ounce) package pitted dates, snipped
	confectioners' sugar

CRUST

Preheat oven to 350°. Blend flour, sugar and butter and place in 9 inch square pan. Bake for 20 minutes.

BATTER

While crust is baking, combine sugars, eggs and vanilla extract. Beat well. Sift together dry ingredients and add to batter. Stir in walnuts and dates.

Pour batter over hot crust. Bake for 20 minutes longer. Cool in pan. Sprinkle with confectioners' sugar. Cut into bars.

1½ DOZEN

 **Egg Kichlach**

3	eggs
	pinch of salt
5	tablespoons sugar
¾	cup oil
1	cup flour

Preheat oven to 375° Beat eggs with salt. Add sugar, beating constantly. Add oil and flour.

Drop batter by scant teaspoons on oiled cookie sheet. Bake for 20 minutes. Remove from cookie sheet at once.

3 DOZEN

Chocolate Nut Bars

FIRST LAYER

½ cup butter
1 egg yolk
2 tablespoons water
1½ cups flour
1 teaspoon sugar
1 teaspoon baking powder
1 cup chocolate chips

SECOND LAYER

2 eggs
¾ cup sugar
6 tablespoons butter, melted
2 teaspoons vanilla extract
2 cups chopped nuts

Preheat oven to 350°. Beat together butter, egg yolk, and water. Stir in flour, sugar and baking powder. Pour batter into greased 13 x 9 inch pan and bake for 10 minutes. Sprinkle chocolate chips over dough and place in oven 1 minute to melt. Spread evenly.

Beat eggs and sugar together, stir in butter and vanilla extract and fold in nuts. Spread mixture over chocolate layer and bake 30-35 minutes. Cut while warm.

24 SQUARES

Forgotten Cookies

2 egg whites, stiffly beaten
⅔ cup sugar
1 cup chocolate bits

Preheat oven to 350°. Add sugar gradually to egg whites and beat well. Fold in chocolate bits.

Drop batter from teaspoon on ungreased cookie sheet. Shut oven off. Put cookie sheet in oven and leave overnight — but don't forget in the morning.

3 TO 4 DOZEN

Hamentaschen Cookies

A Purim tradition.

1	cup sugar
1⅓	cups shortening or margarine
2	eggs
6	tablespoons water
½	teaspoon vanilla extract
4	cups sifted flour
	chocolate bits

Cream together sugar and shortening. Add eggs and continue creaming until smooth. Stir in water and vanilla extract. Add sifted flour, mixing until the dough forms a ball. Wrap in waxed paper and refrigerate overnight.

Preheat oven to 350°. Roll out dough and form circles with cutter or glass. Place some chocolate bits in the center of each circle. Fold 3 edges in to form a triangle. Bake for approximately 15 minutes.

Honey Cookies

1	cup margarine
½	cup sugar
4	tablespoons honey
2½	cups flour, sifted

Cream margarine, sugar and honey. Slowly add flour. Mix to a smooth dough. Chill at least 2 hours.

Preheat oven to 350°. Roll out dough on floured surface; do not roll too thin. Shape with cookie cutters. Bake on ungreased cookie sheets for approximately 15-20 minutes, watching carefully, until golden brown.

Javanese Cookies

1   cup butter
¾   cup sugar
2   cups flour
1   cup coconut

Cream butter and sugar. Add flour and coconut. Shape into 2 rolls and chill in refrigerator or freezer until firm.

Preheat oven to 300°. Cut dough into ¼ inch slices. Bake on cookie sheets for 30 minutes or until light brown. This is a very slow oven, but it is necessary for this cookie.

4 DOZEN

Lemon Bars

CRUST
2   cups flour
½   cup confectioners' sugar
1   cup butter

TOPPING
4   eggs
2   cups granulated sugar
⅓   cup lemon juice
½   teaspoon baking powder
¼   cup flour
     confectioners' sugar

Preheat oven to 350°. Combine crust ingredients in food processor and pulse until well-mixed and dough forms a soft ball. Press into bottom of an ungreased 10 x 14 inch pan. Bake for 20-25 minutes until light brown.

While crust is cooking, mix together eggs, sugar and lemon juice in food processor. When well mixed, add flour and baking powder and pulse a few times until mixed into egg mixture.

Pour filling over crust immediately and return to the oven for 20-25 minutes. Top will be gently set when done. Remove from oven and run knife around edge of pan to prevent sticking. Sprinkle top with confectioners' sugar. Cool and cut into squares.

30 SQUARES

Lemon Almond Cookies

¾   **cup unsalted butter, softened**
1   **cup plus 2 tablespoons sugar, divided**
1   **large egg**
1½   **tablespoons freshly grated lemon zest**
6   **tablespoons finely ground almonds**
1½   **cups flour**

Cream butter and 1 cup sugar with an electric mixer. Beat in egg. Add zest and almonds and mix well. Add flour, a little at a time, beating between additions, until dough is well combined. Cover and chill for 2 hours.

Preheat oven to 350°. Form the dough into walnut size balls and place them 2 inches apart on a lightly greased cookie sheet. Flatten them with the bottom of a glass until they are 2 inches in diameter. Sprinkle with sugar. Bake for 10-12 minutes or until lightly brown around the edges. Cool on wire rack.

Grandma Bea's Famous Mandel Bread

3   **eggs**
1   **teaspoon vanilla extract**
1   **cup sugar**
3   **teaspoons baking powder**
1   **cup oil**
2   **cups Wondra flour**
½   **cup raisins**
½   **cup chopped nuts**
¼-½   **cup semisweet chocolate chips, melted**
½   **teaspoon cinnamon mixed with ½ cup sugar for topping**

Preheat oven to 375°. Mix together eggs, vanilla extract, sugar and baking powder until well blended. Add oil and mix well. Add flour gradually. Fold in raisins and nuts. Fold in melted chocolate to obtain a marble effect. Divide dough into 6 loaves, 3 on each cookie sheet. Sprinkle with cinnamon and sugar. Bake for 25 minutes. Remove from oven and slice each loaf on the diagonal into biscotti sized cookies. Lay slices on their side and return to the oven for 5 minutes.

This recipe calls for Wondra or instant flour, which has a lower protein content than all-purpose flour. You can substitute cake flour if Wondra is unavailable.

Chocolate Chip Mandel Bread

2 cups flour
1 cup sugar
1 teaspoon baking powder
3 eggs
¾ cup oil
1 teaspoon vanilla extract
1 cup chocolate bits
  cinnamon for top

Preheat oven to 350°. Line broiler pan with aluminum foil.

Combine all ingredients except cinnamon. Mix well. Form dough into 2 loaves on broiler pan. Generously sprinkle tops with cinnamon. Flatten loaves slightly and bake on middle rack for 20 minutes.

Remove pan from oven and slice loaf into ¾-1 inch slices. Lay slices on their side and return to oven for 10 additional minutes. Cool.

Rolled Mandel Bread

4 eggs
1 cup oil
1 cup sugar
3 teaspoons baking powder
½ cup orange juice
½ cup lemon juice
  pinch salt
5 cups flour
1 teaspoon vanilla extract
⅓ cup jelly, any flavor
⅓ cup nuts

Preheat oven to 350°. Mix first 9 ingredients together to form dough. Divide dough into 3 sections. Roll each ball out the length of a jelly-roll pan and about the width of ⅓ pan. If dough is too soft to roll out, refrigerate until firmer. Top with jelly and nuts. Roll lengthwise into the shape of a log. Bake for 30 minutes or until brown. Cool slightly.

Slice each log into 1 inch wide slices and place slices on their side on dry cookie sheet. Put back in the oven until lightly browned.

Chocolate chips can also be added before rolling.

278

Mandel Bread

3   eggs
1   cup sugar
1   cup oil
1   teaspoon vanilla extract
1   teaspoon baking powder
3   cups flour
1   cup chopped walnuts
1   cup cinnamon and sugar mix, divided

Preheat oven to 350°. Beat eggs and sugar together until blended. Add oil, vanilla extract and baking powder and mix well. Mix in flour gradually, one cup at a time. Add chopped nuts.

Moisten hands with cold water and separate dough in half. Sprinkle some flour on working surface and mold dough into a long loaf. Place on a greased and floured baking sheet. Sprinkle cinnamon and sugar mix lightly over top of the dough.

Bake for 30 minutes. Remove from the oven and slice the loaf into ½-¾ inch pieces. Turn each piece to one side. Sprinkle with cinnamon and sugar mix. Bake for 5 to 10 minutes. Remove and turn each slice carefully to the other side. Sprinkle with cinnamon and sugar mix. Bake for another 5-10 minutes. Allow to cool.

 Nut Cookies

½   cup butter
5   tablespoons confectioners' sugar
1   teaspoon water
1   cup flour
1   cup chopped nuts
2   teaspoons vanilla extract

Preheat oven to 350°. Cream all ingredients. Shape into small balls.

Bake on ungreased cookie sheet for 20 minutes or until lightly browned. When cool, roll in confectioners' sugar.

2 DOZEN

 **Pecan Shorts**

½   **cup butter**
¼   **cup confectioners' sugar**
½   **teaspoon vanilla extract**
1½   **teaspoons cold water**
1   **cup flour**
1   **cup small pecans**

Mix all ingredients. Shape into a long roll. Chill for 2 hours.

Preheat oven to 350°. Slice roll and bake on cookie sheet for 25 minutes.

40 COOKIES

Poppy Seed Cookies

¾   **cup vegetable oil**
1⅓   **cups sugar**
3   **eggs**
1   **teaspoon vanilla extract**
3¼   **cups flour**
2¼   **teaspoons baking powder**
¼   **teaspoon salt**
⅓   **cup poppy seeds**

Preheat oven to 350°. Line two large baking sheets with parchment paper.

Beat together oil and sugar. Add eggs and vanilla extract, mixing until well blended. Fold or mix in the flour, baking powder, salt and poppy seeds. Cover dough with a towel and let rest approximately 10 minutes.

Dust rolling pin with flour. Roll out ⅓ of the dough, on a well floured board, as thin as possible (⅛-¹⁄₁₆ inch thick). Cut into 2 inch rounds and transfer to baking sheets. Repeat with remaining dough. Bake 12-15 minutes until tops are lightly golden.

Can add lemon zest to dough. Cookies can also be lightly brushed with vegetable oil and sprinkled with sugar before baking.

Miniature Pecan Tarts

CRUST

½	cup butter or margarine, room temperature
¼	pound cream cheese, room temperature
1	cup flour

FILLING

1	egg
1	teaspoon vanilla extract
¾	cup brown sugar
1½	tablespoons butter
1	(1 pound) package pecan halves

Mix together crust ingredients and refrigerate 1 hour.

Preheat oven to 350°. Press dough into miniature muffin tins. Combine ingredients for filling and beat until smooth. Fill shells ¾ full and top each with 2 or 3 pecan halves. Bake for 30 minutes.

24 TARTS

Rugelach

PASTRY

2	cups all-purpose flour, sifted
1	cup sweet butter
1	(8 ounce) package cream cheese

FILLING

⅓	cup sugar
1	tablespoon cinnamon
½	cup walnuts
¼-½	cup raisins
	apricot or raspberry jam, enough to spread

Combine pastry ingredients and mix well. Divide into 4 balls and wrap each in wax paper. Refrigerate at least 2 hours. Combine filling ingredients and set aside.

Preheat oven to 375°. Roll each ball ¼ inch thick and about 10-11 inches in diameter. Cut each circle into 12 wedges. Spread filling on dough. Roll toward the point of the wedge. Bake on a greased cookie sheet for 15-20 minutes, or until brown.

4 DOZEN

Louise's Rugelach

1 cup salted butter
1 cup heavy sweet cream
¾ ounce yeast
3 egg yolks
3-4 cups flour
    pineapple or other jam
    raisins
    chopped nuts
    cinnamon and sugar

Cream butter and cream together. Dissolve yeast in egg yolks. Add flour and egg mixture alternately to cream mixture. Add more flour if dough is too tacky. Shape into a long roll and refrigerate overnight.

Preheat oven to 400°. Cut roll into 8 pieces. Roll each piece out into a circle on a board with cinnamon and sugar. Cut each piece into 8 triangular sections. Put a drop of jam, raisins and nuts, on the wide side of each triangle. Roll up from the wide end. Place point down on a greased cookie sheet. Bake for 15 minutes.

Raspberry Nut Meringue Cookies

1⅔ cups flour
½ teaspoon salt
½ cup brown sugar
¾ cup margarine
2 eggs, separated
1 teaspoon vanilla extract
    raspberry jam
¼ cup sugar
¼ teaspoon cinnamon
½ cup chopped nuts

Preheat oven to 375°. Combine flour, salt and brown sugar. Cut in margarine. Beat egg yolks and add. Add vanilla extract.

Press dough into ungreased 8 inch square pan. Bake for 15 minutes. Cool. Spread raspberry jam on dough.

Lower oven to 325°. Beat egg whites until very stiff. Add sugar and cinnamon slowly. Spread on top of jam and sprinkle with nuts. Bake for 25 minutes. Cut into squares.

2 DOZEN

Easy Rugelach

8   ounces vanilla ice cream
1   cup butter, room temperature
3   cups flour
    chopped nuts
    preserves

Mix first 3 ingredients and refrigerate overnight.

Preheat oven to 375° Roll out dough and fill with nuts and preserves. Bake for 30 minutes. Slice when cool.

Easy Apricot Strudel

1   cup butter, softened
2¼   cups flour
1   cup sour cream
2   cups apricot preserves
1   cup shredded coconut
½   cup chopped walnuts
      confectioners' sugar

Blend butter, flour and sour cream. Shape into ball and refrigerate in covered bowl for 1 hour.

Preheat oven to 450°. Divide dough into fourths and roll each quarter into a 13 x 6 inch rectangle. Spread preserves along length, to width of 1½ inches. Sprinkle coconut and nuts on top of preserves and roll up from long side, like a jelly-roll. Seals edges and ends. Repeat with remaining dough.

Place seam side down on ungreased cookie sheet. Bake for 18-20 minutes until evenly browned. Cool and sprinkle with confectioners' sugar. Slice each roll into about 12 pieces.

4 DOZEN

Sour Cream Strudel

Makes a lovely holiday gift.

1	cup sour cream
1	cup butter, softened
2	cups flour
	pineapple or raspberry preserves.
1	cup sugar
	cinnamon to taste
¾	cup raisins
2	apples
1	cup finely chopped walnuts
1	egg yolk, lightly beaten

Combine sour cream and butter. Gradually blend in flour. Form dough into ball, divide into quarters and refrigerate overnight.

Preheat oven to 425°. Roll out dough, one section at a time (not too thin). Dot each round with preserves and sprinkle each with ¼ of sugar, cinnamon and raisins. Grate ½ apple over each and sprinkle with ¼ cup walnuts. Roll up, brush with egg yolk, and fold ends under. Bake for 20-25 minutes. Slice when cool.

4 DOZEN

Freezes beautifully.

Simply *More* Pies

Blueberry Open Face Pie

1	cup sugar
3	tablespoons cornstarch
	pinch of salt
1	cup water
4	cups blueberries, divided
1	tablespoon butter
	9-inch pie shell, baked
	whipped cream or ice cream

Mix sugar, cornstarch and salt in saucepan. Add water and 1 cup blueberries. Cook and stir over medium heat until thickened. Stir in butter, let cool. Add remaining blueberries. Pour into baked pie shell. Refrigerate. Garnish with whipped cream or serve with ice cream.

8 SERVINGS

No-Roll Pie Crust

1½ cups flour
1   teaspoon salt
2   tablespoons sugar
½   cup vegetable oil
2   tablespoons cold milk

Sift the flour, salt and sugar into an 8 or 9 inch pie plate. Combine oil and milk in measuring cup. Whip with a fork and pour all at once over flour mixture. Mix with fork until flour is completely dampened. Press evenly and firmly to line bottom of pan, then press dough up the sides and partly cover rim. Be sure dough is pressed to uniform thickness. To flute, pinch dough lightly with fingers. Do not use a high fluted edge.

For baked shell: Prick entire surface and bake in preheated 425° oven for 12-15 minutes. Cool and fill as desired.

For unbaked shell: Fill as desired and bake in preheated 400° oven for 15 minutes, then reduce heat to 350° and bake until filling tests done, or follow directions for filling being used.

1 PIE CRUST

 Chocolate Pecan Pie

½   cup butter, melted
1   cup sugar
1   cup white corn syrup
4   eggs, slightly beaten
1   teaspoon vanilla extract
1   cup pecan halves
¾-1 cup chocolate bits
     unbaked pie crust

Preheat oven to 350°. Combine all ingredients. Pour into pie crust and bake for 45-50 minutes.

8 SERVINGS

No Crust Cream Cheese Pie

1	pound cream cheese
3	eggs
⅔	cup sugar
½	teaspoon vanilla extract
1	pint sour cream
3	tablespoons sugar
1	teaspoon vanilla extract

Preheat oven to 350°. Beat cream cheese, eggs, sugar and vanilla extract together until very smooth. Pour into well-greased 9 inch pie plate and bake for 30 minutes. Remove from oven when center of pie reaches level of edge. Cool 20 minutes. Center shrinks as it cools.

Mix sour cream with sugar and vanilla extract and fill center of pie. Return to 350° oven for 10 minutes. Chill.

8 SERVINGS

Chocolate Angel Pie

3	egg whites
1	cup sugar, divided
1	teaspoon vanilla extract
¾	cup graham cracker crumbs
½	cup chopped pecans

CHOCOLATE FILLING

2	ounces high quality semisweet or bittersweet chocolate
5	tablespoons water
2	tablespoons butter
3	tablespoons sugar
1	teaspoon vanilla extract
½	pint heavy cream, whipped

Preheat oven to 350°. Beat egg whites until stiff but not dry. Gradually add ½ cup sugar and vanilla extract. Mix crumbs, pecans and remaining sugar and fold into egg whites. Pour into greased and floured 8 inch pie plate. Bake for 25 minutes. Cool thoroughly. It will fall slightly as it cools.

Melt chocolate in top of double boiler. Add water and blend. Add butter and sugar and mix well. Cool. Stir in vanilla extract and fold into whipped cream. Turn into shell and chill several hours.

6 TO 8 SERVINGS

Pecan Pie

3	eggs
¾	cup sugar
1	cup corn syrup
1	teaspoon vanilla extract
¼	cup margarine, melted
1	cup pecans
9	inch pie shell, unbaked

Preheat oven to 375°. Beat eggs. Add sugar. Mix well. Stir in syrup, vanilla extract, and margarine. Sprinkle pecans on bottom of unbaked pie shell. Pour filling over all and bake 40-45 minutes.

8 SERVINGS

Coffee Toffee Pie

½	cup butter, softened
¾	cup sugar
1	square unsweetened chocolate, melted
2	teaspoons instant coffee powder
2	eggs
	9-inch pie shell, baked
	grated bitter chocolate for garnish

TOPPING

2	cups heavy cream
2	tablespoons instant coffee powder
½	cup confectioners' sugar

Cream butter and sugar. Blend in melted chocolate and instant coffee. Add eggs and beat 5 minutes. Pour into pie shell and chill.

Whip together topping ingredients until stiff. Spread over cooled pie and chill 2 hours. Grate bitter chocolate on top.

Coconut Pie

This pie makes its own crust.

4	eggs, beaten
½	cup flour
¼	teaspoon baking powder
2	cups milk
1	cup coconut
1¾	cups sugar
¼	cup butter
1	teaspoon almond extract

Preheat oven to 350°. Combine all ingredients and mix well. Pour into greased 10 inch pie plate. Bake for 1 hour until golden brown and firm. It makes its own crust and is lovely served warm and even better with ice cream on top.

8 TO 10 SERVINGS

Key Lime Pie

CRUST

1¼	cups cinnamon graham crackers
⅓	cup melted unsalted butter

FILLING

3	egg yolks
1	(14 ounce) can sweetened condensed milk
½	cup plus 2 tablespoons Key lime juice
2	teaspoons grated lime zest, preferably from Key limes
	whipped cream for garnish

Preheat oven to 350°. Mix crust ingredients together and press into 10 inch pie pan. Combine filling ingredients. Pour in pie crust and bake 30 minutes.

Top with a dollop of whipped cream.

8 TO 10 SERVINGS

Heath Candy Ice Cream Pie

1   box vanilla wafers
½   gallon ice cream, any flavor
6   Heath candy bars (toffee coated
       with chocolate), frozen
1   (8 ounce) jar hot fudge sauce

Make crust of vanilla wafers along sides and bottom of 10 inch pie plate. Fill with ice cream and top with Heath bars, chopped while frozen. Keep in freezer until a few minutes before serving. Spoon 1 tablespoon of hot fudge sauce over each slice and serve.

8 TO 10 SERVINGS

Lemon Ginger Pumpkin Pie

1   cup or more crushed gingersnaps
½   cup chopped pecans
½   teaspoon cinnamon
⅓   cup shortening
1   (15 ounce) can pumpkin
2   eggs, beaten
2   tablespoons lemon juice
¼   cup melted margarine
¾   cup white sugar
¼   cup brown sugar
1   cup evaporated milk

TOPPING
1   cup heavy cream
2   tablespoons sugar
½   teaspoon powdered ginger

Preheat oven to 425°. Combine gingersnap crumbs, pecans and cinnamon in large mixing bowl. Cut in shortening with pastry blender or two knives until mixture is uniform.

Bake 5 minutes. Remove from oven.

Reduce heat to 350°. Combine pumpkin, eggs, lemon juice, margarine, sugars and milk and beat until smooth. Spoon into crust. Bake for 40 minutes.

Beat topping ingredients until thickened to a whipped topping consistency. Garnish or spread over pie and serve.

8 SERVINGS

Pear Pie

More delicate than apple pie.

6	cups pared and sliced firm pears
¾	cup sugar
½	teaspoon nutmeg
	cinnamon
2	tablespoons flour
⅓	tablespoon butter
	pastry for 2 crust pie

Preheat oven to 425°. Mix the pears with sugar, nutmeg, cinnamon and flour. Spoon mixture into pastry-lined pie pan. Dot filling with butter. Cover with top crust. Bake for 35-45 minutes until browned and bubbly.

Sour Cream Pumpkin Pie

Red Rooster

1	(9 inch) pie shell, baked
1	envelope unflavored gelatin
¼	cup cold water
3	eggs, separated
⅓	cup sugar
1¼	cups pumpkin purée, canned or homemade
½	cup sour cream
½	teaspoon salt
1	teaspoon cinnamon
¼	teaspoon cloves
¼	teaspoon nutmeg
¼	teaspoon ginger
¼	cup sugar
1½	cups heavy cream
1	cup confectioners' sugar
1	teaspoon vanilla extract
½	cup chopped pecans

Soften gelatin in water. Beat egg yolks with ½ cup sugar until thick and lemon colored. Add pumpkin, sour cream, salt and spices. Cook over medium heat, stirring constantly. Remove from heat and stir in softened gelatin until dissolved. Cool. Beat egg whites until frothy. Add ¼ cup sugar gradually, beating until peaks form. Fold into pumpkin mixture. Set aside. Whip cream with confectioners' sugar and vanilla extract. Spoon half of pumpkin mixture into pie shell. Spread half of whipped cream mixture on top. Repeat. Sprinkle with pecans. Chill 2 hours before serving.

8 SERVINGS

Strawberry Tart with Almond Nut Crust

CRUST

5   ounces finely ground blanched almonds

½   cup unsalted butter, at room temperature

4   tablespoons sugar

1½   cups flour

1   small egg, beaten

½   teaspoon vanilla extract

FILLING

3   pints ripe strawberries

1   (6 ounce) jar red currant jelly

1   tablespoon plain gelatin

¼   cup orange liqueur

Mix crust ingredients together until well blended. Press into 9 inch tart pan with a removable bottom, taking care to keep the thickness of the crust uniform. Chill for 30 minutes.

Preheat oven to 350°. Bake crust for 15-20 minutes to a light golden color. Cool before filling.

Hull strawberries and arrange them upside down in the tart shell. Prepare a glaze by melting jelly, gelatin and liqueur in a saucepan. Stir over low heat until mixture is clear. Spoon or brush over berries.

Walnut Fudge Pie

It is very rich and chewy.

½   cup butter

3   (1 ounce) squares unsweetened chocolate

2   eggs

1   cup sugar

½   cup flour

1   teaspoon vanilla extract

½   cup coarsely chopped walnuts or pecans

   pinch of salt

   whipped cream or ice cream

   hot fudge sauce as garnish

Preheat oven to 325°. Melt butter and chocolate in top of double boiler. Cool. Add remaining ingredients and mix well. Pour into greased 9 inch pie plate. Bake for 20 minutes. Cool and refrigerate.

Serve with whipped cream or ice cream and fudge sauce.

6 TO 8 SERVINGS

Apricot Mousse

2   (30 ounce) cans apricots
    water
2   (3 ounce) packages apricot gelatin
2   tablespoons orange liqueur
2   cups heavy cream, whipped
2   packages ladyfingers
    macadamia nuts, optional

Drain apricots, reserving juice. Add water to juice to make 3½ cups liquid. Heat liquid to boiling, add gelatin and stir to dissolve. Purée apricots in blender and add to gelatin mixture. Add liqueur. Chill until mixture starts to thicken. Beat cream slightly and fold in whipped cream.

Line bottom and sides of 10 inch springform with ladyfingers. Pour in apricot mixture. Refrigerate until set, about 4 hours. Decorate with apricot halves, nuts and dabs of whipped cream.

12 SERVINGS

Lemon Chiffon Ice Box Dessert

6   eggs, separated
1½   cups sugar, divided
1½   packages ladyfingers
¼   cup cold water
3   lemons
1   envelope unflavored gelatin
¼   teaspoon salt
    whipped cream
    grated nut or coconut

Beat egg yolks well. Add ¾ cup sugar. Add juice and grated rind of 3 lemons. Dissolve gelatin in cold water and add to lemon mixture. Cook over hot water until thick. It will continue to thicken as it cools.

Beat egg whites until stiff and gradually add ¾ cup sugar and salt. Fold egg whites into cooled lemon mixture. Line sides and bottom of 9 inch springform pan with ladyfingers. Pour in lemon mixture. Refrigerate.

Garnish with whipped cream and grated nuts or coconut.

10 SERVINGS

Chocolate Mousse Cake

½   **pound high quality semisweet or bittersweet chocolate**

3   **tablespoons cold water**

1   **cup pasteurized egg whites**

1   **pint heavy cream, divided**

2-3   **packages ladyfingers**

4   **tablespoons confectioners' sugar or to taste**

1   **teaspoon vanilla extract**

Grease 9 inch springform pan with butter. Line sides and bottom of pan with ladyfingers. Combine chocolate and water and microwave in 20 second intervals, until melted. Stir. Beat egg whites until stiff. Set aside. Whip ½ pint heavy cream in clean bowl. Set aside.

Fold egg whites thoroughly into chocolate mixture. When well blended, fold in whipped cream. Gently pour mousse mixture into prepared pan. Refrigerate overnight or freeze.

When ready to serve, remove sides of springform pan. Whip remaining cream with confectioners' sugar and vanilla extract and garnish cake.

May substitute sliced sponge cake for ladyfingers.

Frozen Strawberry Meringue Torte

A light dessert for Passover.

1½   **cups almond macaroons**

2   **teaspoons margarine, melted**

½   **cup chopped pecans or walnuts**

2   **egg whites, at room temperature**

1   **cup sugar**

3   **cups fresh sliced strawberries, divided**

1   **tablespoon lemon juice**

1   **(10 ounce) package frozen strawberries**

3   **tablespoons frozen orange juice concentrate**

1   **tablespoon currant jelly**

Preheat oven to 350°. Process macaroons, margarine and nuts in food processor until crumbly. Press into 10 inch springform pan. Bake 7-10 minutes. Cool.

Beat egg whites on low speed with mixer. Add sugar, 2 cups sliced strawberries and lemon juice. Increase speed to high and beat until stiff peaks forms, about 10-15 minutes. Pour into cooled crust and freeze.

Make sauce by puréeing frozen strawberries, orange juice concentrate, remaining 1 cup sliced strawberries and currant jelly.

Remove torte from springform pan and slice. Pour a little sauce over each slice and serve.

16 SERVINGS

Crust can be omitted and meringue can be placed in individual parfait glasses.

Apple Crisp

4	large Golden Delicious apples, cored, peeled and chopped
¼	cup sugar
¼	teaspoon cinnamon
1	cup brown sugar
1	cup flour
1	cup quick or rolled oats
½	cup unsalted butter, chopped confectioners' sugar, optional

Preheat oven to 350°. Put apples in 8 or 9 inch square baking pan. Mix the sugar and cinnamon and sprinkle over apples. Combine the brown sugar, flour and oats in a mixing bowl. Cut in the butter with a pastry blender or 2 knives until the mixture resembles coarse crumbs. Sprinkle the oat mixture evenly over the apples. Bake for 40-45 minutes until the topping is golden and the filling is bubbling. Let cool to just warm. Sprinkle with confectioners' sugar if desired.

6 SERVINGS

Apple Brown Betty

6	cups apples, peeled and sliced
1	teaspoon cinnamon
1-2	tablespoons lemon juice
1	cup flour
1	cup sugar
1	teaspoon baking powder
	pinch salt
1	egg
¼	cup butter, melted

Preheat oven to 375°. Layer apples in buttered 8 inch square pan. Sprinkle with cinnamon and lemon juice. Combine flour, sugar, baking powder, salt and egg. Mix until crumbly. Sprinkle on top of apples. Drizzle melted butter on top of crumbs. Sprinkle with cinnamon. Bake 1 hour.

6 SERVINGS

Norwegian Apple Tart

1 cup sweet butter
1 cup sugar
1 cup flour
1 (3½ ounce) can slivered almonds
6 apples, peeled, cored and thinly sliced
  heavy cream

Preheat oven to 325°. Cream butter until fluffy. Add sugar gradually. Add flour and mix well. Stir in almonds.

Arrange sliced apples in greased 2 quart soufflé dish. Spread batter over apples. Bake for 35 minutes until crust is golden. Serve warm with cream.

6 TO 8 SERVINGS

Apricot Crisp

2 (30 ounce) cans apricot halves, drained
2 tablespoons water
1 tablespoon lemon juice
½ cup packed light brown sugar
½ teaspoon cinnamon
  dash of nutmeg, optional
¼ teaspoon salt
¾ cup flour
⅓ cup butter or margarine

Preheat oven to 350°. Arrange apricot halves in greased shallow 1½ quart baking dish. Mix water and lemon juice. Pour over apricots.

Combine sugar, spices and flour. Cut in butter with a pastry blender until finely blended. Spoon evenly over apricots. Bake for 40 minutes.

8 TO 10 SERVINGS

Mixed Berry Cobbler

4	cups assorted berries
2	teaspoons fresh lemon juice
½	cup sugar, divided
¾	cup plus 2 tablespoons flour
¼	teaspoon salt
1½	teaspoons baking powder
2	tablespoons unsalted butter, chilled and cut into small pieces
½	cup heavy cream

Preheat oven to 400°. Place berries and lemon juice in a bowl. Toss with ⅓ cup sugar and 2 tablespoons flour. Set aside.

In food processor with metal blade, process ¾ cup flour, salt, baking powder, 1½ tablespoons sugar and butter until mixture resembles peas. Slowly add cream and process just until dough comes together.

Fill ovenproof casserole with berries. Dot fruit with dough in clumps. Sprinkle with 2 teaspoons sugar. Bake for 20 minutes until bubbly and golden brown.

Serve with ice cream or whipped cream.

8 SERVINGS

Fruit Cobbler

¼	cup butter or margarine, softened
⅔	cup brown sugar
½	cup flour
½	teaspoon baking soda
1	teaspoon cinnamon
½	cup quick oats
1	tablespoon water
3	cups fruit

Preheat oven to 350°. Mix dry ingredients until grainy. Place ½ crumbly mixture on bottom of greased 8 inch square pan. Top with fruit. Any fruit combination works: seasonal berries, peaches and raspberries, peaches and blueberries. Add water to remaining mixture and mix well. Sprinkle mixture on top of fruit. Bake 20-35 minutes. Best served warm, but leftovers are a favorite breakfast the next day.

6 SERVINGS

Recipe is easily doubled in a 13 x 9 inch pan.

Purple Plum Crunch

Fantastic dessert

FILLING

4-5	cups fresh Italian plums, pitted and quartered
3	tablespoons flour
½	teaspoon cinnamon
¼	cup packed brown sugar

TOPPING

1	cup flour
¾	cup sugar
¼	teaspoon nutmeg
¼	cup brown sugar
1	teaspoon baking powder
1	egg, well beaten
½	cup butter, melted

Preheat oven to 375°. Pit and quarter plums. Toss with flour, cinnamon and brown sugar. Place in 2 quart rectangular glass baking dish. Make topping by combining flour, brown sugar, baking powder, nutmeg, sugar and egg with fork until crumbly. Sprinkle over plums. Pour cooled butter evenly over topping. Bake for 40 minutes. Serve warm.

Rhubarb Crunch

1	cup flour
¾	cup cornmeal
1	cup brown sugar
½	cup butter, melted
1	teaspoon cinnamon
4	cups trimmed and cut rhubarb
1	cup sugar
1	cup water
½	teaspoon vanilla extract
2	tablespoons cornstarch

Preheat oven to 350°. Mix flour, oatmeal, brown sugar, melted butter and cinnamon until crumbly. Press half of mixture into bottom of 7 x 12 inch pan. Add rhubarb. Mix remaining ingredients and pour over rhubarb. Sprinkle remaining crumbs on top. Bake for 1 hour.

Strawberry Rhubarb Puff

2 (16 ounce) packages frozen rhubarb, thawed
2 (10 ounce) packages frozen strawberries, thawed
1¼ cups sugar, divided
2 cups flour
3 teaspoons baking powder
1 teaspoon salt
⅓ cup vegetable oil
⅔ cup milk
   butter
1 teaspoon cinnamon

Preheat oven to 450°. In ungreased 9 inch square pan, mix rhubarb, strawberries and 1 cup sugar. Place in oven to get hot.

Put flour, 2 tablespoons sugar, baking powder and salt into bowl. Pour oil and milk into measuring cup (do not stir together). Pour all at once into flour mixture. Stir until mixture leaves side of bowl and forms a ball. Drop dough by 9 spoonfuls onto hot fruit. Make an indentation in each biscuit and dot with butter.

Mix 2 tablespoons sugar and 1 teaspoon cinnamon and sprinkle on biscuits. Bake for 25-35 minutes and watch carefully. Do not let it brown too much.

9 SERVINGS

Raspberry Ice Cream

1 tablespoon grated lemon peel
1 tablespoon lemon juice
1 (10 ounce) package frozen raspberries, thawed
⅔ cup condensed milk
1 cup heavy cream, whipped

Combine lemon peel, juice and raspberries in blender. Blend 20 seconds on high. Reduce speed to low and pour in milk.

Fold berry mixture into whipped cream, using rubber spatula.

Pour into ice cube tray and cover securely with wax paper. Freeze 2-3 hours until firm.

6 SERVINGS

Chocolate Fudge Bread Pudding
with White Chocolate Rum Anglaise Sauce

Chef Rich Kunsch at Ledgemont Country Club in Seekonk, Massachusetts

4	tablespoons butter, melted and divided
3	cups heavy cream
1	cup brown sugar
½	cup cocoa powder
4	large eggs, lightly beaten
1	cup buttermilk
1	teaspoon ground cinnamon
1	cup (6 ounces) chocolate chips
6	cups bread cubes, ½ inch cubes
	confectioners' sugar for dusting
2½	cups white chocolate rum anglaise

Preheat oven to 300°. Brush 10 x 14 inch baking dish with 2 tablespoons butter. In a small pot, bring heavy cream to a simmer. Remove from heat and stir in brown sugar and cocoa powder to dissolve.

In a large bowl, whisk together cream mixture with eggs and buttermilk. Add cinnamon, chocolate chips and bread cubes. Stir in remaining 2 tablespoons of melted butter.

Pour into prepared baking dish. Place in center of oven and bake 1-1¼ hours until firm. Remove and cool on a rack until warm before cutting into squares. To serve, plate with 3 tablespoons anglaise and dust with confectioners' sugar.

12 SERVINGS

Using a combination of bread along with chocolate cake, cupcakes or brownie cubes with give you a richer pudding.

White Chocolate Rum Anglaise Sauce

1	cup heavy cream
2	ounces white chocolate chips
2	tablespoons dark rum
1½	cups vanilla pudding

Place white chocolate in a small mixing bowl. In a small sauté pan, bring cream to a boil. Pour over white chocolate and whisk until thoroughly melted. Add rum and pudding and whisk to incorporate. Chill until ready to serve.

Caramel Apricot Rice Pudding

½   **pound dried apricots**

¼   **cup butter or margarine, melted**

1   **cup light brown sugar**

3   **cups cooked and hot long grain white rice**

4   **eggs, beaten**

1   **cup sugar**

1   **teaspoon salt**

2½   **teaspoons vanilla extract**

1   **quart milk, scalded**

¼   **teaspoon nutmeg**

½   **teaspoon cinnamon**

1½   **cups or less, according to taste, heavy cream, whipped**

     slivered almonds

     unsweetened chocolate, shaved

Preheat oven to 350°. Cook apricots until tender as package directs; drain. Pour melted butter into 3 quart casserole and sprinkle with brown sugar. Arrange apricots, rounded side down, in a single layer over brown sugar and butter mixture. Spoon in rice.

Beat eggs until light and foamy. Stir in sugar, salt and vanilla extract. Slowly stir in milk. Pour milk mixture over rice and apricots. Sprinkle with nutmeg and cinnamon.

Set casserole in a pan of hot water. Bake for 1-1¼ hours or until silver knife inserted in center comes out clean. Cool. At serving time, decorate with whipped cream, chocolate and almonds.

12 SERVINGS

Pumpkin Pudding

1   **(15 ounce) can pumpkin purée**

1   **(12 ounce) can evaporated nonfat milk**

2   **large eggs, beaten**

¼-½   **cup sugar**

2-4   **teaspoons cinnamon**

¼   **teaspoon ground ginger, optional**

¼   **teaspoon ground cloves, optional**

     whipped cream

Preheat oven to 350°. Mix all ingredients together and pour into 8 inch square casserole. Bake for approximately 30 minutes. Don't overbake; the center should be slightly wiggly.

Serve warm with whipped cream or refrigerate for later.

6 SERVINGS

Grape Nut Custard

½-¾ cup Grape Nuts
½ cup sugar
4 eggs
2 teaspoons vanilla extract
1 quart milk
½ cup raisins, optional

Preheat oven to 350°. Mix Grape Nuts and sugar. Add eggs beaten with vanilla extract. Slowly stir in milk. Stir in raisins, if desired. Pour into baking dish and set pan into large pan of water. Bake on bottom rack of oven for 1 hour.

8 SERVINGS

Panna Cotta

3 small envelopes unflavored gelatin
4 cups whipping cream
4 cups half-and-half
2 cups sugar
1 vanilla bean, split in 2 and scraped
  finely grated zest of 1 lemon
  chocolate sauce or raspberry purée

Dissolve gelatin in 1 cup cold water in a small bowl. Combine the whipping cream, half and half, sugar, lemon zest and vanilla bean, including scrapings in a 3 quart pot. Bring just to below the boiling point. Remove from heat, discard the vanilla bean and stir in the dissolved gelatin. Pour into individual 1 cup molds, cover and refrigerate 2 hours or until set. Unmold and serve on chocolate sauce or raspberry purée with a garnish of fresh berries.

10 SERVINGS

Can double yield by using ½ cup molds.

Crème Brulée

4   **cups whipping or heavy cream**

1   **vanilla bean, split lengthwise**

       pinch salt

8   **large egg yolks**

¾   **cup plus 2 tablespoons sugar**

8   **tablespoons packed light brown sugar**

Preheat oven to 300°. Place (8) ¾-cup ramekins in a roasting pan. In a saucepan over low heat, combine cream, vanilla bean and salt. Warm for 5 minutes.

In a large bowl, combine the egg yolks and sugar. Pour in the hot cream and stir gently to combine. Strain the custard into a pitcher and skim off any bubbles. Pour the custard into the ramekins, filling them to the rim. Place the roasting pan in the oven and carefully pour warm water into the pan until it reaches halfway up the sides of the ramekins. Loosely cover pan with aluminum foil. Bake 1¼ hours until set. Remove ramekins from the water bath and cool. Cover individually and refrigerate for at least 3 hours or up to 2 days.

When ready to serve, preheat the broiler. Uncover the ramekins and place them on a baking sheet. Top each with 1 tablespoon brown sugar and, using a spatula or knife, spread the sugar evenly over the custards. Broil the custards until the sugar caramelizes, 30 seconds to 2 minutes. Serve immediately or refrigerate up to 4 hours.

8 SERVINGS

 # Zabaglione

Perfect solution for using egg yolks when you used the whites!

6	**egg yolks**
6	**tablespoons sugar**
⅔	**cup imported Marsala wine**

Beat egg yolks. In top of double boiler, gradually add sugar and wine while beating. Place over boiling water and whisk until mixture begins to thicken and foam. Remove from heat.

Serve warm as sauce over strawberries, or plain in individual wine glasses.

4 TO 6 SERVINGS

Simply *More* and Then Some

The 1962 Annual Meeting and Luncheon celebrated
the 65th anniversary of the Women's Association.

The dedication of the Miriam Hospital brought a new sense of purpose to the Women's Association which expanded its role and sought creative ways to fulfill its mission of providing Public Relations, Education, Fundraising, and Volunteerism.

Our newsletter, *Miriam Examiner* was born in 1956 and continues to inform and educate our membership. Special events also raised funds for the hospital. Gala Concerts held in honor of Leonard Bernstein and the New York Philharmonic in 1966 and Andre Previn and the London Philharmonic in 1973 provided new intensive care units for the hospital. Our Annual Equipment Event has raised funds to purchase needed medical equipment each year since 1926, when the women purchased the linens for the original hospital on Parade Street. Guest speakers have educated our members and the public about health issues, including the effects of smoking on health, which resulted in the 1963 ban of the sale of cigarettes anywhere in the hospital, an action which attracted positive national attention. Today, The Miriam Hospital is totally smoke-free.

And in 1975, The Miriam Hospital Association produced a cookbook, *Simply Delicious,* which sold out through 3 printings, the last of which resulted in a national mail order business. In total, our 1975 cookbook earned $80,000 in profits for The Miriam. Mothers and grandmothers have passed their cookbooks down to a new generation. *Simply Delicious* has been unavailable since 1988 and is still often requested.

To date, the Miriam Hospital Women's Association has donated hundreds of thousands of dollars in revenue from our Gift and Coffee Shops. Our named funds have purchased textbooks for the physicians' library and music CDs for patient use, artwork to brighten patient surroundings, educational materials to aid in the prevention of heart disease, special funds to provide equipment and essentials for patients, and contributions to fund wigs and prostheses for those undergoing treatment for cancer. We even provide refreshments to comfort patients and their families in the hospital's waiting rooms. Our most successful brick "Walkway to Health" program supports the Emergency Heart and Cancer Centers for the hospital.

 ## "A Bit of Grog"

Johnson and Wales University, College of Culinary Arts

3   oranges stuck with cloves
½   gallon cider
1   fifth apple brandy
    cinnamon sticks

Preheat oven to 350°. Bake oranges 20-35 minutes until they ooze and begin to color. Heat cider until hot. Open brandy — immerse bottle in hot water until piping hot. Put oranges in meat pot or flameproof bowl. Pour ½ of brandy over oranges and ignite. It will burn with a lovely blue flame. Extinguish by pouring cider over.

Serve in punch cups with cinnamon sticks.

12 TO 15 SERVINGS

 ## Champagne Punch

1   (6 ounce) can frozen orange juice
2   (6 ounce) cans frozen pineapple juice
1   (10 ounce) jar cherries and juice
1   (10 ounce) package frozen raspberries or strawberries
1   pint lemon sherbet
1   pint lime sherbet
1   bottle champagne
1   bottle club soda
4   cups ice cubes

Mix together all ingredients except ice cubes. Add ice cubes when everything is defrosted.

20 SERVINGS

Bloody Mary Big Easy

Rue De L'Espoir Restaurant in Providence, Rhode Island

BLOODY MARY MIX

1	quart tomato juice
1	quart vegetable juice
1	cup lemon juice
2	teaspoons cracked black pepper
2	teaspoons celery salt
2	teaspoons Worcestershire sauce
2	tablespoons horseradish
6	drops Tabasco sauce

SPICY COATING MIX

¼	teaspoon cayenne pepper
1	teaspoon chili powder
1	teaspoon garlic powder
1	teaspoon paprika
1	teaspoon onion powder
1	teaspoon salt
1	teaspoon black pepper
1	teaspoon cumin
	vodka
	hot cherry peppers for garnish

Mix juices, black pepper, celery salt, Worcestershire, horseradish and Tabasco together. Add additional horseradish and Tabasco sauce if you prefer Bloody Mary mix to be spicier.

Mix spices for the coating mix together in a shallow bowl.

Take an old fashioned glass and turn the rim of the glass in ice, then dip glass into spice mixture to coat rim. Fill the glass with ice. Pour in 1½ ounces vodka and fill with Bloody Mary mix and shake. Garnish with hot cherry pepper.

10 TO 12 SERVINGS

Old Fashioned Lemonade

1	lemon
½	cup sugar
1	quart water
	ice

Roll lemon until soft. Slice thin. Add sugar and let stand one hour. Add water and ice.

 # Raz Punch

2	(10 ounce) packages frozen raspberries, thawed
2	(6 ounce) cans frozen limeade
4	cups water
½	cup sugar
2	(1 liter) bottles lemon-lime soda, chilled
	ice cubes

Sieve berries and discard seeds. Combine berries, limeade, water and sugar. Mix well. Chill. At serving time, add soda and ice.

30 SERVINGS

Use well chilled medium dry wine or champagne in place of water.

 # Sangría

½	cup superfine sugar
1	cup cold water
1	lime, thinly sliced
1	orange, thinly sliced
12	ice cubes, approximately
1	bottle red wine
2	cups soda water, approximately

Combine sugar and water in a small saucepan. Cook over moderate heat, stirring almost constantly until sugar is dissolved. Just before sugar boils, remove from heat. Add lime and orange. Cool. Add fruit and macerate for at least 4 hours at room temperature.

Fill a pitcher with about a dozen ice cubes. Add the macerated fruit and ½ cup of the syrup. Fill pitcher with wine and soda. Swizzle.

Put a slice of lime and a slice of orange in each glass before serving.

ABOUT 1 QUART

Susan's Secret Applesauce

8 McIntosh apples
½ cup cinnamon red hot candies
½ cup water
¼ teaspoon nutmeg

Quarter apples and place in a large pot. Bring to a boil and then simmer until soft. Remove apples with a large slotted spoon. Place in a food mill over a large bowl and turn until all sauce has strained into the bowl; the mill captures the skin, core and seeds, so there is no need to peel or core.

Add cinnamon candies to the warm sauce and stir constantly until they melt. Add nutmeg. Add extra sugar to taste if necessary.

Amazing Cranberry Sauce

2 cups sugar
1 cup water
1 pound fresh cranberries, washed
⅓ cup orange marmalade
   juice and zest of 1 orange
½ cup slivered blanched almonds
⅓ cup orange liqueur

Bring sugar and water to a boil and cook for 5 minutes. Add cranberries and cook until skins burst, about 5 minutes. Stir in marmalade, orange zest and orange juice. Remove from heat and cool. Add almonds and liqueur.

4 CUPS

David's Charoses

Not just for Passover. Great served as an appetizer with Brie cheese and crackers.

1	tart green apple, peeled and cored
¾	cup pitted prunes
½	cup dried apricots
2	cups dry red wine
1	cup golden raisins
½	cup sugar
⅓	cup toasted walnut halves
⅓	cup sliced almonds
1	teaspoon honey
⅓	cup coarsely chopped pecans

Cut apple, prunes and apricots into ¼ inch pieces. Place in large heavy pot with wine, raisins and sugar. Boil until sugar is dissolved. Reduce heat and simmer 20-25 minutes until almost all of the liquid is absorbed and the mixture is syrupy. Stir in walnuts and almonds. Cool. Store covered in refrigerator.

Bring honey to a boil in a small skillet. Add the pecans and stir until well coated. Transfer to a bowl and cool.

Serve charoses in a bowl either sprinkled with pecans or with the pecans mixed in.

Chutney

Goes well with curry dishes.

4	large onions, quartered
1	pound dried apricots
1	pound raisins, chopped
¼	cup almonds, ground
2	teaspoons ginger
1	garlic clove, minced
4	cups vinegar
	pinch cayenne
	salt and pepper to taste
2	cups sugar

Boil onions until tender and chop. Boil apricots until soft.

Mix all ingredients together and cook over medium heat for 30 minutes, stirring frequently.

Cool and pack into sterilized jars.

2 QUARTS

Peach Chutney

Ideal with curry dishes and grilled chicken and fish.

4	quarts peaches, peeled and finely chopped
1	cup raisins
1	cup chopped onion
1	clove garlic, minced
1	cup chopped sweet red pepper
2½	cups brown sugar
5	cups vinegar
¼	cup mustard seeds
2	tablespoons ground ginger
2	teaspoons salt

In large kettle, cook all ingredients over low heat for 40 minutes or until thick, stirring often to prevent sticking.

Ladle mixture into hot sterilized jars, leaving ¼ inch headspace. Seal.

4 TO 5 QUARTS

Ginger and Rhubarb Strawberry Compote

1½	pounds rhubarb
1	cup sugar
	grated rind of 1 orange
1½	pounds strawberries
3	tablespoons chopped crystallized ginger

Trim rhubarb, removing any peel that comes off easily. Cut into 1½ inch pieces. Combine with sugar and orange rind and bring slowly to a boil, covered, in a non-aluminum saucepan. Reduce heat and simmer gently for 15 minutes.

Meanwhile wash and stem strawberries. If they are large, cut in half lengthwise. Add the strawberries and ginger to the rhubarb and continue cooking for about 5 minutes, until berries are soft but hold their shape.

Cool and chill.

4 CUPS

 # Fruit Curry

1	(20 ounce) can pineapple chunks
2	(15 ounce) cans pear halves
2	(15 ounce) cans peach halves
2	(15 ounce) cans apricot halves
⅓	cup butter, melted
¾	cup packed brown sugar
4	teaspoons curry powder

Preheat oven to 300°. Drain all fruit thoroughly. Mix butter, sugar and curry powder together. Place fruit in a baking dish and pour butter mixture over fruit.

Bake for 1 hour.

Nice served with corned beef and chicken.

 # My Own Duck Sauce

1	(12 ounce) jar plum jam
½	cup chutney, finely chopped
5	teaspoons vinegar
½	cup water
2	teaspoons sugar
2	tablespoons preserved ginger, finely chopped

Combine all ingredients in a saucepan and place over low heat. Bring to a boil. Reduce heat and simmer 5 minutes.

Cool and pack in jars.

 # Horseradish

Warning: Be ready to cry!

1	cup grated horseradish root
⅓	cup white vinegar
½	teaspoon salt
1	teaspoon sugar
	grated beet root for color, if desired

Peel horseradish root with vegetable peeler. Grate or cut into cubes and process cubes in food chopper or blender.

Combine ingredients and pack in jars. Store in refrigerator.

Maria's Mustard

2 cups dry white wine
1 cup chopped onion
2 cloves garlic, minced
1 (6 ounce) can dry mustard
2 tablespoons honey
1 tablespoon vegetable oil
2 teaspoons salt
   few drops Tabasco sauce

Combine wine, onion, and garlic in small saucepan and bring to a boil. Reduce heat and simmer 5 minutes.

Pour mixture into bowl and cool. Strain into dry mustard in a small saucepan, beating constantly with a wire whisk until very smooth.

Blend remaining ingredients into mustard mixture. Heat slowly, stirring constantly, until mixture thickens. Cool.

Pour into jar. Cover and chill at least 2 days to blend flavors. Keep refrigerated.

2 CUPS

Tartar Sauce

1 cup mayonnaise
2 tablespoons chopped sweet pickle
1 teaspoon chopped chives
1 teaspoon chopped parsley
1 teaspoon chopped shallots or scallions
1 teaspoon chopped green olives
¼ teaspoon salt
   dash of pepper
2 teaspoons dry sherry, optional

Combine all ingredients and refrigerate until ready to use.

1 CUP

Bread and Butter Pickles

½ cup salt

ice water to cover vegetables

30 medium cucumbers, thinly sliced
(1 gallon)

8 medium onions, thinly sliced

2 large red or green peppers, cut in
fine strips

5 cups sugar

5 cups vinegar

1 teaspoon whole cloves

2 tablespoons mustard seeds

1 teaspoon turmeric

Dissolve salt in ice water and pour over vegetables. Let stand for 3 hours.

Combine remaining ingredients and bring to a boil. Drain vegetables and add to marinade. Heat to boiling point but do not boil.

Pack into sterilized jars and seal. Let pickles stand 6 weeks before using.

8 TO 10 PINTS

Dill Pickles

8 pounds pickling cucumbers
(3-4 inches long)

8 stems dill

8 teaspoons pickling spices

8 cloves garlic, peeled and cut in half

3 medium onions, sliced thinly

4 quarts water

2 cups vinegar

1 cup pickling salt

1 teaspoon alum

Wash cucumbers. Place 8 one quart canning jars and lids in boiling water for 10 minutes to sterilize. Remove jars from water. In each jar, place 1 stem dill, 1 teaspoon pickling spice, 1 clove garlic, a small handful of sliced onion, and cucumbers to fill the jar. Pack tightly.

In a large pot, bring water, vinegar, pickling salt and alum to a rapid boil over medium heat. Fill jars with boiling brine to ½ inch from the top of the jar. Wipe rims clean with a damp towel and seal the jars.

Store pickles at least 8 weeks before opening. Store in refrigerator after opening.

8 QUARTS

Toorshie (Mixed Pickles)

4	pounds green tomatoes
3	pounds green peppers
1	large head cauliflower
2	packages carrots
2	bunches celery
1	head cabbage
1	bunch fresh dill
3-4	hot peppers
2	heads garlic
2	quarts water
1½	quarts vinegar
¾	cup un-iodized salt
	celery leaves

Wash vegetables and cut into medium size pieces. Mix in a large bowl.

Using about a dozen quart jars, fill each with a couple sprigs of dill, a couple of pieces of garlic, 1 inch piece of hot pepper and mixed vegetables. Push down to pack tight.

Mix brine by combining water, vinegar and salt. Pour brine over vegetables to top of jar to prevent excess amount of air. Add celery leaf on top and cap.

Let stand 2 months before using.

12 QUARTS

Fabulous Fudge

1	(12 ounce) package semisweet chocolate chips
¾	(14 ounce) can condensed milk
½	cup chopped walnuts

Melt chocolate bits in top of double boiler. Add condensed milk and beat thoroughly. Add nuts.

Line 8 inch square pan with waxed paper. Pour in fudge and chill until hardened. Cut into bite size pieces.

48 PIECES

# Hot Fudge Sauce

½   cup butter
2   (1 ounce) squares unsweetened chocolate
2   cups confectioners' sugar
1   (5⅓ ounce) can evaporated milk
1   teaspoon vanilla

Melt butter and chocolate in a double boiler. Add small amounts of sugar and milk alternately. Simmer 10 minutes over direct heat. Add vanilla.

Serve over ice cream.

Matzo Toffee

A Passover treat.

3   pieces matzo
1   cup unsalted butter
1   cup dark brown sugar
1   (12 ounce) package chocolate chips
1¼ cups chopped pecans

Preheat oven to 400°. Line the bottom and sides of a baking sheet with foil and dust with vegetable cooking spray. Arrange matzo pieces to cover the sheet, leaving as many whole as possible and using smaller pieces to fill in.

In a small saucepan, melt butter and brown sugar. Simmer 2 minutes and then pour over matzo to cover. Bake 6 minutes on the middle rack.

Remove from oven. Sprinkle chocolate chips evenly over the top. Return to the oven for 1-2 minutes to melt chocolate. Remove from oven and spread the chips to completely cover. Sprinkle with pecans.

Place in freezer for 20 minutes. Remove toffee from the pan and break into pieces. Store in freezer in an airtight container.

If not making for Passover, try a sleeve of saltines or graham crackers instead of matzo.

Pecan Brittle

2 cups white sugar
2 cups brown sugar
½ cup light corn syrup
½ cup water
⅛ teaspoon salt
¼ cup butter, softened
⅛ teaspoon baking soda
1½ cups coarsely chopped pecans

Combine sugars, corn syrup, water and salt. Cook and stir until drop of mixture forms brittle threads when dropped into cold water (300°F on candy thermometer). Remove from heat.

Add butter and baking soda, stirring just until mixed. Add pecans and pour immediately onto greased heatproof surface. Smooth out to a thin layer and score in squares, if desired.

Just before candy is completely cool and hardened, loosen and break into squares or rough pieces.

Sugared Walnuts

¾ cup sugar
4 tablespoons honey
½ teaspoon ginger powder
1 pound shelled walnuts, quartered
matzo meal

Heat sugar, honey and ginger until syrupy. Add walnuts and cook 3-5 minutes, mixing constantly. Do not let mixture boil.

Empty onto wet board and with wet hands form mixture into an even layer. Sprinkle with matzo meal and let cool. Cut into small pieces and dip bottoms into matzo meal.

To make softer candy, add more honey.

Simply *More* for Kids

In 1996, the Miriam Hospital Women's Association sponsored a fashion show
to benefit the Women's Wellness program for women with AIDS.

In this year of 2009, The Miriam Hospital Women's Association celebrates its 113th year of continuous service. Our membership today is almost 800 strong. Many of our members can trace their family involvement in The Miriam and The Miriam Hospital Women's Association through three generations. Others are newcomers to our beautiful state and have found a warm welcome and satisfaction through helping The Miriam grow and maintain its excellence.

The Miriam Hospital has also continued to grow and expand. Today, Miriam Hospital has 247 licensed beds, is affiliated with the Warren Alpert School of Medicine at Brown University and is an integral part of the Lifespan Health System. The Miriam has received the Magnet Recognition Award for Excellence in Nursing Services three times and has been nationally recognized as a top hospital in cardiovascular care. Important medical research, with NIH funding, takes place in our Center for Aids Research and at the Center for Preventative and Behavioral Medicine. Annually, the hospital has over 15,000 patient discharges, over 100,000 emergency department and outpatient visits, and conducts over 10,000 surgeries.

In June 2007, the Victor and Gussie Baxt Building opened. This new facility includes 10 state-of-the art operating rooms including advanced robotics, a radiology suite offering the latest diagnostic imaging and interventional technologies, 36 private patient rooms, conference rooms and a gift shop and cafeteria. The Victor and Gussie Baxt building represents the first step in the Miriam Hospital Campaign for the Next Generation, and *Simply More Delicious* is proud to have designated its proceeds towards that campaign.

Strawberry Banana Milkshake

1	cup skim milk
½	ripe banana
⅓	cup low fat cottage cheese
½	cup frozen strawberries

Blend milk, banana and cottage cheese until smooth. Add frozen strawberries. Blend well.

1 SERVING

Sunrise Smoothie

⅔	cup orange juice
1	banana
1	cup frozen strawberries
	ice cubes
1	scoop protein powder, optional

Blend orange juice and banana in blender. Add protein powder, if desired. Slowly add frozen strawberries, a few at a time, blending often between additions. Add ice for additional thickness and coldness. Blend well.

1 SERVING

Pear Pops

1	(15 ounce) can pear slices
1	(8 ounce) container plain yogurt
3	tablespoons honey
½	teaspoon lemon juice
	popsicle or craft sticks.

Combine ingredients in blender until fully mixed. Pour into cups or popsicle molds. Add sticks to hold them. Freeze.

Cinnamon Toast

1 teaspoon cinnamon
1 tablespoon sugar
2 slices bread
1 tablespoon butter or margarine,
   softened

Mix cinnamon and sugar together in a small bowl until it is all one color. Spread butter evenly over each slice of bread. Place on a small piece of aluminum foil. Sprinkle the entire surface with the cinnamon and sugar mixture. Place in toaster oven and cook until top is crispy and bubbly. Remove from oven and allow to cool for a few minutes before eating.

1 SERVING

French Toast

2 eggs
⅓ cup milk
6 slices bread
2 tablespoons butter or margarine
   cinnamon and sugar
   syrup

Combine egg and milk in a shallow bowl or pie plate. Mix with fork until well blended. With fingers or a fork, dip bread into egg mixture to coat both sides.

Spray a skillet with vegetable cooking spray or coat with butter or margarine. Warm skillet over medium heat. Place two dipped bread slices at a time into pan and cook until golden brown, approximately 2-3 minutes. Flip to the other side and cook another 2 minutes.

Serve with cinnamon and sugar or syrup.

3 TO 4 SERVINGS

Monkey Bread

2	tablespoons cinnamon
½	cup brown sugar
1	cup white sugar
½	cup butter or margarine
1	loaf frozen challah dough, defrosted

Preheat oven to 350°. Mix cinnamon and sugar in a medium size bowl. Melt butter or margarine in another bowl. Grease a nonstick Bundt pan. Pull off pieces of bread dough about the size of a quarter and roll into a ball. Dip into margarine and then into cinnamon-sugar mixture. Drop balls into pan.

Bake for 35-45 minutes until desired toastiness. Cool in pan for 10 minutes and invert onto serving dish. Serve warm, by either slicing or just pulling off a piece.

8 SERVINGS

Refrigerated cans of biscuits can also be used. Just cut each biscuit into 4 pieces.

Baked Chicken Tenders

2	boneless skinless chicken breast (about 1 pound)
	salt and pepper
1	egg
¼	cup milk or water
2	cups bread crumbs, seasoned or unseasoned

Preheat oven to 375°. Cut each chicken breast into strips about 1 inch wide. Season with salt and pepper.

Beat egg and milk together in a shallow bowl. Put bread crumbs in another bowl. Dip chicken strips into egg mixture to fully coat. Roll dipped chicken into bread crumbs to coat all over. Place on a baking sheet. Bake for 12-15 minutes. Serve with your favorite dipping sauce.

4 SERVINGS

Use panko (Japanese) bread crumbs for a lighter, crispier crust.

Hot Dog Fingers

1   (8 ounce) can crescent style
    refrigerated rolls
8   hot dogs

Preheat oven to 325°. Unroll dough. Place 1 hot dog on the shortest side of each triangle. Roll dough around hot dog. Place on ungreased cookie sheet. Bake 15-18 minutes until golden brown.

8 SERVINGS

To use cocktail size hot dogs, cut each triangle of dough lengthwise into 3 narrow triangles and wrap around each hot dog. Reduce baking time to 12-15 minutes.

Quesadilla

2   (6-8 inch) flour tortillas
¼   cup cooked cubed chicken or cooked
     beans
½   cup grated jack or Cheddar cheese
     chopped tomatoes, optional
     chopped scallions, optional
     sliced black olives, optional
     salsa

Place 1 tortilla on microwave safe plate. Sprinkle chicken, cheese and desired vegetables on top. Cover with other tortilla. Microwave for 30 seconds until cheese begins to melt.

Heat a non-stick skillet to medium-hot. Spray with vegetable cooking spray. Slide warm quesadilla into skillet. Cook until lightly browned on bottom, about 1 minute. Spray top with vegetable cooking spray and flip over. Cook until second side is golden brown, about 1 minute more. Transfer to a plate and cut into wedges with a pizza cutter. Serve with your favorite salsa, if desired.

1 SERVING

Baked Macaroni and Cheese

3   cups macaroni or other pasta
2   tablespoons cornstarch
1   teaspoon salt
½   teaspoon dry mustard, optional
¼   teaspoon pepper
2½ cups milk
2   tablespoons margarine
1   (8 ounce) package shredded
     Cheddar or Monterey Jack cheese,
     divided

Cook pasta to al dente according to package directions. Drain.

Preheat oven to 375°. In a medium saucepan, combine cornstarch, salt, mustard and pepper. Put over a low heat and stir in milk until smooth. Increase heat to medium high, add the margarine, and stir constantly until the mixture comes to a boil. After it has boiled for 1 minute, remove from heat and stir in all but ¼ cup cheese.

Combine the cheese mixture and pasta and then pour into a greased 2 quart baking pan. Sprinkle with remaining cheese. Bake uncovered for 25 minutes until hot and bubbly.

4 TO 6 SERVINGS

Add a (10 ounce) package of frozen broccoli that has been cooked and drained to the cheese mixture.

Matzo Pizza

A favorite for many kids during Passover.

1 matzo
2-3 tablespoons marinara or pizza sauce
   sliced tomatoes, optional
   sliced mushrooms, optional
   sliced peppers, optional
¼ cup grated mozzarella cheese
   sprinkle basil, optional

Preheat oven or toaster oven to 375°. Line baking sheet with foil and place matzo on top. Spread matzo with sauce. Add vegetable toppings, if desired. Sprinkle entire matzo with shredded cheese. Sprinkle with basil. Bake for about 10 minutes until cheese melts.

1 SERVING

Broiled Veggies

fresh green beans, washed
broccoli, cut into spears
olive oil
kosher salt

Preheat oven to broil. Place a layer of desired vegetables on a baking sheet. Drizzle with olive oil and toss each piece gently. Sprinkle with kosher salt.

Broil in oven for 5-10 minutes, until vegetables start to darken. Serve immediately.

The salt brings out the sweetness in the vegetables.

Apple Kugel

2	eggs
1	cup flour
1	cup sugar
¾	cup oil
1	teaspoon baking powder
1	teaspoon vanilla
5	apples, peeled and sliced
	cinnamon to taste

Preheat oven to 350°. Beat the eggs, flour, sugar, oil, baking powder and vanilla together. Mix in the apples slices and stir. Pour into 8 inch square baking pan and top with cinnamon.

Bake for 1 hour. Allow to cool slightly before serving.

4 TO 6 SERVINGS

Homemade Cinnamon Apple Sauce

6-8	McIntosh or other cooking apples
¾	cup water
½	teaspoon cinnamon
¼-½	cup sugar

Peel, core and coarsely chop apples. Place apples in a saucepan with water and cinnamon. Bring to a boil over medium heat. Cover, reduce heat and simmer 10 minutes, stirring occasionally. Add sugar to taste. Simmer another 3-5 minutes to desired smoothness.

4 TO 6 SERVINGS

For a simple fall dessert, serve over a scoop of ice cream and sprinkle each serving with 1 tablespoon granola.

Easy Ice Cream Cake

16   ice cream sandwiches

1   (16 ounce) container frozen non-dairy whipped topping

1   (12 ounce) jar hot fudge topping, room temperature

     sprinkles or chopped nuts for garnish

Unwrap 8 ice cream sandwiches. Lay side by side in a 9 x 13 inch baking dish.

Spread evenly with half of the hot fudge topping, and then half of the whipped topping.

Unwrap the other 8 ice cream sandwiches and make another layer on top of the whipped topping. Spread the rest of the hot fudge sauce on top of the ice cream sandwiches and then spread the whipped topping on top of that. Garnish with chopped nuts, sprinkles, or grated chocolate bar.

Cover and freeze at least 1 hour before servings. Remove from freezer 10 minutes before serving. Cut into squares. Keep uneaten portions covered and frozen.

16 SERVINGS

You can also use caramel topping and add fresh sliced strawberries and nuts before the second layer of ice cream sandwiches.

Easy Mint Brownies

1   box fudge brownie mix plus
      ingredients needed for mix
28   pieces Andes chocolate mints

Prepare brownies as directed on box for chewy or fudge brownies in a 13 x 9 inch pan. While baking, unwrap mints and set aside. When brownies are done, remove from oven and place mints on top. Allow to sit for 5 minutes or until melted. Swirl mints with knife to cover and ice the brownies. Let cool and cut into squares.

18 SERVINGS

Trifle

1   round angel food cake
1   (21 ounce) can cherry pie filling,
      divided
2   (3½ ounce) boxes vanilla pudding
      milk
1   (12 ounce) can Mandarin oranges,
      drained and divided
1   (12 ounce) can freestone peaches,
      drained and divided
2-3   bananas, sliced and divided
1   cup whipped cream or whipped
      topping
      strawberries for garnish

Prepare pudding according to package directions.

Slice angel food cake into 3 layers. Tear one layer into pieces and place in bottom of large glass bowl. Spoon ⅓ of pudding over cake. Spoon ½ can cherry pie filling over pudding. Add ⅓ of fruit (oranges, peaches and bananas). Repeat layers of torn cake, ⅓ pudding, remaining pie filling and remaining fruit. Add the final layer of torn cake. Top with whipped cream and garnish with strawberries or slivered almonds. Chill before serving.

8 TO 12 SERVINGS

Any variety of fruit or pie filling can be used. Choose your favorites.

Edible Fish Tank

2-4 boxes blue gelatin

1-2 cups diced strawberries

6-8 different colored Swedish fish candy

gummi aquatic creatures, such as octopus, optional

Make gelatin according to package directions. Use as many gelatin packages as are needed to fill large fish bowl or brandy snifter. Refrigerate approximately ½ hour until partially set. Layer diced strawberries as coral or rocks on bottom of the fish bowl. Spoon gelatin on top. Press fish, and other aquatic candies, into bowl close to side. Refrigerate until completely set.

12 TO 16 SERVINGS

This could also be made in clear plastic cups with a 1-2 fish in each cup for individual servings.

Dirt

1 large package chocolate sandwich cookies

2 large boxes instant chocolate or vanilla pudding

2 cups milk

2 cups frozen nondairy whipped topping

gummi worms

Crush cookies in a food processor or in a zip-top plastic bag using a rolling pin.

Mix pudding and milk together. Beat well until thickened. Stir in cool whip. Stir in about ½ of crushed cookies.

Assemble dirt in a clean, plastic flower pot or in paper cups for individual servings. Spoon in pudding mixture, planting gummi worms in dirt as you go. Top with remaining cookie crumbs and leave one worm hanging halfway out. Add plastic or paper flower if desired.

8 TO 10 SERVINGS

Chocolate Minglers

1	cup chocolate chips
¼	cup peanut butter
6	cups Crispix cereal
½	cup peanuts, optional
1	cup confectioners' sugar

Place chocolate chips in large microwaveable bowl. Melt on high for 1 minute. Stir. Cook another 30 seconds or until melted. Stir. Add peanut butter and stir until smooth. Stir in peanuts, if desired. Gently stir in cereal until all is coated in chocolate.

Place confectioner's sugar in a large zip-top bag. Add coated cereal. Seal bag and shake until cereal is evenly coated. Store in airtight container in refrigerator.

16 SERVINGS

White Chocolate Snack Mix

3	(10 ounce) packages white chocolate chips
4	tablespoons canola oil
4-6	cups Crispix
2-4	cups crispy wheat cereal squares
1	(15 ounce) package thin pretzel sticks
4	cups mixed nuts

Melt chocolate and oil in double boiler. Do not microwave. Mix in remaining ingredients. Spread on 4-5 wax paper lined cookie sheets and cool. Break into pieces.

No Cook Fudge

1 cup margarine, melted
1 teaspoons vanilla
3 tablespoons cocoa powder
1 (16 ounce) box confectioners' sugar
1 cup peanut butter
   walnuts, optional

Mix ingredients in a large bowl, beating with an electric mixer until well blended.

Pour into an ungreased 8 inch square pan. Garnish with walnuts if desired. Refrigerate until set, at least 20 minutes. Cut into 1 inch squares.

64 PIECES

Lollipops

A great treat to make with an adult. It gets very hot!

1-2 tablespoons sweet butter
1   cup sugar
½   cup light corn syrup
⅔   cup water
    food coloring
    flavoring
12 popsicle or craft sticks

Line a cookie sheet with foil and grease with butter. Set sticks on foil apart from each other.

Measure sugar, corn syrup and water directly into a pot. Stir ingredients and heat over medium flame, but do not stir again while heating. Cook for approximately 25 minutes; the mixture will be boiling and keep getting thicker. The color will change to light straw. Watch constantly to avoid burning.

Test to see if syrup is ready. Carefully drizzle a little bit into a glass of very cold water. The drizzle should harden, making noise; it will be like glass. Add color and flavoring. Stir quickly and spoon onto tops of sticks. You must work fast, because mixture hardens quickly. Allow lollipops to cool completely before touching to prevent burned fingers. Clean up easily by letting hot water run into pot and spoon in sink.

12 LOLLIPOPS

Photo Credits

TO BEGIN WITH DIVIDER PAGE

The charter members of The Miriam Hospital Association in 1907 at the home of Mrs. Betsy Woolf. Back row left to right, Mrs. Jack Shein, Mr. and Mrs. Sam Tatz, Mrs. Betty Woolf, Mrs. Theresa Feldman. Front row left to right, Mrs. Bleumer Lisker, Mrs. Mary D. Grant, Mrs. Amelia Dolberg, Mrs. Sarah Rotke, Mrs. Max Silverstein.

VEGETARIAN ENTREES DIVIDER PAGE (BACK)

Committee for Miriam Hospital Strawberry Festival, Taken on Mrs. Charles Brown's lawn, June 1939. Mesdames Kahnovsky, Leo Cohen, William Cohen, Samuel Markoff, Nathan Hilfer. Second row, Mesdames Mellion, Horvitz, Goldman, Shakovsky, Grant, Smith, Meyers, Rosen, Temkin, Brown, Felder, Klemer. Third row, Mesdames S. Ernstof, J. Ernstof, L. Smira, Lovett, Leibo, Webber, Kenison, Hornstein, Sass.

AND THEN SOME DIVIDER PAGE

May 1962. Foreground Mesdames Minnie Seefer, Rosalea Cohn, Fannie Brown, Sarah Smith, Mildred Field.

Thanks to the chefs and establishments:

Al Forno
Bacaro
Café Zelda
Capriccio's
Eastside Marketplace
Johnson and Wales
   University College of
   Culinary Arts

Ledgemont Country Club
Melissa Petitto, Chef
   to the Stars
New Rivers
Redlefsen's
Red Stripe

Rhode Island Convention
   Center
Rue De L'Espoir
Tom's Market
University of Rhode Island*
Whole Foods Market

This beautiful cookbook would not have been possible without the beautiful artwork of Faye Stolzman, cover artist, and Maria Alfie, the artist whose drawings graced *Simply Delicious* as well as the pages of this book.

In addition, we would like to thank

Susan Adler Kaplan for her editing expertise.

Soozie Sundlun at East Greenwich Photo and Studio for taking wonderful photographs of the artwork.

Anne Sherman and the Rhode Island Jewish Historical Association for the safekeeping of the historic photographs and for her assistance in combing through hundreds of photos to find the ones we used.

We regret that we were not able to include all submitted recipes due to duplications and space limitations, but your suggestions contributed to the overall quality of this book. We sincerely hope that no one has been inadvertently overlooked; if so, please accept our sincere apologies.

*SNAP-ED Family Nutrition Program Hotline (877)FOOD-URI(366-3874)

Contributors

The Miriam Hospital Women's Association thanks the countless volunteers who have contributed to this book. We sincerely appreciate all of you who contributed recipes or memories, tested and evaluated recipes, as well as all of you who wrote, edited, compiled, proofed, marketed and sold this cookbook. Thanks as well to those whose efforts are yet to come as *Simply More Delicious* continues to be read and enjoyed.

Betty Adler
Debra Alpert
Huda Alsabe
Jenifer Arruda
Elizabeth Atalay
Charlotte Bailey
Linda Baker
Randi Beranbaum
Karen Bergel
Mitzi Berkelhammer
Mish Blacher
Amy Bloom
Kim Borek
Ira Brandstein
Zita Brier
Jeffrey Brier
Wendy Buckler
Leslie Chazan
Sherry Cohen
June Condon
Bettina Crisafulli
Katie Damon
Annette D'Augelli
Lisa Davis
Judy Deutsch
Isabel Dias
Celeste DiMascalo
Grace Dugan
Ellie Elbaum
Robin Engle
Dana Falco
Mary Ferreira
Mary Flynn
Donna Frank
Ellie Frank
Susan Froehlich
Mary Gagnon
Sharon Gaines
Mickey Gardella
Diana Glashow

Debra Goldfarb
Amy Goldstein
Carol Griffin
Arnold Herman, MD
Debra Herman, PhD
Marcia Hirsch
Kathleen Hittner, MD
Denise Josephs
Margie Kaplan
Susan Adler Kaplan
Sheila Kaufman
Rosemary Khosrovani
Nancy Kirsch
Mary Kitzes
Glenda Labush
Barbara Lavine
Diane Lazarus
Lenore Leach
Margaret Lederer
Kathy Barbone Lee
Joyce Leven
Lisa Letourneau
Carol Levinger
Maybeth Lichaa
Terry Lieberman
Monica Lightman
Marianne Litwin
Lori Lowinger
Tracy Mahoney
Margaret Malo
Celeste Mascolo
Judy Matt
Ro Mede
Elle Merchant
Carolyn Merriman
Kim Millette
Melissa Miller
Jenifer Mowry
Jane Nelson
Lisa Nulman

Tina Odessa
Elaine Odessa
Susan Odessa
Cathy Oresman
Irene Pappas
Sarika Parikh
Beth Rabin
Belle Rampone
Sheila Riebe
Bea Rosen
Linda Rubenstein
Myrna Rubell
Cynthia Rupp
Rose Sagan
Ruth Saltzman
Dana Salvadore
Harriet Samors
Leslie Sax
Evelyn Seigle
Barbara Sheer
Mindy Sherwin
Willeen Snow
Leila Sock
Sue Suls
Lori Swanton
Stacie Tracey
Wilma Traylor
Karen Trinkle
Deborah Varrieur
Sidney Voelker
Pamela Vogel
Renee Vogel, MD
Ronnee Wasserman
A.J. Wasserman
Lisa Waterman
DeeDee Witman
Dolores Zompa
Rissy Zwetchkenbaum

Simply More Delicious would not have been possible without the hard work of those who published *Simply Delicious,* the first cookbook of the Miriam Hospital Women's Association. It is not only a cherished community favorite, but it provided an amazing starting point from which to begin – including recipes, layout and design, and a faithful following of supporters. So once again, we thank the contributors to *Simply Delicious.*

Regina Abrams
Eleanor Adler
Barbara Agostinelli
Maria Alfie
Esther Alter
Roslyn Applebaum
Harriet Baron
Jacqueline Barrett
Gussie Baxt
Brenda Bedrick
Ida Baretta
Frances Berger
Lillian Bernstein
Marcia Bigney
Marcia Blacher
Nancy Blackman
Karen Blickstein
Deborah Blitz
Judy Blumhagen
Evelyn Botvin
Janet Braunstein
Zita Brier
Gloria Brody
Sylvia Brown
Bertha Burgess
Dawn Campbell
Helen Caslowitz
June Chason
Pat Chiarello
Beverly Cohen

Bettina Crisafulli
Marilyn Danger
Rose Deitch
Sharon Del Deo
Sylvia Denhoff
Virginia Derosiers
Dora Diamond
Charlotte Dick
Mildren Doll
Alice Eichenbaum
Ellie Elbaum
Barbara Eliot
Rose Fabricant
Sidney Factor
Marcia Feinberg
Frances Fain
Martin Felder
Velma Felder
Terri Feldman
Irma Finberg
Carol Friedland
Mary Garr
Ellen Geltzer
Evelyn Gerstenblatt
Sonia Ghertler
Yetta Glicksman
Ruth Goldberg
Maxine Goldin
Norma Goldman
Rebecca Goldman

Bonnie Goldowsky
Diana Goldstein
Sophie Goldstein
Ruth Goodwin
Frances Greene
Davida Greenstein
Joan Grober
Anne Grossman
Esther Grossman
Hazel Grossman
Dories Gurland
Julie Gutterman
Rita Herman
Helene Hill
Cora Himmel
Elaine Hoffman
Melvin Hoffman
Eleanor Horvitz
Harriet Horvitz
Ruth Horvitz
Carolyn Issenberg
Celia Izeman
Paula Izeman
Beverly Jacobson
Betsy Jacobson
Pauline Jacobson
Rose Jacobson
Phyllis Joachim
Ann Jones
Judi Josephson

Berle Kadish
Sue Kahn
Carol Kaplan
Susan Kaplan
Gertrude Katz
Norma Kaufman
Judy Keeley
Rose Kelman
Georgette Kershaw
Shirley Kestenman
Mary Kitzes
Elaine Klein
Celia Klemer
Delores Kone
Muriel Krasnoff
Elaine Kroll
Beverly Kwasha
Glenda Labush
Dorothy Lampal
Mollie Langer
Tillie Langer
Anna Laprey
Naomi Laufer
Barrie Lax
Sandi Lax
Lenore Leach
Sara Leach
Carol Levinger
Barbara Levine
Nan Levine
Reva Lewis
Shirley Lewis
Alice Liffman
Rita Listengart
Elizabeth Lofthouse
Judy Logan
Sally Ludman
Betty Macktez
Sadra Maldavir
Edith Mancoll
Roslyn Markoff
Rita Martin
Jemma Martino
Melba Meister
Dorothy Mensch
Dotti Meyer
Pam Meyers

Sara Miller
Linda Mittleman
Frieda Morris
Susan Morris
Jane Nelson
Bernice Novogrodski
Phoebe Nulman
Susan O'Brien
Patti Okun
Ruth Page
Evelyn Parness
Sandra Perley
Ethel Perry
Gertrude Podrat
Jen Pollock
Marietta Porrazzo
Lotte Povar
Marie Presel
Carol Pressman
Rebecca Primiano
Anne Quinn
Elaine Rakatansky
Ellen Reeves
Joan Reeves
William Reeves
Anne Ress
Rose Roitman
Judy Rosenbaum
Sue Rosenfield
Joan Rottenberg
Susan Rotundi
Linda Rubenstein
Ethel Runstein
Elaine Sachs
Isadora Safner
Gerry Salter
Anna Samdperil
Harriet Samors
Ellen Saxl
Lorna Schiffman
Sylvia Schoenbaum
Jeanette Schoenberger
Barbara Schwartz
Dorothy Schwartz
Lillian Schwartz
Linda Schwartz
Esther Scoliard

Lea Scott
Jeanette Segool
Minnie Seefer
Beatrice Shore
Rachel Siegel
Tovia Siegel
Susan Slepkow
Helen Smith
Carol Sofro
Ruth Spiegle
Gloria Spivack
Barbara Spraragen
Libby Stein
Beverly Sugarman
Carlyn Summer
Joanne Summer
Lisa Tamura
Janet Tarpey
Larry Thibert
Marjorie Thornton
Sophie Torgan
Cynthia Triedman
Belle Tuck
Bella Weinstein
Isabelle Weinstein
Esther Weltman
Edna Wharton
Gloria Winston
Dorte Witoszka
Herta Wolfson
Marilyn Woronov
Beulah Wuraftic
Marjorie Yashar
Elinor Zelkind
Fay Zura

RESTAURANTS

Arboretum
Great House
Red Rooster
Johnson and Wales School of
    Culinary Arts

Index

DIPS AND SPREADS

E

EGGPLANT

EGGS

ESCAROLE

F

FIGS

FISH

FROSTINGS AND ICINGS *(see Desserts)*

FRUIT *(see also individual listings)*

G

GRITS

I

ICE CREAM *(see Desserts)*

K

KIDS

KUGELS

L

LAMB

LEMONS AND LIMES

M

MANGOES

MUSHROOMS

N

NUTS

O

P

T

TARTS *(see Desserts)*

TORTES *(see Desserts)*

TOFU

TOMATOES

V

VEAL

VEGETABLES *(see also individual listings)*

VEGETARIAN

Z

ZUCCHINI *(see also Squash)*

Simply More Delicious

The Miriam Hospital Women's Association
164 Summit Avenue
Providence, Rhode Island 02906
http://cookbook.miriamhospital.org
Telephone (401)793-3520

Please send my cookbooks to:

Name _____

Address _____

City State Zip _____

Phone _____

E-mail _____

BOOK PRICES

Quantity	Cost
1 book	$25.95 + $1.82 tax + $8.23 postage and handling = $36.00
2 books	$51.90 + $3.63 tax + $12.47 postage and handling = $68.00
3 books	$77.85 + $5.45 tax + $13.70 postage and handling = $97.00
6 books	$155.70 +10.90 tax + $14.40 postage and handling = $181.00

I would like to order _____ cookbook(s). Total amount enclosed: _____

Please make check payable to MHWA and send to the address above.

- -

Join the Miriam Hospital Women's Association.

❑   My annual dues of $30 are enclosed.

❑   I would like to find out more about the Women's Association. Please have
someone from the Membership Committee contact me.

Name _____

Address _____

City State Zip _____

Phone _____

Best time to call _____

RETURN TO:
MHWA 164 Summit Avenue Providence, RI 02906